REINCARNATION

REINCARNATION

© Copyright 2019 by the United States Spiritist Council

Scripture quotations are from the ESV Bible (The Holy Bible, English Standard Version), copyright © 2001 by Crossway Bibles, a publishing ministry of Good News Publishers. Used by permission. All rights reserved.

ISBN 978-1948109130
LCCN 2019940381
Proofreading: Jussara Korngold
Book design: Helton Mattar Monteiro
Cover design: HML

International data for cataloging in publication (CIP)

D3376 Delanne, Gabriel, 1857–1926
Reincarnation / Gabriel Delanne. Translator: Helton Mattar Monteiro. – New York: United States Spiritist Council, 2019.
382 pp.; 21.59 cm.

Original title: Documents pour servir à l'étude de la réincarnation (Paris, Éditions de la B.P.S, 1924).

ISBN: 978-1948109130

1. Reincarnation. 2. Spiritism. 3. New Spiritualism. I. Title.

LCCN: 2019940381   DDC 133.93   UDC 133.7

1st edition, 1st print – May 2019

All rights reserved to
United States Spiritist Council
http://www.spiritist.us – info@spiritist.us
Book portal: https://is.gd/ussf1

Manufactured in the United States of America

No part of this book may be reproduced or transmitted in any form or by any means, electronic or mechanical, including photocopying, recording, or by any information storage and retrieval system, without the prior permission in writing from the copyright holder.

The name "United States Spiritist Federation" is a trade mark registered of the United States Spiritist Council.

GABRIEL DELANNE

REINCARNATION

"TO BE BORN, TO DIE, BE REBORN AGAIN AND INCESSANTLY PROGRESS; THAT IS THE LAW."
Allan Kardec

TRANSLATED BY H. M. MONTEIRO

UNITED STATES SPIRITIST FEDERATION
NEW YORK
2019

About the Author ...

Born in France in 1857, Gabriel Delanne, together with Léon Denis, turned out to be one of the main exponents of Spiritism after Allan Kardec's sudden death in Paris, in 1869.

His contribution to the study of mediumistic and animistic phenomena from a scientific standpoint is invaluable, as attested by his many books and articles dealing mainly with the immortality of the soul.

As a child, he met Kardec who was a personal friend of his father's, whereas his mother was a writing medium. This early contact left an indelible impression on him, an eletrical engineer by profession, which would last all his life as a respected investigator of psychical phenomena.

When he disincarnated in 1926, he was heard to say, "Friends, keep in mind that Delanne has never feared death."

Reincarnation was his last book, crowning a distinguished and prolific career.

USSF

Contents

Introduction 1

1. A HISTORICAL LOOK AT THE THEORY OF SUCCESSIVE LIVES

India 9
Persia and Greece 10
The Neoplatonic School 13
Judea 14
The Romans 16
The Druids 17
The Middle Ages 18
Modern Times 18
An inquiry by Dr. Calderone 21

2. SCIENTIFIC BASES OF REINCARNATION · PROPERTIES OF THE PERISPIRIT

Apparitions of the Living 26
Apparitions of the Deceased 31
Induced apparitions 36
Experiments held at the International Metapsychic Inst. 45
Report by Mr. Gabrielli 48
Logical necessity for the existence of the perispirit 57
Where and how did the perispirit acquire its functional properties? 61

3. THE ANIMAL SOUL, AN ESSAY ON THE UNITY OF THE LAWS OF LIFE THROUGHOUT THE ORGANIC SCALE

Necessity for earthly incarnations 65
Animal evolution 69
Formation and gradual development of the spirit 73

Passage of the intelligent principle throughout the animal series 75

4. ANIMAL INTELLIGENCE

The calculating horses 79
A dog named Rolf 87
Lola 96
Zou 99

5. SUPERNORMAL FACULTIES IN ANIMALS AND THEIR INDIVIDUAL PRINCIPLE

A likely case of clairvoyance 107
Phantom of a dog seen by a cat 108
Phantoms collectively perceived by humans and animals 108
Visions of human phantoms not relatable to any telepathic coincidence and perceived collectively by humans and animals 109
Vision first perceived by an animal instead of a human 109
The apparition of Palladia, *visual, auditory, collective* 111
Haunted places 112
The survival of animals after death 116
Apparition of a dog 117
Visions of animal phantoms not relatable to any telepathic coincidence and perceived collectively by humans and animals 118
A ghost dog 121
The laughing dog 122
Apparitions of animals in experimental seances 125
Visible materializations of animal forms 126
Nevi 127

6. THE INTEGRAL MEMORY

Integral memory 133
Other cases of ecmnesia 141
History of Louis V 146

Latent memory 151
Vision through crystal ball 154
Cryptomnesia 156

7. EXPERIMENTS IN MEMORY RETRIEVAL

Study of seances where alleged revelations about the subject's or participants' past lives have occurred 168
Unforeseen revelation 171
Subliminal novel or reminiscence 174
Tenacious hatred 178
Reincarnation in England 180
Can reincarnation be proved? 180
Successive lives 183
The medium Hélène Smith 186
Awakening of the past during trance 194
A complex case of reminiscing 196
A resuscitation of the past 202
An atonement 205
Summary 206

8. HEREDITY AND CHILD PRODIGIES

Child prodigies 209
Musicians 214
Painters 219
Scholars, writers and poets 220
Mental calculators 222

9. REMINISCENCE STUDY

Feelings of déjà vu 227
Visions of unknown places by subjects during sleep 233
Haunted by the living 234
Likely reminiscences among children 239
Little girl speaking a special idiom in which French words are found 239
Are these dormant memories roused? 241

10. RECOLLECTIONS OF PREVIOUS LIVES

Trianon 261
Awakening of recollections 263
The case of Laure Raynaud 266
In Genoa a death certificate is found which would be that of Mrs. Raynaud 274
Excerpt from the death certificate of the parish of San Francesco d'Albaro, Genoa 276
One of Dr. Durville's subjects, Mrs. d'Elphes, completes the evidence given by Mrs. Raynaud 277
Curious statements 283

11. OTHER FACTS INVOLVING REMEMBRANCE OF PAST LIVES

Excerpt of an inquiry by Dr. Calderone, reported by Dr. Moutin 298
Memory of a previous life 304

12. CASES OF REINCARNATION ANNOUNCED IN ADVANCE

A new proof of reincarnation 310
Upcoming reincarnation announced twice in advance 312
Recalling a song as learned in a previous life 315
Reincarnations announced in Spiritist seances 317
The twin girls of Dr. Samona 327
A few remarks 349

13. OVERVIEW OF ARGUMENTS IN FAVOR OF REINCARNATION

The soul is a transcendental being 352
The perispirit and its properties 353
Where and how could the perispirit have acquired its properties? 356

| Human reincarnation and the integral memory 359
| Heredity and child prodigies 363
| Reminiscences 365
| True recollections of past lives 366
| Reincarnations announced in advance 368

14. CONCLUSION

| Forgetting the past.. 374
| The problem of the existence of evil 376
| Progress 377
| Moral consequences 379

Photo credits 382

Introduction

Blaise Pascal once said that, "The immortality of the soul is a matter which is of so great consequence to us and which touches us so profoundly that we must have lost all feeling to be indifferent as to knowing what it is."[1] This need to know our destiny has been the concern of innumerable generations, since all the great revolutions that transformed societies were accomplished by religious reformers. However, in our day, uncertainty about this important subject reigns in the minds of the majority of our contemporaries, because religion having lost much of its moral authority has seen its evocative power grow weaker. With spiritualistic philosophers, the soul, eager for truth, is shown wandering in the dark maze of abstract metaphysics, often self-contradictory and sometimes downright incomprehensible.

The 19th century was remarkable for the extraordinary development of positivistic research in all branches of science. The new knowledge which we thus have acquired has revolutionized our conditions of existence, and improved our material life in proportions which would have seemed unthinkable to our great grandfathers. And yet we have been able to accuse science of failing all our hopes, for if it triumphs in the domain of matter, it has remained voluntarily aloof of what is most important for us to know, namely, to say whether we have an immortal soul and, if so, what becomes of it after death; and, even more so, whether it exists before birth. But if science was unable to build, it was a powerful instrument of destruction.

---

1 [Trans. note] Blaise Pascal (1623–1662), "Pensées" in *Great Books of the Western World: Pascal*, vol. 33 (Ed. by R. M. Hutchins. Chicago: Encyclopaedia Britannica, Inc., University of Chicago, 1952), p. 206.

The discoveries of astronomy, geology, and anthropology have lifted the veil of our origins and, in the light of these great natural revelations, religious fictions about the origins of Earth and the human race have faded away, just as legends do when confronted with history. On the other hand, intense criticism on the part of exegetes has removed from the Bible its character of divine revelation, in such a way that many sincere spirits now refuse to submit to its authority. This decay of faith is also the result of an antagonism that exists between religious education and reason. The ancient conceptions of Heaven and Hell are outdated, for one does not understand an eternity of suffering as punishment for a lifetime that lasts less than a second vis-à-vis the immensity of time; and that one cannot conceive of an idle and blissful happiness whose eternal monotony would be a veritable torment. To shed new light on a subject as anciently controversial as that concerning the existence of the soul, we must resolutely abandon the field of sterile philosophical discussions –which in most cases only lead to contradictory solutions – and instead address this issue through observation and experimentation.

The soul exists substantially; if it is really different from the body, it must be possible to find proof of its independence from the organism in its manifestations. Now, these proofs exist, and it is easy to be convinced of this when one studies impartially the facts classified today under the names of clairvoyance, telepathy, premonition, exteriorization of the sensibility or the motricity, and out-of-body experiences. For a long time, science remained skeptical in face of these phenomena in which it did not believe, and it took the persevering efforts of Spiritists for seventy years to guide independent researchers in such novel ways. Yet justice was done at last, when Professor Charles Richet placed on the desk of the Academy of Sciences, in March 1922, his *Traité de Métapsychique* [*Treatise on Metapsychics*], which is a formal recognition of the indisputable reality of the phenomena of which I listed above. If that famous physiologist is still opposed to a spiritual interpretation of the facts, it is only timidly that he fights such an explanation. However, many illustrious scholars have not shown his scruples about the phenomena, since William Crookes, Alfred Russell Wallace, F. W. H. Myers, Oliver Lodge, Cesare Lombroso, and so many others, fully accept the theory of spirituality, as the only one which can fit all cases. The British Society for Psychical Research (SPR), composed of leading scientists and eminent psychologists, has controlled (i.e., supervised) thousands of observations since the year 1882, and conducted thorough and faultless experiments. Also, thanks to the popularization of hypnotic processes, the literate public is becoming increasingly familiarized with such phenomena which reveal the existence of a human soul in us.

However, it is not enough to establish that the thinking being is a reality; it is necessary to prove, too, that the individual self survives death, and that with the same abundance of positive demonstrations as those which ascertains one's existence during physical life. Spiritists have responded to this expectation by showing that the relations between the living and the dead are established through several forms of writing, typtology (i.e., spirit-rapping), spirit sight and hearing, etc. They have used photography, weight scales, imprints and casting molds to establish the objective reality of the ghosts that appear during materialization seances. The momentary corporeality of these apparitions is irrefutable since all these documents subsist permanently after the phantoms have vanished.

All the objections against these phenomena as being the result of fraud, hallucinations, etc., have been refuted by repeated inquiries undertaken all over the world by most qualified scientists and, in face of the mass of accumulated documents, it can now be affirmed that the materiality of the facts is no longer disputable. Doubtless, the struggle against bias will be long still, for we see united, in a motley coalition, priests and materialists, who also feel threatened by this new science (Spiritism). Still, the demonstrative force of Spiritism is so great that it has conquered millions of adherents from all walks of society, and is pushing up and down the ruins of the past.

Not being able to further extend myself on the subject of these varied proofs and demonstrations, I refer the reader wishing to learn more about it to already published books.

The fact remains that the existence of our human soul during life is beyond doubt, and that it survives the disintegration of the body, retaining with it in the Hereafter all the faculties and powers it possessed here below. Now the question is whether the soul preexisted birth and what evidence can be gathered to support the theory of preexistence. Such evidence is of two types, namely:

    1) Philosophical arguments
    2) Scientific observations

Let us take a quick look at these two aspects of the issue.

Belief in the plurality of existences has been accepted by the most eminent minds of antiquity in forms that at first seemed somewhat obscure, but which, in the long run, have been clarified in an understandable way. Because Christianity rejected this theory, humans today are not very familiar with this idea, so eminently rational. We will see that there are some irresistible arguments in its favor, if we want to reconcile the intellectual and moral inequalities that still exist on Earth, by endorsing an immanent justice explanation.

If we accept that the soul of a human being is not coming for the first time to Earth, and that it has not suddenly come into existence, then we are led to suppose, going back to the origins of humankind, that it previously went through the animal kingdom, which it traveled throughout, since the beginning of life in the globe. We shall see that the discoveries of science strongly support this way of thinking, for it is possible to ascertain, by the filiation of living beings, a progressively higher correlation between material organisms and increasingly developed forms of psychical faculties.

It is at this point that we bring into play the experiments of Spiritism, in order to try to give this philosophical theory an experimental basis, in other words, in order to make it enter the realm of science. The following is a brief summary of the most salient points of this demonstration.

Experimentation proves that the soul is inseparable from a fluidic body called the perispirit. This envelope contains in it all the laws that govern the organization and maintenance of the material body, at the same time as those governing the psychological functioning of the spirit. The materializations of spirits show us this formative and plastic power at work and, make us suppose that what takes place, momentarily and abnormally, in a Spiritist seance, occurs slowly and naturally at the moment of birth. From then on, each being brings with him/her their own power of development, while only the form, that is to say the internal and external structural type of the organism, is modified by the laws of heredity which can disturb more or less its functioning. I tried to sketch this demonstration more than thirty years ago, in my book *Évolution Animique* [*Animistic Evolution*], and in a memoir presented at the International Spiritualist Congress, held in London in 1898.

If the preceding assertions are correct, we should find in the animal series the same phenomena as encountered in human beings, and be able to control them experimentally. I will expose the physiological and psychological proofs that we have about this point, and we will see that if documents are still too scarce to be absolutely convincing, they however are of sufficient value to be taken very seriously.

Another series of arguments may be drawn from the testimony of the spirits themselves, and I shall take great care not to neglect this source of information, while making all necessary reservations as to the credit we should give to affirmations of this nature. There exists indeed a rather great divergence on this subject among spirits which manifest themselves in different parts of the world. Discarnate spirits of Latin countries (France, Italy, Spain, etc.) teach the theory of successive lives almost unanimously, and it was thanks to them that Allan Kardec adopted this theory, which he had previously opposed. Conversely, in Anglo-Saxon countries, most spirits reject this hypothesis. We must not be too frightened by this disagreement, because on the spiritual plane, as on Earth, opinions are greatly divided regarding the major laws of nature, and among them as with us, only the most educated and advanced end up demonstrating the merits of their opinions. In the past twenty years it has been found that reincarnation is now accepted by a large number of spirits from the United Kingdom and the United States.[2] I came to the conclusion that this theory had hitherto been left aside by the spiritual guides, to avoid clashes with old beliefs which could have compromised the development of Spiritism. Today, when this tenet has millions of followers in the New World (North, Central and South Americas), this danger no longer exists and the theory of successive lives is gaining ground every day.

Two types of proof of reincarnation can be found in Spiritist communications:

1) Those from spirits claiming to remember their past lives;
2) Those in which spirits announce in advance what their reincarnations here below will be, even specifying their gender and particular features through which one should be able to recognize them.

I shall carefully discuss these documents and we shall see that many of them survive all criticism.

There are still two sets of evidence concerning successive lives. First there are those provided by human beings who remember having already lived on Earth. About this matter,

---

2 See William F. BARRETT, *On the Threshold of the Unseen* (New York: E. P. Dutton & Co., 1917), ch. xxiii, "... Reincarnation," p. 284.

a comparison of these phenomena with those of paramnesia (disordered memory, confusion of facts and fantasy) will allow us to keep only unassailable documents. Then there are those which are deduced from the existence of child prodigies. Because psychic heredity is inadmissible, since we know that the soul is not generated by the parents, hence reincarnation would be the only logical explanation of these apparent anomalies.

These facts, so neglected hitherto by philosophers, have a considerable importance: if we wish to examine them carefully and deduce their consequences, that will result in almost certainty of the theory of successive lives, and we will understand the great evolution of the human soul, from the lowest forms to the highest degrees of supernormal and moral life. This tenet has a philosophical and social significance of considerable importance for the future of humankind, because it lays the foundation for an integral psychology that fits wonderfully to all contemporary sciences in their loftiest conceptions.

So let us study it with impartiality so that we can see that it is not a mere scientific theory, but more than this: a magnificent and irrefutable truth.

A HISTORICAL LOOK AT THE THEORY OF SUCCESSIVE LIVES

ANTIQUITY OF BELIEF IN SUCCESSIVE LIVES · INDIA · PERSIA · EGYPT · GREECE · JUDEA · THE NEOPLATONIC SCHOOL OF ALEXANDRIA · THE ROMANS · THE DRUIDS · THE MIDDLE AGES · IN MODERN TIMES: THINKERS AND PHILOSOPHERS THAT HAVE ACCEPTED THIS TENET · A INQUIRY ON THE SUBJECT CARRIED OUT BY DR. CALDERONE

INDIA

THE BELIEF IN SUCCESSIVE LIVES (or reincarnation) is also called palingenesis, from two Greek words *palin* 'again' + *genesis* 'birth'.[3] What is truly remarkable is that, from the dawn of civilization, it had been formulated in India with a precision that the intellectual condition of that distant time could hardly have foreshadowed. Indeed, from the earliest antiquity, the peoples of Asia and Greece believed in the immortality of the soul and, better still, some were concerned to know whether this soul was created at the time of birth or already existed prior to that.

I will briefly review the opinions of authors that have studied this issue. India is very probably the intellectual cradle of humanity, and it is indeed quite remarkable that one finds in the *Vedas* and in the *Bhagavad Gita* passages such as this:

---

3 For the historical part, please refer to André PEZZANI's very well accomplished book, *La Pluralité des Existences de l'Âme* [*The Plurality of Existences of the Soul*]; see also T. PASCAL's book *Évolution Humaine* [*Human Evolution*]; Charles BONNET's *La Palingénésie*; and BALLANCHE's *Essai de Palingénésie Sociale* [*Essays on Social Palingenesis*].

> "The soul is neither born nor dies; it has neither been nor will it be created, because it is unborn and eternal. It is ever-youthful, yet ancient. It is not destroyed when the body is destroyed. ... Knowing the soul to be indestructible, eternal, birthless and immutable, how can a person kill or cause anyone to be killed?"
>
> "As a person adopts new garments, discarding those that are old and worn, similarly, the soul continues to adopt new bodies, leaving those that are old and useless...."
>
> "... I have passed through many births. I can remember all of them, whereas you, O Arjuna, cannot."[4]

Here Vedic precepts affirm the eternity of the soul and its progressive evolution through multiple reincarnations, the object of which is the destruction of all desire and every thought of personal reward. In fact, continues the instructor (it is still the heavenly voice which is talking):

> "The great souls who become My associates in My divine pastimes, having reached Me, are never again born into transitory existence, which is the abode of suffering."
>
> "O Arjuna, from the plane of Lord Brahma downwards, all planes or their residents are subject to return. But ... there is no rebirth after reaching Me."

Persia and Greece

In Zoroastrianism, the religion of ancient Persia, we find a very high conception: that of a final redemption granted to all created beings, after having undergone expiatory tests which are inexorable and will eventually earn the human soul its final happiness. To be condemned to an eternal hell would be in total contradiction with the goodness and kindness of the Author of all beings.

---

4 [Trans. note] All excerpts are from the *Srimad Bhagavad-gita: The Hidden Treasure of the Sweet Absolute* (Trans. Sri S. Das. W. Bengal: Sri C. S. Math, 2006).

Pythagoras was the first to introduce in ancient Greece the tenet of the rebirth of the soul, which he had learned during his travels to Egypt and Persia. He had two philosophical doctrines: one reserved for initiates who attended the Mysteries, and another one destined for the people at large. The latter one gave rise to the erroneous concept of metempsychosis. For the initiates, the ascension was gradual and progressive, without regression into lower forms; whereas for the people in general, little evolved as they were, it was taught that evil souls were supposed to be reborn in the body of animals, as clearly stated by his disciple Timaeus of Locri in the following passage:[5]

> "It is for the same reason that transient (belief-based) penalties of soul transformation (or metempsychosis) must be established, so that timid souls (of men) pass (after death) into the bodies of women to be exposed to contempt and insults; the souls of murderers into the bodies of ferocious beasts to (receive) their punishment; indecent and obscene ones into pigs and wild boars; those of inconstant and feather-brained persons into birds which fly in the air: those of lazy, sluggish, ignorant and mad persons into the forms of aquatic animals."

Among the Greeks, it all is quite remarkable that Herodotus, in speaking of the doctrine of the Egyptians, foresaw the necessity of the passage of the soul through the animal stages, although attributing to it a character of penalty which confirmed the error of metempsychosis. However, the "Father of History" believed that pure souls could evolve in other orbs of heaven. He says that the high priests of Mithra, in Persia, represented the transmigrations of souls in celestial bodies under the mysterious symbol of a ladder or staircase with seven steps, each made of a different metal, which symbolized the seven orbs to which the days of the week were dedicated, but arranged in reverse order as follows, as

---

[5] TIMAEUS OF LOCRI in Greek and French, by the Marquis d'ARGENS, Berlin, 1763, p. 252. My translation.

reported by Celsus: Saturn, Venus, Jupiter, Mercury, Mars, the Moon, and the Sun.

Therefore, in Greek antiquity there were two teachings, one for the crowd, the other one for the wise to whom truth was revealed after they had undergone the initiation process which was called "mysteries." Aristophanes and Sophocles alluded to the Mysteries as "the hopes of death." Porphyry also said:

> "At the moment of death, our soul must be as it was during the celebration of the mysteries; that is to say, free from passion, envy, hatred and anger."[6]

Through this we see the importance of the Mysteries as a moralizing and civilizing force in ancient times. Indeed, they secretly taught the following:

1) The unicity (oneness) of God
2) The plurality of worlds, and the rotation of the Earth as later affirmed by Copernicus and Galileo.
3) The multiple, successive lives of the soul.

Plato adopts the Pythagorean idea of palingenesis. He based it on two main reasons set forth in his book *Phaedo*. The first is that, since death succeeds life in nature, it is logical to accept that life succeeds death, for nothing can be born out of nothing. Should the beings that we see dying never return to life, everything would end up being absorbed by death. The second premise proposed by the great philosopher is based on reminiscence, since, according to him, to learn is to remember. Now, he said, if our soul remembers having already lived before and descending into a body, why should we not believe that, on leaving it, it will be able to successively animate several other bodies?

---

6 [Trans. note] See A. Pezzani, *La Pluralité des Existences de l'Âme* (Paris: Didier, 1865), p. 81.

Rising higher still, Plato[7] affirms that the soul, once free from imperfections and attached to divine virtue, becomes somehow holy and no longer returns to Earth. But before reaching this evolution level, for a thousand years souls return to Hades; and when they are to come back here to Earth, they drink the waters of Lethe, which make them lose all memory of their past lives.[8]

THE NEOPLATONIC SCHOOL

The Neoplatonic school of Alexandria taught reincarnation by further specifying the conditions of this progressive evolution for the soul. Plotinus, the first of these philosophers, returns to the subject many times in the course of his *Enneads*. "It is a dogma recognized throughout antiquity," he says, which was then universally taught, that if the soul makes mistakes, it is condemned to expiate them by suffering punishments in the dark gloomy regions of hell. Then it is admitted to pass onward into a new body, in order to start all over again. In chapter 8 of the second *Ennead*, he further elaborates his thought in the following sentence:

> "The gods are ever looking down upon us in this world ..., for their providence is never-ending; they allot to each individual his appropriate destiny, one that is in harmony with his past conduct, in conformity with his successive existences."[9]

Iamblichus synthesizes the tenet of successive lives as follows:

> "What appears to us to be an accurate definition of justice does not also appear to be so to the Gods. For we, looking

---

7 See PLATO, *The Spirit of Laws* vol. I (Trans. T. Nugent. London: Printed for J. Nourse and P. Vaillant , 1773), book x.

8 [Trans. note] Lethe was a river in Hades, the abode of the dead.

9 [Trans. note] Excerpted from Théophile PASCAL, *Reincarnation: A Study in Human Evolution* (Trans. Fred Rothwell. London: T. P. Society, 1910), ch. IV, p. 214.

at that which is most brief, direct our attention to things present ... But the powers that are superior to us know the whole life of the Soul, ... looking at the offenses committed by souls in former lives: which men, not perceiving, think that they unjustly fall into the calamities which they suffer."[10]

Thus, according to him, neither chance nor fatality, but an inflexible justice, regulates the existence of all beings; and, if some individuals are overwhelmed with affliction, it is not by virtue of any arbitrary decision by divine decree, but as an unavoidable consequence, to them, of faults committed previously. Later on it will be seen that the spirit that returns to Earth sometimes freely accepts painful trials, no longer as punishment, but to reach more quickly a higher degree of evolution.

JUDEA

The idea of past lives was generally accepted among Hebrews.

"Elijah, says St. James the Less, was no different from any of us; he did not have any predestination decree other than that which we ourselves possess. His soul, when God sent him to Earth, had already reached a very eminent degree of perfection, which drew him, in his new life, to ever more potent and higher graces."[11]

Belief in soul rebirths is indicated in a veiled manner in the *Bible*, although much more explicitly in the *Gospels*, as is easily ascertained by the passages below.

Indeed, the Jews believed that the return of Elijah to Earth was to precede that of the Messiah. That is why, in the Gospel, when asked by his disciples if Elijah came back, Jesus answers them in the affirmative by saying:

---

10 [Trans. note] *Op. cit., ibid.*, p. 215.
11 [Trans. note] PEZZANI, *La Pluralité des Existences de l'Âme* (Paris: Didier, 1865), book 2, ch. 1, "Jean-Baptiste," p. 105.

"Elijah has already come, and they did not recognize him, but did to him whatever they pleased." (Matthew 17:12 ESV)

Then the disciples understood, says the evangelist, that he was speaking to them of John the Baptist. On another occasion, having encountered a blind man from birth, who was begging, Jesus was asked by his disciples about him:

"Who sinned, this man or his parents, that he was born blind?" (John 9:2)

So they thought he could sin before being born? And yet Jesus did not object to such an odd question; and, without reprehending them, as it seems he would surely have done, had they been in error, he merely gave them the following reply:

"It was not that this man sinned, or his parents, but that the works of God might be displayed in him." (John 9:3)

In the Gospel of John, Nicodemus, who was a Jewish senator and a Pharisee, asks Jesus for explanations on the dogma of future life. Jesus answered him:

"Truly, truly, I say to you, unless one is born again he cannot see the kingdom of God." (John 3:3)

Nicodemus is upset by this answer because he took it in its coarse sense.

Nicodemus said to him, "How can a man be born when he is old? Can he enter a second time into his mother's womb and be born?" Jesus answered, "Truly, truly, I say to you, unless one is born of water and the Spirit, he cannot enter the kingdom of God...."
"Do not marvel that I said to you, 'You must be born again.' The wind blows where it wishes, and you hear its sound, but you do not know where it comes from or where it goes...."
Nicodemus said to him, "How can these things be?" Jesus answered him, "Are you the teacher of Israel and yet you do not understand these things?" (John 3:4–5, 7–8)

This last observation of Christ shows that he is surprised that a master in Israel does not know reincarnation, because it was taught as a secret doctrine to intellectuals of that time. One of the proofs that can be given that there were teachings hidden to the masses, are those collected in the various books which constitute the *Kabbalah*.

In the secret teachings reserved for initiates, one proclaimed the immortality of the soul, the successive lives, and the plurality of the inhabited worlds. These doctrines are found in the *Zohar*, written by Rabbi Shimon ben Yochai, presumably around AD 121, but only known in Europe by the end of the 3rd century AD. On the other hand, the transmigration of souls, if we believe St. Jerome, was long taught as an esoteric and traditional truth that should be entrusted to a small number of elect ones. Origen accepted as a logical necessity the preexistence of the soul to explain certain passages of the Bible, without which, he says, one could accuse God of iniquity. These conceptions, though repulsed by the ecclesiastical councils, were preserved, even in the clergy, by independent minds like Cardinal Nicholas of Cusa, and among the philosophers, by the followers of the occult sciences, who transmitted these traditions under the seal of secrecy.

The Romans

Among the Romans who drew most of their knowledge from the Greeks, Virgil clearly expresses the idea of palingenesis in the following terms:

> "All these [souls], when they have traveled round the circle of a thousand years, God summons in mighty throng to the river of Lethe, that so, forgetful of the past, they may go back to visit again the vault of the sky, and begin without reluctance to return to the body."[12]

---

12 [Trans. note] VIRGIL, *The Works of Virgil* (Trans. J. Lonsdale, Samuel Lee. London and New York: Macmillan, 1872), "Æneid," book VI,

Another poet, Ovid, also says that his soul, when purified, will inhabit the globes that populate the firmament, thus extending the concept of palingenesis to other worlds in interplanetary space.

THE DRUIDS

The Gauls, my ancestors, practiced the religion of the Druids and believed in the oneness of God, and in successive lives. About them, Julius Caesar once wrote:

> "They (the Druids) in particular want to inculcate this idea, that souls do not die, but pass from one body to another."[13]

The Roman soldier and historian Ammianus Marcellinus reports that in accordance with Pythagoras's opinion, they affirmed that souls are immortal and that they will animate other bodies. That is why, when they burned their dead, they threw in the pyre some letters which they addressed to their parents or to their deceased friends, as if these latter were to receive and read them. The Druids taught that there are three circle: the first one is Ceugant, which belongs only to God; the second is the circle of Gwynfid, the abode of happiness; and then there is Abred, or circle of migrations, which comprises Earth and the other planets. The Earth was considered a place of passage for one to rise to higher worlds. The idea of preexistence, and not of metempsychosis, is clearly formulated by the bard Taliesin, when he says:

> "I have been a viper in the lake, ... a spotted adder on the mountain, a star, a priest. This was long, long ago; since then, I have slept in a hundred worlds, revolved in a hundred circles."[14]

724–751, p. 174.

13 [Trans. note] Julius CAESAR, *The First Six Books of Caesar's Commentaries on the Gallic War* (Trans. P. Bullions. New York: Pratt, Oakley & Co., 1859), book VI, p. 191, notes 13–14; p. 256.

14 [Trans. note] T. PASCAL, *Reincarnation: A Study in Human Evolution* (Trans. Fred Rothwell. London: T. P. Society, 1910), "The Celts."

The Middle Ages

Through the whole Middle Ages, the teaching of palingenesis (rebirth) remained veiled, for it was severely proscribed by the then all-powerful church. These tenets were confined to secret societies, or transmitted orally among initiates who were engaged in occult sciences.

Modern Times

It was necessary to wait for modern times, and with them, the freedom of thinking and discussing publicly, for this truth of successive lives to be reborn and widely disseminated.

One of the most eminent philosophers of the 17th century, Leibniz, in studying the problem of the origin of the soul, accepts that the intelligent principle, in the form of monads, was able to develop going through the animal scale.

Pierre Samuel Dupont de Nemours, a profound thinker of the 18th century, accepts by the mere force of reasoning, like Charles Bonnet, that the soul released from the body is always united to a spiritual form that allows it to retain its individuality, and that after a stay on the spiritual plane, it returns to Earth to improve itself by acquiring higher and higher moral qualities. P. S. Dupont de Nemours, like Leibniz, supposes that the intelligent principle passed through all living species before reaching humanity. The philosopher Gotthold E. Lessing wrote:

> "Why should not every individual man have existed more than once upon this world? ... Is this hypothesis so laughable merely because it is the oldest? ... Why may not even I have already performed all those steps of my perfecting which bring to man only temporal punishments and rewards."[15]

---

15 [Trans. note] G. E. Lessing, *The Education of the Human Race* (Trans. F. W. Robertson. 3rd ed. London: H. S. King & Co., 1872), pp. 76–77, par. 94–96.

Also to be noted are Ballanche, Schlegel, and Saint-Martin, who all express, each in his own fashion, ideas similar to those of P. S. Dupont de Nemours on the subject of palingenesis. J. Constant Savy, who lived at the beginning of the 19th century, does not admit the idea of eternal hell, because a punishment of this sort would be a blind and implacable revenge, since it would punish by everlasting tortures the faults of a single life which, however long it might have been, represented only a few moments vis-à-vis eternity. He accepts the theory of successive lives, for, he says, the immortality of humans consists in a progressive march; where they prepare the life in which they enter by the one they leave. Finally, since there are two worlds, one necessarily material and the other necessarily intellectual, these two worlds, which make up the coming life, must have harmonious relations with ours. By evolving themselves, humans will move into the world forward.

Spiritualistic philosophers such as Pierre Leroux and Charles Fourier have accepted the plurality of existences of the soul.

But Fourier, with his systematic and adventurous spirit, imagines periods of intertwined human and extraterrestrial lives. Thus, according to him, there are exactly eight hundred and ten existences, divided into five periods of unequal extent, encompassing eighty thousand years!

Alphonse Esquiros affirms that each of us is the author and also the doer, so to speak, of his/her future destinies. Ignorant or degraded beings who have failed to bring forth their souls return to a woman's womb to put on a new body and fulfill a new earthly existence. Such reincarnation is done by virtue of a great law of balance, which brings all beings back to the exact punishment or reward for their works. These rebirths on Earth are limited and the purified soul will then live in higher worlds.

In his beautiful book, *Terre et Ciel*, Jean E. Reynaud gives a superb explanation of the necessity for successive lives occurring first on Earth and then in other worlds scattered in the infinite.

In spite of the absence of any memory of our past existences, we always come after ourselves, always carrying in ourselves the principle of what we will become later, and we always advance. Reynaud supposes that when we reach perfect life we will recover the integral memory of all our past, and this will be for us a grandiose spectacle, since it will encompass the whole course of our earthly knowledge. So to be born, it is not to start, but only to change one's bodily frame.[16]

Pelletan and Henri Martin were Reynaud's disciples.

If we accept, as the Druids already did, that the ascending evolution of the soul takes place in the infinite cosmos, the plurality of inhabited worlds becomes a logical consequence of the plurality of existences. This was clearly highlighted by my eminent friend Camille Flammarion in the middle of the 19th century. The following sums up his views on the subject:

> "If the intellectual world and the physical world form an absolute unity, and the set of sidereal humanities form a progressive series of thinking beings, from the lower intelligences below, just out of the infancy of matter, up to the divine, powerful entities that can contemplate God in Its glory, and understand Its sublimest works, everything is explained and all harmonizes. Earthly humanity finds its place in the lower levels of this vast hierarchy, and the unity of the divine plan is thus established."[17]

In 1857, Allan Kardec published *The Spirits' Book* in which he expounded all the philosophical reasons which led him to accept the theory of successive lives; and the dissemination of this great truth in countries such as France, Italy, Spain,

---

16 [Trans. note] See Jean REYNAUD, *Terre et Ciel* [*Earth and Heaven*] (Paris: Furne, 1854).

17 [Trans. note] C. *Flammarion, La Pluralité des Mondes Habités* [*Plurality of Inhabited Worlds*] (14th ed. Paris: Didier, 1869), livre v, p. 263.

Portugal, among other countries of this language group, is mainly due to his writings. I will come back later to the powerful arguments which he listed, and which should be able to convince any fair-minded individual. It is worth noting that the tenet of successive lives was popularized in the 19th century by the general public, by novelists such as Balzac, Théophile Gautier, George Sand, and by the great poet Victor Hugo.

An inquiry by Dr. Calderone

An inquiry conducted by Dr. Calderone,[18] director of the Italian periodical *Filosofia della Scienza* in 1915, proved that many thinkers and philosophers have adopted the magnificent theory of palingenesis (rebirth).

Dr. J. Maxwell, author of the book *Metapsychical Phenomena* (London, 1905) expressed himself in these terms:

> "To me the theory of reincarnation seems well worth accepting.... It explains Evolution and Heredity. It is imbued with morals. It is a source of energy and at the same time it helps the development of societies by the feeling it instills of a necessary hierarchy."

But J. Maxwell does not believe that it can be scientifically demonstrated. I will try to prove the opposite in the course of this book.

Dr. Moutin on his part admits the possibility of successive lives, but he conceives them as being accomplished on the far lands of heaven instead of being confined to Earth. Col. Rochas d'Aiglun believes in the evolution of human beings, and he honestly admits that his experiments with hypno-magnetic subjects to induce a regression of memory to previous lives did not yield any positive results. Nevertheless he believes in the principle of successive lives, as he

---

18 See the *Revue Scientifique et Morale du Spiritisme*, issues of August and September 1913.

admits the existence of God, by reasoning. Dr. Gustave Geley positively asserts it when he says:

> "Dear friend, you know that I am a reincarnationist, and have been so for three reasons: because the tenet of palingenesis seems to me perfectly satisfactory from a moral standpoint; absolutely rational from a philosophical standpoint; and from a scientific standpoint, likely, or better still, probably true."

Charles Lancelin, a magnetizer, in his response to the inquiry, affirms his belief in reincarnation, because he considers that subconsciousness is the result of all our previous consciousnesses.

Spiritist writer Léon Denis of course replied in the affirmative, especially since he claims to have obtained from mediums who were unknown to one another, consistent details of his past lives. Through introspection, he believes in the reality of these revelations, because they conform to his analytical study of his own character and psychic nature.

In Italy, Professor Tummolo is a strong advocate of the reincarnationist idea. Mr. Enrico Carreras admits that early stages of scientific evidence have already been obtained.

César de Vesme, director of the French journal *Annales des Sciences Psychiques*, remains undecided, but he is inclined to suppose that one day we will succeed in setting up experiments which will enable us to penetrate the mystery of our lives.

It is to the establishment of these early stages of scientific demonstration that this book is dedicated; and I hope it will not be deemed worthless in the building of a future science regarding the human soul.

In France, this is how we saw Paul Bodier's *La Villa du Silence*; *Réincarné*, by Dr. Lucien Graux; *Le Fils de Marousia*, of Mr. Gobron; *Un Mort Vivait parmi Nous*, of Jean Galmot, among other titles, appear almost immediately one after the other, all presenting the belief in rebirths through more or less likely fiction.

Palingenesis has sometimes inspired poets of the caliber of Théophile Gautier, Gerard de Nerval and Jean Lahor.[19] Here is a sample that clearly exemplifies Lahor's talents and beliefs:

"Just as deep inside the forests and chaste waterfalls
A pale moonbeam shimmers through gloom and darkness,
The memory of each of my past lives still lingers and calls,
Flickering within my heart as if doomed to forgetfulness."

"I feel a world in me of confused thought,
Somehow I feel that I have lived before,
Having wandered in forests with deep verdure inwrought,
While for love the brute in me still yearns ever more."

"During winter, when evening falls, I feel in a daze,
That once as animal or plant I suffered pain,
As Adonis lying in his grave, eyes in a glaze,
Whose heart revives when all turns green again."

"When my spirit longs for pure light,
A whole past keeps it chained and torn;
I feel the first darkness hold me tight,
Earth was so dark when I was born."

"My soul has slumbered for too long and stifled its flame;
I struggled to climb from night's womb into the light of day!
I would like to be pure, were it not for the original shame;
The old blood of the brute still runs in my veins today!"

However interesting and convincing they may be, these philosophical conceptions should now necessarily be submitted to objective criteria and analytical experimentation, in order to consider the great law of successive lives from a scientific perspective.

Hence, first and foremost, I will set forth the facts that irrefutably corroborate the existence of the soul – its true nature being so different from what religions and philosophies have taught us in this regard.

---

19 Sometimes spelled LAHORE; it was a pseudonym of French physician Henri CAZALIS.

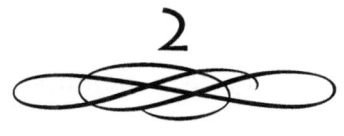

SCIENTIFIC BASES OF REINCARNATION · PROPERTIES OF THE PERISPIRIT

SPIRITISM SCIENTIFICALLY DEMONSTRATES THE EXISTENCE OF THE SOUL AND THE PERISPIRIT · IT IS INSEPARABLE FROM THE THINKING PRINCIPLE · DEMONSTRATION OF THIS GREAT TRUTH BY STUDYING THE MANIFESTATIONS OF THE SOUL DURING LIFE AND AFTER DEATH THE PERISPIRIT IS THE MATRIX FROM WHICH THE HUMAN BODY IS BUILT · IT MAINTAINS AND REPAIRS THE ORGANISM · IT CANNOT BE A PRODUCT OF MATTER · IT CARRIES ON WITH IT INTO THE SPIRITUAL WORLD THIS ORGANIZING FEATURE WHICH WOULD BE USELESS SHOULD IT NOT RETURN TO EARTH · WHERE COULD IT HAVE ACQUIRED SUCH PROPERTIES? · ON EARTH OBVIOUSLY · IT IS LOGICAL TO ADMIT THAT IT HAS PASSED THROUGH THE ANIMAL STAGES

THE GREAT MERIT of spiritualistic magnetists (starting with Mesmer) and Spiritists is to have attempted to move the study of the human soul from the realm of psychology into that of scientific observation, by studying objective manifestations of the thinking being. Throughout the 19th century, mainstream philosophy was confined to the field of introspection, systematically neglecting the facts, which were so numerous and interesting, involving extrasensory actions of the human being.

Yet thanks to the British Society for Psychic Research (SPR), it has now been established that telepathy is an indisputable reality, that clairvoyance,[20] whether during sleep or in the waking state, is very real, and finally that the prediction of the future has been repeatedly observed. These newly-known faculties belong to the soul and cannot

---

20 [Trans. note] Throughout this book, *clairvoyance* means *clear seeing* or *remote viewing*, and not the perception of things or events in the future.

be explained by any physiological property of the body. Such findings are of considerable importance, but these discoveries are all surpassed by that of the fluidic body of the soul which Spiritists call the *Perispirit*. The existence of a spiritual body had been suspected all the time, since the Hindus already called it the *Linga Sharira* (subtle body); the Hebrews, *Nephesh*; the Egyptians, *Ka* or *Bai*; the Greeks, *Ochema*; Pythagoras, the subtle chariot of the soul or *Eidolon*; the British philosopher Ralph Cudworth, the *Plastic Medium*; and among Occultists, the *Astral Body*.

This double of the body has been reported by trance mediums who saw it coming out of one's material body at the moment of death, or disengaging themselves when they were exteriorizing themselves in out-of-body experiences. It is this intermediary principle between spirit and matter which individualizes the soul, which enables it to preserve its consciousness and its memories after death, as well as during life. It also maintains one's body type, sustaining it and repairing it for the whole duration of a lifetime. Therefore, I will briefly recall the different kinds of proofs we possess to establish the reality of this suprasensible organism, still so unknown to current science.

APPARITIONS OF THE LIVING

I summarized, in the first volume of my book *Les Apparitions Matérialisées des Vivants et des Morts* [*Materialized Apparitions of the Living and the Dead*],[21] a number of authentic cases which demonstrate that, during life, the soul can come out of its physical body to show itself at a distance with a second body identical to the first, and, in some instances, temporarily retaining the same properties. It is no longer a question of more or less questionable theories: this is Nature itself speaking. Among a hundred other proofs, let me quote

---

21 G. DELANNE, *Les Apparitions Matérialisées des Vivants et des Morts* (Paris: Librairie Spirite, 1909), tome I, p. 266.

one reported by the illustrious British journalist William Stead: for more than an hour he saw the materialized double of one of his friends who, at the time, was actually lying, away in her bedroom.

The doppelganger was strong enough to push a door, hold a book, and walk. The fluidic double was so identical to the fleshly body that the sitters did not suspect that they were in presence of the materialized apparition of a living person.

There are many other similar cases, and one cannot but call the attention of researchers to these spontaneous manifestations. Here no medium was needed. It is in one's own organism that the spirit found sufficient strength to give to its spiritual body the appearance of matter. Now, to walk, to hold a book, the phantom must be well organized. It is essential that it is equipped with an extra-physiological apparatus which plays the same role as the physical limbs. The lady in Stead's account, with her phantom hand, held a book offered to her, exactly as she would with her ordinary hand – this is a fact, not a hypothesis.

Likewise,[22] when the phantom of a passenger wrote on a blackboard the directions which were to save the ship in distress on which his physical body was asleep, he was still acting as he would have done to write in normal life; that is, he had a grasping organ that allowed him to hold the chalk. He directed the movements of the chalk by conveying upon it the different movements necessary to produce the drawing of a graphic. In a word, there was a real duplication of the physical body, and it must have extended to the smallest details of his anatomical constitution, since the acts he performed were the same. I will also recall that Mrs. Annie Eva Fay's double,[23] in the famous Crookes and Varley experiment, appeared between the curtains of a cabinet, also holding a book in her hand that she gave to one of the sitters, while all the time, her body of flesh and bone, in lethargy,

---

22 *Op. cit.*, tome I, p. 275.
23 *Op. cit.*, tome I, p. 400.

was traversed by an electric current which ensured that she kept still and had never moved.

The deduction immediately imposes itself upon us that there exists in each of us a second body, identically similar to the first, and which can separate from it momentarily replace it, in order to allow the exteriorized soul to come into contact with the outside world. When referring to the bilocation case of Alfonso de Liguori, who attended Pope Clement XIV during his last moments in Rome, while his servants noticed the same day that the venerable prelate remained asleep far away, in his cell of Arienzo, an Italian town and commune near Naples, Joseph-Pierre Durand, a physician of high philosophical caliber, wrote the following:[24]

> "If the fact in question and the facts or so-called similar facts which are daily described in publications of scientific telepathy are verified and proved; if, in a word, we are forced to admit them, whatever it costs us; well, to me a consequence seems to derive thereof with the most limpid and irresistible evidence, namely, that one's apparent physical nature is associated to an occult physical nature which is functionally equivalent to it, although of a quite different constitution. It is that the living organism that we see, and anatomists dissect, also has a double (that is, if it itself is not instead the double of the other one), an occult organism which neither the scalpel nor the microscope can reach, and which for that purpose is none the less provided – better than the other perhaps – with all the organs necessary for the double effect, which is the whole raison d'être of one's vital organization, of collecting and transmitting to consciousness impressions from without, and allowing one's psychic activeness to act upon the surrounding world and modify it in turn."

The above is, in a pithy form, an inescapable conclusion to which one cannot raise any objection.

---

[24] J. P. DURAND, *Le Merveilleux Scientifique* (Paris: Félix Alcan, 1894), p. 61.

Indeed, in his latest book, *De l'Inconscient au Conscient* [*From the Unconscious to the Conscious*], Dr. Gustave Geley has also arrived at the following conclusions, after pointing out all the obscurities found in mainstream physiological teaching:[25]

> "It is necessary and sufficient, indeed, to understand everything, the mystery of the specific form, the embryonic and postembryonic development, the constitution and maintenance of the personality, the organic repairs and all the other general problems of biology, to admit a notion – not new, certainly, but envisaged in a new way – of *a dynamism superior to the organism which is actually conditioned by it*."[26]
> "This is not just the guiding idea as proposed by Claude Bernard, a sort of abstraction, an incomprehensible metaphysical-biological entity. It is rather a concrete notion, that of a controlling and centralizing dynamism, dominating intrinsic contingencies, the chemical reactions of the organic milieu as well as the ambient influences of the external environment."

Allan Kardec, many decades ago, already taught this duplication of the organism, which we verify today with all the luxury of precautions required by the scientific method. If, indeed, the scalpel and the microscope are powerless to reveal the existence of the perispirit, photography, on the one hand, is able to detect the presence of the exteriorized phantom of a living person, even when invisible to the eye, as we have perfectly authentic examples; just as we have, on the other hand, the experiments conducted by Col. Rochas d'Aiglun let us witness the exteriorization of the subject's sensibility and motricity. Such objective phenomena fortunately brought into play scientific experimentation in a field that seemed reserved exclusively for observation, while at the same time, removing any shadow of uncertainty as

---

25 G. GELEY, *De l'Inconscient au Conscient* (Paris: Félix Alcan,, 1919), p. 51.
26 See my book, *Évolution Animique* (Paris: Chamuel, 1897), in which I ascribe to the perispirit this psychodynamic mechanism.

to their true cause. In all cases, it is the human soul, and it alone, which intervenes, because, when one wants to replicate the experiment, one can choose the place, the time, and the conditions; and the subject who acts can sometimes even remember what happened while he/she was seeing it from a distance. The subject has the feeling of being transported to the very spot where he/she was visible; and they are not mistaken, for they can accurately describe the unknown things that were at the places he/she visited abnormally.

Better still, in sittings with the Italian sensitive Eusapia, for example, we observe a synchronism between the physical movements of the fleshly body and those of the fluidic body: the physical and physiological effort has been transported at a distance, and there remain objective traces of this extracorporeal action. These are displaced furniture, pressure exerted on recording gages and, above all, the precious result of imprints and casting molds that make it possible to realize, by sight, the nature of the acting cause.[27]

In presence of such observations the complete inanity of Catholic, Occultist, and Theosophical theories involving foreign beings for the explanation of such phenomena become even more evident. When Mr. Siemiradsky finds that the imprints left on lampblack by the fluidic hand – that one has felt or that one saw operating – are identical to the skin patterns of Eusapia's hand, one must have a wild imagination and a total lack of scientific spirit, to imagine that it is a demon that had fun in this little trick. Similarly, when one gets a hollow mold of her face in clay, as I myself[28] have seen, there is no need for infernal cohorts for an explanation. There is no miracle, no foreign intervention, but only the action

---

[27] For corroboration, see Professor Botazzi's experiments, in volume I of my book *Les Apparitions Matérialisées des Vivants et des Morts*. See also the work of Dr. W. J. Crawford published in *Revue Métapsychique*, no. 4, year 1921.

[28] G. Delanne, *Les Apparitions Matérialisées des Vivants et des Morts* (Paris: Librairie Spirite, 1909) tome I, p. 452 *et seq.*

of the fluidic body, of which these phenomena demonstrate the existence with overwhelming force.

If one really seeks the truth, away from any preconceived idea, it is necessary to follow the facts step by step and not to multiply the causes without necessity. When one finds in the human being sufficient reason for a phenomenon, it is unscientific to try to interpret them by extraneous causes – especially when these are purely hypothetical – as is the case of demons, angels, larvae, astral shells, elementals, among other entities hitherto imaginary.

It follows directly from observation and experimentation that the human individual is able, in special circumstances, to separate into two parts: on the one hand, we see the physical body, generally inert, immersed in deep sleep; on the other, a second body, an absolute duplicate of the first, which acts intelligently far away, leading any observer to infer that intelligence accompanies the double and that it is not a mere virtual image, an effigy without consciousness.

Apparitions of the deceased

What is most remarkable is that the duplication is observed in perfectly alive persons as well in those who are about to die, or finally those who deceased, having disappeared from our objective world a long or a short time ago. The phantoms of the dead are as numerous as those of the living. They have exactly the same outward appearances and often the same objective reality as the doubles of material life, which logically lead us to ascribe to them the same cause: the human soul; from which an important fact categorically derives, namely, that death does not annihilate it. It is a proof of survival that is revealed to us by our observation of natural phenomena; and each day that goes by increases the enormous mass of reported cases that we already have.

There exist in the Proceedings of the Society for Psychical Research (SPR) two memoirs on the apparitions of the dead, one by Edmund Gurney completed by F. W. H. Myers, and another by Mrs. Sidgwick, in which it is possible to examine all kinds of apparitions.

There are telepathic hallucinations proper, those which the seeing individual himself/herself fabricates; then, also, there are clairvoyant visions; and finally collective apparitions, as is the case with the phantoms of the living. We know that one can obtain, through experiments, the same series of phenomena between two living operators, one of whom, without warning the other, acts on himself/herself to appear to the latter.[29] Here there can be no doubt as to the cause of the phenomenon: it is the agent,[30] and the agent alone, that is the author of the apparition for which he/she has fixed the day and the hour at his/her pleasure. Sometimes the agent could recollect his/her displacement, and was able to specify the details of what he/she observed while the percipient was seeing the fluidic double.

After death – I repeat it again and again – absolutely similar facts take place.[31] The apparitions of the dead have characteristics identical to those of the phantoms of the living, and if it is really the human soul that produces them, then the most legitimate induction would be to ascribe the phantoms of the dead to the same cause, that is to say, to the soul which bodily death has not destroyed. It continues its life and still has a substantiality that perpetuates its earthly type. Hallucination must be excluded for explaining when the vision of a deceased person, when one of the following characteristics is present:

1) The phantom, if known to the percipient, shows through particular marks or features unknown to the seeing

---

29 *Op. cit.*, tome I, ch. v, "Essai d'apparitions volontaires," p. 199.

30 We call *agent* the person whose phantom is seen, while the *percipient* is the person who experiences the vision.

31 See the three volumes of C. FLAMMARION, *Death and Its Mystery – Before Death*; "– At the Moment of Death"; "– After Death" (Trans. E. S. Brooks, L. Carroll. London and New York: T. Fisher Unwin Ltd., The Century Co., 1922–1923),

subject, that it looked so during his/her lifetime (wounds, scars, special clothing, etc.). It is obvious that if a vision is merely clairvoyant, it is necessary for the one who produces it to be present there, otherwise it would never take place.

2) The apparition is that of a person the percipient has never seen before; however, his/her description of the phantom is sufficiently precise to establish its identity. It would be absurd to attribute to chance the fairly faithful reconstruction of an individual so that it can be recognized. The individual's personality must therefore be present, it is not a mere image, as some colorful cliché, because such manifestations show an intentional character that is indicative of an intelligence at work.

3) The apparition gives information whose accuracy is later corroborated, or it narrates a real fact *totally unknown to the percipient*.

4) Photographs of the apparitions were accidentally or voluntarily obtained.

5) Several witnesses have successively or simultaneously witnessed and been affected by the manifestation of the materialized being.

6) Last but not least, both animals or pets and humans have collectively perceived the apparition.

All these facts are inexplicable except by the direct action of a discarnate being. Telepathy between the living, or delayed telepathy, does not apply to these phenomena, which are direct demonstrations of the self's immortality.

As a result, relations between the living and the dead are natural facts occurring spontaneously when physical and intellectual circumstances allow. There is no supernatural nor amazing nor miraculous intervention: it is only an *animistic*[32] phenomenon, of the same kind as that which takes place among the living. If the exteriorization of the subject proves

---

[32] [Trans. note] In Spiritism *animistic* (from *animism*) specifically refers to a phenomenon or action coming from one's own soul itself, as opposed to a *mediumistic* one, which should come from a discarnate spirit.

the existence of the perispirit during life – and photographs and imprints of the double do not leave any doubt about it – the same facts obtained after the death of the operating agent establish with the same force the persistence of the perispirit.

This is the tangible evidence that observation has brought. Let us not forget that it such experiments were made by very demanding and meticulous scholars when it comes to the choice of testimonies, who discuss the tiniest details and include in their collection only stories that seem absolutely flawless. It is conceivable then that someone such as Dr. Joseph-Pierre Durand could have written again on this subject:[33]

> "If the distinct and independent existence of an occult physique and physiology, besides the physique and physiology such as we know them, may logically intervene in scenes of active telepathy, in which the actors are living, then this is a peremptory material demonstration furnished by telepathic actions which, in spite of the intense dismay of science and the outrage of philosophical prejudice, our reason is constrained and forced to attribute to the dead. For if on the other hand, someone would still imagine, in desperation, some other cause to the telepathic miracle, I do not know what new property of the brain cell could possibly exist to produce all the phantasmagoria of telepathy without the help of any organ whatsoever or any apparent vehicle. This is the plank of salvation to which our rationalism is no longer able to hold on; especially when the human brain, which could at least save appearances, turns out to be no more than a disorganized and putrefied pulp, or even just a handful of dust lying in an empty skeleton skull."

God is my witness that Spiritists have affirmed practically the same thing for over half a century, and that it is not of slight advantage to be in accordance with such a scientific mind as that of Joseph-Pierre Durand, one of the fathers of

---

[33] J. P. DURAND, *Le Merveilleux Scientifique* (Paris: Félix Alcan, 1894), p. 61.

hypnotism and a leading physiologist. Let me now resume the quoted excerpt:

> "And it is precisely that which the Society for Psychical Research, in London, and the editorial staff of the *Annales Psychiques*, in Paris, commanded by Professor Charles Richet, have found, after organizing a vast investigation on the phantoms of living persons, also known as phantasms of the living. They found that phantoms of this class, the only ones scientifically admitted at first, proved to be pitifully rare,[34] whereas, on the other hand, it was by legion that phantoms of the dead came out of that investigation. And that is not all, such phantoms of the other world, which have no brain, and, consequently, no brain cells, present themselves with a singularly paradoxical oddity, somehow being the most alive of all, because they are, to say the least, the noisiest and most restless phantoms; and it is no wonder that they are in charge of doing things such as these: jostling furniture, forcing doors open, breaking dishes, breaking tiles, hitting and hurting people, to the great and natural despair of the tenants and owners."[35]

One cannot escape the facts which, once meticulously analyzed, place us in presence of posthumous beings which have a psychical body, since this latter can act upon matter. However, it was necessary to be able to examine more closely these phantoms to know their nature, because natural apparitions are too fleeting, or occur under circumstances which are so exciting for witnesses that it is difficult for them to preserve sufficient composure to carefully note all features and details.

---

[34] There is some exaggeration here, since the phantoms of the living are as numerous as those of the dead. See on this subject the three volumes of C. FLAMMARION, *Death and Its Mystery*.

[35] See C. FLAMMARION, *Haunted Houses* (New York: Appleton & Co., 1924); and C. LOMBROSO, "Haunted Houses," in *The Annals of Psychical Science*, April–June 1909, p. 187.

Induced apparitions

Spiritists were the first to organize experimental seances in specific places, on selected days, and surrounded by the necessary precautions so as to successfully observe apparitions. From the day when it became known that mediums could be used for materialization, a vast inquiry was organized, which was successful in more than one way.

Do not think that induced apparitions were accepted from the outset by all experimenters. Even among Spiritists, furious polemics started between those convinced and skeptical ones. All the suppositions that still persist today addressed issues such as these: Is it credible that a spirit, that is to say, a being whose essence is immaterial, would take on a coarse fleshly body? Where would the spirit have picked it up? Why did it appear wearing draperies and sometimes – horror of horrors – with a frock coat or hat? Was it not proof that the sitters were either hallucinated or shamefully deceived by impostors? These objections, and many others, did not detain the researchers. Precautions against fraud were innumerable. Sometimes the medium was tied up in his/her chair, which was fastened to the floor with the ends of the rope being held outside the cabinet by one of the sitters. At other times, the subject was inserted in a bag carefully closed around the neck by a braid, to which knots were attached, and these were then sealed. Other times still the medium was locked up in a cage and, despite everything, the apparitions circumvented the shackles which were supposed to retain them. Some experimenters even went to the extreme of nailing sensitive Florence Cook's hair to the floor. In the end, people realized that, with real mediums, all these measures were perfectly useless; the beings that appeared and disappeared before the audience, or melted before their very eyes, have enough power to play with our precautions, because very often they released the medium from those bonds, without a single knot being undone,[36] and without any possibility of anyone finding out how they did it.

Those willing to take the trouble to examine the rich annals of Spiritism will be able to convince themselves that, under other names, all the current hypotheses and theories were discussed by those pioneering researchers. At first the trance imagination of the medium was used, with the temporary creations which were shown to the sitters being ascribed to it. It was a suggestion that the subject (the agent) sent up to those who, after a long wait in the darkened place, were predisposed to such hallucinations. Incidentally, Franz Hartmann did not have the primeurs of this invention. However, this hypothesis had to be modified when it became certain that the phantoms were objectively real. Then it was pretended that everything was perfectly understood and explainable as an exteriorization of the double, and by its transfigurations. The mediums supposedly drew from the subconsciousness of the sitters the types on which they modeled their fluidic bodies, in order to give them the appearance of one or more deceased persons known to some person among the participants. This is where modern scholars who have not studied these phenomena enough stand today; notice, for example, how Professor Charles Richet in his latest book, *Traité de Métapsychique* (Paris, 1922), baptizes the phantom "ectoplasm," which is merely a phenomenon of ideoplasty of matter exteriorized by a medium.

Esopsychism, Ideoplasty, Psychodynamism, Panpsychism, etc., are only different denominations for the same thing. Despite the ingenuity of their intellectual acrobatics, these theories are far from sufficient to explain all cases. It sometimes happens that the apparition expresses itself or writes in a language unknown to the medium and to the sitters – and here is the shipwreck of *esopsychism* as a theory. In other

---

36 See *Revue Métapsychique*, November–December 1922, p. 362.

circumstances, there are two, three, four phantoms talking and moving at the same time, or giving a concert where each one holds its part – so here, one must say goodbye to *ideoplasty*, unless arbitrarily endowing it with miraculous powers. Finally, certain identities have unmistakably established their independence as beings, as it has occurred in cases of spontaneous apparitions.

The fact that official, mainstream science advances with the greatest circumspection in such little explored territory seems fair enough; after all, it is science's duty not to venture out until it has exhausted all natural (or so-called natural) possibilities before admitting such an unforeseen cause. But its representatives show bad grace in passing judgment too categorically before having sufficient experience. We, Spiritists, who have preceded them a great deal, have the right, on the basis of our past, to be astonished at their haughtiness, to reproach them for their ignorance of results previously obtained, to tell them that their interpretations are erroneous; and they will eventually recognize it when they have acquired more experience. I know that progress is only made in stages, that it takes a long time for public opinion to get used to novelties, so it is without impatience that I await the arrival of new spirit mediums, with which we can continue these exciting discoveries. Since the phenomena are real and have already occurred everywhere, it is certain that we will see them again; and that we shall triumph one day, because truth always prevails.

As we shall see in a moment, nowadays this is already happening.

Now, coming back to the main subject of the present study, it could be seen by means of spirit photography (obtained by Crookes, Aksakov, and celebrated chemist Boutlerow, among others), that phantoms have real forms; that during the materialization, they possess all the characteristics of living beings like body size, volume, etc.; their limbs, both arms and legs, are identical to ours. They can walk, talk, write.

When one takes their hand, it produces the impression of an ordinary human hand. But this was not yet enough to study the differences between the medium and the apparition. It was necessary to be able to see the latter often enough, and in fairly good conditions, to note the peculiarities which make it an individuality distinct from that of the medium. The Crookes experiments – to cite just one authentic example – meet all these requirements.

I recall the famous scientist's own words. William Crookes operated at his home, within locked doors.[37]

> "Before concluding this article I wish to give some of the points of difference which I have observed between Miss Cook and Katie. Katie's height varies ; in my house I have seen her six inches taller than Miss Cook. Last night, with bare feet and not 'tip-toeing,' she was four and a half inches taller than Miss Cook. Katie's neck was bare last night ; the skin was perfectly smooth both to touch and sight, whilst on Miss Cook's neck is a large blister, which under similar circumstances is distinctly visible and rough to the touch. Katie's ears are unpierced, whilst Miss Cook habitually wears earrings. Katie's complexion is very fair, while that of Miss Cook is very dark. Katie's fingers are much longer than Miss Cook's, and her face is also larger. In manners and ways of expression there are also many decided differences."[38]

To appreciate the value of such differences, it is good to remember that in the hundreds of cases of duplication of the living that have been verified, always and everywhere it has been observed that being which is exteriorized is a perfect reproduction of the agent's physical body. It is a rule which, to my knowledge at least, does not suffer from any exception. When one gets imprints or casts of a double of the living, either with sensitives Eglinton or

---

37 G. DELANNE, *Les Apparitions Matérialisées des Vivants et des Morts* (Paris: Librairie Spirite, 1911), tome II, p. 493.

38 [Trans. note] W. CROOKES, *Researches in the Phenomena of Spiritualism* (London: J. Burns, 1974), "Spirit forms," p. 107.

Eusapia, it is an exact anatomical copy of the real body that the molding shows. The tiniest details of the fluidic limb are visible. The protrusions produced by the muscles, veins or bones, the epidermic patterns, all come as if one had operated on a fleshly subject. Therefore, scientifically, because of the discrepancies reported, one is not allowed to see in Katie's phantom the double of Miss Cook, and until proven otherwise, I am inclined to believe that they are two separate individuals.

Here are some other differences. In terms of size, Crookes was able to ensure, through an ingenious process, that his previous appreciations were accurate, by operating as follows:

> One of the most interesting of the pictures is one in which I am standing by the side of Katie ; she has her bare foot upon a particular part of the floor. Afterwards I dressed Miss Cook like Katie, placed her and myself in exactly the same position, and we were photographed by the same cameras, placed exactly as in the other experiment, and illuminated by the same light. When these two pictures are placed over each other, the two photographs of myself coincide exactly as regards stature, etc., *but Katie is half a head taller than Miss Cook, and looks a big woman in comparison with her.* In the breadth of her face, in many of the pictures, she differs essentially in size from her medium, and the photographs show several other points of difference." (My emphasis.)
>
> "But photography is as inadequate to depict the perfect beauty of Katie's face, as words are powerless to describe her charms of manner. Photography may, indeed, give a map of her countenance; but how can it reproduce the brilliant purity of her complexion, or the ever-varying expression of her most mobile features, now overshadowed with sadness when relating some of the bitter experiences of her past life, now smiling with all the innocence of happy girlhood when she had collected my children round her, and was amusing them *by recounting anecdotes of her adventures in India?"* [39] (My emphasis.)

---

39 [Trans. note] *Op. cit.*, "The last of Katie King," pp. 109–110.

The apparition thus asserts that she lived before, since she is dead now; in a word, that she is a spirit. Why doubt her word?

Nonsense! – some skeptics like Mr. T. Flournoy would say – do not trust appearances. Katie may very well be only a subconscious character created by Miss Cook, a split personality, an ideal type that the latter creates and exteriorizes by transfiguring her double. Really, with all due respect, when it comes to Spiritist manifestations, it seems that the best critics lose the plot completely. It must first be established that the transfiguration is a phenomenon resulting from the will of the medium, by the way, something that has never been proven. From the fact that the mind is able to act upon the psychical force to give it the appearance of reality, it does not at all result that it is able to modify itself. A sculptor can model clay at will clay to shape semblances of humans or animals, but would be completely hopeless if trying to use this faculty to change the shape of his/her own nose. It is therefore an unjustifiable objection made by those who see in the medium merely the author, conscious or not, of the apparition. This interpretation reveals its whimsical character when one examines the issue more thoroughly. It would be necessary to endow the medium with an unparalleled creative power, with a truly miraculous spontaneous generating power, to instantly produce an individual who differs so deeply from the medium from a physiological standpoint. Here is some additional evidence, always borrowed from Crookes:[40]

> "Having seen so much of Katie lately, when she has been illuminated by the electric light, I am enabled to add to the points of difference between her and her medium which I mentioned in a former article. *I have the most absolute certainty* that Miss Cook and Katie are two separate individuals so far as their bodies are concerned. Several little marks on Miss Cook's face are absent on Katie's. Miss Cook's hair is

---

40 [Trans. note] *Op. cit.*, "The last of Katie King," p. 110.

so dark a brown as almost to appear black; a lock of Katie's *which is now before me*, and which she allowed me to cut from her luxuriant tresses, *having first traced it up to the scalp and satisfied myself that it actually grew there*, is a rich golden auburn."[41] (My emphasis.)

The above would already suffice, were it not for an even better description:

"On one evening I timed Katie's pulse. It beat steadily at 75, whilst Miss Cook's pulse a little time after, was going at its usual rate of 90. On applying my ear to Katie's chest I could hear a heart beating rhythmically inside, and pulsating even more steadily than did Miss Cook's heart when she allowed me to try a similar experiment after the seance. Tested in the same way Katie's lungs were found to be sounder than her medium's, for at the time I tried my experiment Miss Cook was under medical treatment for a severe cough."[42]

However improbable these phenomena may appear, they are nevertheless real, for, Professor Charles Richet, after having himself observed identical phenomena to those described by William Crookes, was compelled to write *fifty years on*, in spite of his instinctive repugnance for the subject:[43]

"Spiritualists have blamed me for using this word 'absurd'; and have not been able to understand that to admit the reality of these phenomena was to me an actual pain ; but to ask a physiologist, a physicist, or a chemist to admit that a form that has a circulation of blood, warmth, and muscles, that exhales carbonic arid, has weight, speaks, and thinks, can issue from a human body is to ask of him an intellectual effort that is really painful. *Yes, it is absurd ; but no matter —— it is true.*" (My emphasis)

---

41 C. RICHET too was able to cut and preserve the hair of an apparition. See his book *Traité de Métapsychique*, p. 649.

42 [Trans. note] *Op. cit.*, "The last of Katie King," p. 110–111.

43 Richet was able, too, to cut and preserve a lock of hair of an apparition See C. RICHET, *Thirty Years of Psychical Research* (Trans. S. de Brath. New York: Macmillan, 1923), ch. III, pp. 476 and 544.

Now, coming back to William Crookes: the apparition has a heart and lungs! These have a physiological mechanism which differs from that of the medium, Miss Cook; and without making any suppositions, the following must be naturally deduced: those were two different organisms, since, at the same moment, one was healthy and the other ill.

I ask in all sincerity, where is the true scientific spirit? Is it with those who forge the most outlandish hypotheses, or with those who never go beyond what the most rigorous observation allows them to see? It seems to me that the answer to this question leaves no doubt. It is a thousand times more unlikely to imagine that Katie is a creation of Miss Cook than to believe that she is what she says herself, in other words, a spirit. I myself once found, in presence of Professor Charles Richet, that the phantom of Bien-Boa exhaled carbonic acid, since, by blowing into a balloon containing a solution of barite, it produced under our very noses and eyes a precipitation of carbonate of baryta.

If further proofs of the phantom's independence were needed, they would be found in the conversations that the medium Florence Cook had with the spirit Katie during the last days of her mediumship, and the day of the last seance. Unless you support obvious absurdities such as, for example: one can be simultaneously conscious and unconscious and simultaneously in one's own body and in another, with completely different ideas and a personality antagonistic to one's own. The end of Crookes's report demonstrates with the most powerful evidence that Katie was an individuality distinct from the medium and sitters. Listen to the moving story of the last conversation between the spirit and the medium:

> "Having concluded her directions, Katie invited me into the cabinet with her, and allowed me to remain there to the end. After closing the curtain she conversed with me for some time, and then walked across the room to where Miss Cook was lying senseless on the floor. Stooping over

her, Katie touched her, and said, "Wake up, Florrie, wake up! I must leave you now." Miss Cook then woke and tearfully entreated Katie to stay a little time longer. "My dear, I can't; my work is done. God bless you," Katie replied, and then continued speaking to Miss Cook. For several minutes the two were conversing with each other, till at last Miss Cook's tears prevented her speaking. Following Katie's instructions I then came forward to support Miss Cook, who was falling on to the floor, sobbing hysterically. I looked round, but the white-robed Katie had gone. As soon as Miss Cook was sufficiently calmed, a light was procured and I led her out of the cabinet."[44]

Let us not forget that it is a respected member of the British Royal Society, and one of the greatest scientists and scholars of our age, who is affirming such things. If I chose to quote William Crookes right away, it is because I did not have to fight beforehand to establish the authenticity of his testimony. Yet there are many others who, in their own way, are also as conclusive. Lack of space prevents me from including in this study all the developments it entails, however I again refer the reader to volume II of my book *Les Apparitions Matérialisées des Vivants et des Morts* [*Materialized Apparitions of the Living and the Dead*], where many experiments from all corners of the world are thoroughly narrated and commented. As we can see above, the materialized apparitions of spirits of the dead are autonomous beings which have a heart, a brain, lungs, muscles, nerves, and an intelligence separate and independent from those of the medium; and which, albeit disincarnate, still possess an *earthly* physiological mechanism.

This is where Spiritist experiments have proved to be so valuable. Spontaneous apparitions, as I have already said, are generally fleeting and occur under conditions that are too charged with emotion to warrant a detailed observation by witnesses. Conversely, in materialization seances organized

---

44 [Trans. note] W. Crookes, *Researches in the Phenomena of Spiritualism* (London: J. Burns, 1974), "The Last of Katie King," p. 111.

within a homogeneous group and counting on a good medium, it is possible to properly see the apparition. We can, as Crookes, Aksakov, Charles Richet and I myself did, photograph the same phantom to which we have just talked, which gives you indisputable proof of its real presence. Better still, it is possible to obtain casting molds of hands, feet, and faces, such as those obtained by Reimers, Oxley, Ashead, Ashton, Prof. W. Denton, Epes Sargent and more recently, in 1921, at the International Metapsychic Institute of Paris, all taking the most severe measures for scientific control.

These casts indisputably have established the absolute objective reality of the fleeting phantoms. These are absolute proofs, and it is interesting to note that quite recently I was able to obtain some in Paris.[45]

Here are some details about these recent experiments.

Experiments held at the International Metapsychic Institute[46]

In 1920, at the International Metapsychic Institute of Paris, with Franek Kluski, a nonprofessional and completely unselfish medium, a series of quite conclusive experiments took place.

Among various manifestations and other phenomena, a perfectly recognizable materialization of the late sister of Count J. Potocki occurred.

But it became even more interesting when one obtained molds of limbs materialized under conditions of control which exclude any idea of fraud or deceit. The experiments were under the control of Professor Charles Richet; the Count de Grammont, member of the Academy of Sciences; and Dr. Gustave Geley.

---

45 [Trans. note] G. Delanne was a scientifically qualified experimenter.
46 Founded by Mr. Jean Meyer and recognized as being of public utility; located at 89, Niel Avenue, Paris.

There was constant light throughout the seances and the hands of the medium were held continuously, right and left, by controllers who were also watching without interruption the position of the medium's legs and feet.

The molds were of varied nature. Here are some highlights of the specimens obtained: a child's foot casting mold admirably sharp in its contours, going to the top of the torso; another one shows the lower region of an adult's face in which one distinguishes the upper lip, the lower lip, the underlying fossa and a bearded chin, with something like a wart on the left of the lower lip.[47]

To make sure that it was indeed with his own paraffin that the casts were produced, unbeknownst to anyone, Dr. Geley had dissolved cholesterin in it – by taking a little of the paraffin so prepared, borrowing it from a mold, and dissolving it in chloroform with sulfuric acid added, a red precipitate was produced which ordinary paraffin does not yield. For the sake of precaution, Dr. Geley had colored this paraffin again in blue. Here is what happened:[48]

> "The blue dye, having been placed in excess and not entirely dissolved, formed lumps disseminated here and there in the vessel, above the paraffin. Now, in the mold of the foot, at the level of the third toe, one of these lumps is present, incorporated in the paraffin which has solidified over it. It has the size of a big glass pinhead and is dark blue. The lumps are identical to those remaining in the container. It was therefore driven by the ectoplasm stirring paraffin and incorporated into the mold."

> "This evidence, unforeseen and not sought, is very convincing. Finally, immediately after the seance, I took some small fragments on the edges of the foot mold. I put them in a test tube and dissolved them in chloroform. Then I added sulfuric acid: the red tint, characteristic of the presence of

---

47 This casting mold is closer to those obtained of Lilly and Akosa, whose photographs are found in my book *Les Apparitions Matérialisées des Vivants et des Morts*.

48 See *Revue Métapsychique*, no. 5, 1921, p. 226–271.

cholesterin, grew, increased and gradually faded. A comparison test made with pure paraffin was negative. The liquid remained colorless; the slightly yellowish hue of the sulfuric acid (yellowish by oxidation of the cork closing the bottle) was in no way modified."

"The proof is absolute: all molds were made with our paraffin and during the seance. We can affirm this categorically by relying not only on the experimental modalities, the precautions taken and the testimony of our senses, but also on the presence of the blue tint, identical in the molds and the container; on the accidental incorporation of a lump of blue color in the mold of the foot; and finally on the chemical reaction detecting the presence of cholesterin. The weigh is also concordant."

For the record, two casting molds of hands were obtained in the sitting of November 8th, 1920 (1st seance), two others in the sitting of November 11th (2nd seance), only one on November 15th (5th seance), two on December 27th (10th seance), and two on December 31st (11th and last seance).

Such molds could not possibly be produced by fraudulent means, for the following reasons:

1) A soft rubber glove filled with air would present deformations in the final result.

2) If instead the rubber was hard, it could not come out of the paraffin casting without breaking it or deforming it, which by the way never occurred.

3) As for the hypothesis of using an artificial hand made of a human limb, by means of a fusible material such as sugar, for example, although it could have melted into the water leaving a paraffin mold behind. But then the total weight of paraffin water would have been greater than the original weight, and the deception would have been promptly discovered.

Therefore it is well established that the materializations have been forced to volatilize in order to leave the mold intact, as they did, of a part of the phantoms.

Moreover, here is the report of the experts Gabrielli (father and son), who proves beyond a shadow of a doubt the incontestable authenticity of the molds obtained at the Metapsychic Institute.

Report by Mr. Gabrielli

"I, the undersigned, Charles Gabrielli, expert molder, resident at 6, Cheroy Street, Paris, hereby certify that, having appraised paraffin molds filled with plaster which had been entrusted to me for this purpose by Dr. Geley, Director of the Institut Métapsychique International [Metapsychic Institute] ..."

(Followed by a detailed description of the molds.)

"After a quick inspection in Dr. Geley's laboratory, we took these pieces to our workshop for further study. We were immediately struck by the following three details:

1st) The operation of pouring the plaster into the paraffin molds reveals technical faults which prove objectively, apart from any other considerations, the lack of professional competence on the part of the operator, at the same time as his good faith. For example, in document No. 1, the ends of the fingers remained full of air, which is clearly visible by transparency. The plaster could not reach these ends. This defect, which an experienced moulder had very easily avoided, is the formal proof that the plaster has been cast into the molds, and that the piece is not a plaster mold which has been plunged into melted paraffin. Moreover, the plaster did not completely fill the paraffin molds. On the paraffin wax plots that overflow plaster, we find the impression of anatomical details of which we will speak later. So no doubt about how the documents submitted for our examination were obtained; these are definitely paraffin molds that have been filled with plaster.

2nd) The second detail noticed by us is that of the extreme thinness of the paraffin layer constituting the molds. The walls are nowhere over one millimeter in thickness. They have the thinness of a sheet of paper. This thinness is such that we can see through the paraffin layer, over the underlying plaster, all the anatomical details, folds of the skin, furrows, lines, and nails.

3rd) The third remark is the lifelike finesse of the anatomical details. We positively feel life beneath these strange and disappointing molds. Evidence shows that those are, obviously, *living hands* that have been used for these molds

We find not only all the anatomical details, but also traces of muscular contractions that can be explained only by voluntary movements. There are wrinkles on the skin that leave no doubt about it.

After this first examination, we proceeded to the demolding by using a jet of steam which allowed us to remove the paraffin, scales by scales, without altering the underlying plaster. We found on the plaster all the details perceived through the paraffin layer. From our careful and lengthy inspection, we are able to conclude as follows:

Casting molds so perfect, with such fine details, with signs of active muscular contractions, and skin folds, could only have been obtained on a living hand.

These are original, firsthand casts, and not overmoldings. We have then investigated how it would be possible to obtain, by the most diverse processes, moldings analogous to those which we had just examined. We have specially studied the two methods indicated by Dr. Geley, in the *Revue Métapsychique*, No. 5.

1st) The method of demolding by section of a part of paraffin molds and joints, after the exit of the operating hand, had certainly never been used in the parts that we have examined.

a) Indeed, we did not note any traces of welds, scrapings, or any of the inevitable deformations typical of this process. There are no fittings in the gloves that Dr. Geley has submitted to us. There are here and there breaks or collapse, in places, of the molding gloves – breaks and sags explained by the extreme fragility of these gloves – but there is nothing that looks like a joint, or which could be confused with a joint.

b) In any case, the operation of demolding a living hand would not have been possible with such thin gloves. These molding gloves would have been infallibly broken at the slightest attempt of removal. This is something that can be easily assured by anyone. The exit of a living hand from a paraffin mold having a thickness of less than a millimeter is an impossibility.

c) Even with thick molds, the demolding of a living hand from some of the pieces we examined, even after the base section, would have been impossible; this was the case of pieces 1, 4, 5, and 6.

2nd) The other method indicated by Dr. Geley in the *Revue* consists in the use of a fusible and soluble hand (sugar, gelatin or other).

This hand would be dipped in a bath of paraffin, then dissolved in a bucket of cold water, thus yielding a complete paraffin mold, without any joints, and as thin as one would like. This procedure would be very ingenious, but, in our opinion, it has never been used for the specimens submitted to us, for the motive already explained above:

An overmolding cannot offer the same fineness of details as a firsthand molding. Delicate traces would inevitably disappear in overmoldings. A specialist artist will never confuse a firsthand molding with an overmolding. In our opinion, we formally and unreservedly declare that the pieces we have studied are, we repeat, casts of living hands. We wondered whether the hands of corpses could have been used in this specific case. We concluded in the negative. Traces of muscular contractions prove that they were living hands. Other than that, it would have been impossible to get hands of corpses out of casting molds like these, whatever the artifice employed.

We have made many attempts to artificially produce, by the most diverse means, casting gloves similar to those which had been submitted to us. They completely failed. We conclude that it is impossible for us to understand how Dr. Geley's paraffin molds were obtained. It is for us a complete mystery.

Signed: GABRIELLI père;
Victor GABRIELLI fils."[49]

Here, then, are faced with recent experiments which, after forty-seven years, confirm those conducted by Reimers, Oxley and Ashton.

Elsewhere, Mr. Nogueira de Faria published a book entitled *O Trabalho dos Mortos* [*The Work of the Dead*],[50] in which he relates the many experiences of materialization that took place at Mr. Eurípedes Prado's, a pharmacist in Belém do Pará, Brazil. The medium was the latter's wife. These seances took place under the most rigid control, with Mrs. Prado often locked in a cage while the spirits materialized outside.

Some experiments took place in other premises with the same success, involving members of the same circle, among others the music conductor Ettore Bosio, at whose home the phenomena occurred with the same intensity as at the Prados'.

Control was exerted by doctors, such as Lauro Sodré and João Coelho, former governors of the state of Pará in Brazil; Misters José Teixéira and Matta Bacellar (a homeopathic physician); Antonio Porto de Oliveira (a psychiatrist and nervous disease specialist); Ferreira de Lemos (an ophthalmologist); J. Aben-Athar (director of the Pasteur Institute); R. Chaves (a physician and forensic scientist, director of the anthropometric service); J. Pinheiro Sozinho (director of the agriculture school); V. de Mendonça (a specialist in the studies of hypnotism and magnetism); G. Gurjão (a senator); G. Vieira, Auzier, Bentes, Pereira de Barros, Pontes de Carvalho (all doctors); Manoel Coimbra (director of the school of pharmacy); and three members of the Superior Court of Justice of the state, two magistrates, several lawyers,

---

49 [Trans. note] Originally published in *Revue Métapsychique*, January–February 1921, p. 16.

50 [Trans. note] N. de FARIA, *O Trabalho dos Mortos* (6th ed. Rio de Janeiro: FEB, 2002).

Mr. Horiguchi (a minister from Japan), engineers, journalists, the famous poet Eustachio de Azevedo, and the already mentioned maestro Ettore Bosio.

As I cannot dwell here on the details of the seances, I would like to refer the reader to the reports published in the *Revue Métapsychique*.[51]

It suffices to point out that, on several occasions, paraffin casts of hands and feet were obtained from the materialized spirits of João and a young girl, Raquel Figner.

> "In the seance of September 28, 1919, in presence of several people, including two doctors, there was a fluidic formation in the dark: a spirit entity called João, by means of paraffin and water, gave a hand mold of curved fingers and a branch of roses of the so-called angelic species.[52] On April 17, 1920, with people present, both the cabinet and the cage were checked. Half-light. Suddenly, from a white cloud there emerged a clear face, then the whole body of a girl, "that's the entity Anita," said the medium. Anita approached Mr. Prado and kissed his hand. She then greeted the other people. Dressed in white. Long hair. She immediately works with the paraffin and stretches her arm a few times, to show the rest of the operations. The mold will be perfect. She will have added some modeled flowers to it.
> Finally, she knelt and sang a hymn ...
> On April 30, 1920, it is a child's hand that is molded.
> June 14, 1920, in presence of Mr. Horiguchi, minister of Japan in Brazil; Dr. V. de Mendonça; and fifteen other witnesses. Semidarkness. Use of the fan to help cool the molds quickly. Typtological messages inviting Dr. Mendonça to approach the cage for strict control, along with the Japanese minister. Apparition of Spirit João which shakes hands with the doctor and Mr. Horiguchi.

---

51 See *Revue Métapsychique*, year 1922, no. 2; year 1923, no. 1.

52 Bear in mind that, for this seance, as for all those commented herein, the witnesses, attaching the greatest importance to rigorous control of the access ways to the room where the phenomena took place, have safeguarded against all deceit by a series of precautions which the author of *O Trabalho dos Mortos* recalls several times throughout his book.

In the sight of all those present, the spirit works the paraffin, makes three people touch its hand gradually 'gloved'. Once the mold is finished, he hands it to an assistant, who gives it Mr. Horiguchi.
Another mold is produced.
Departure of Spirit João that replaces Anita. Prayer on knees. Stay of a quarter of an hour. Hand pressure. Withdrawal. João returns. Prayer. Then the spirit entity goes back to the medium and comforts it."

The International Metapsychic Institute having opened an inquiry about these seances, seven doctors answered it by affirming the reality of the phenomena obtained in the Prados' and maestro Bosio's groups, where Mrs. Prado also gave some seances.

These attestations are accompanied by a letter from Mr. Frederico Figner who had the joy of seeing his deceased daughter Raquel perfectly materialized and obtain an excellent casting of one of her feet in paraffin.

Now it is no longer possible to deny that the objectified fluidic body is similar in all respects, and even anatomically identical, to ours. It is positively a three-dimensional being that has an earthly morphology. It is not a duplication of the medium, because it differs from the latter physically and intellectually. The spirit that is therein, which is formed under the eyes of the attendants, whether at Villa Carmen or in Dr. Gibier's laboratory, when it reappears in our objective world, instantly takes up all its earthly attributes. These are not created at that moment, they preexisted, albeit in the latent state, because the conditions of life in the hereafter are not like ours, because they do not exist to cater for physical necessities similar to those of the earthly environment.

Sir William Crookes was not the only one to have the privilege of auscultating materialized phantoms. Dr. William Hitchman, president of the Liverpool Anthropological Society, also had this opportunity. In a private circle, with a nonprofessional medium who did not even want his name revealed, he was able to photograph the apparitions and submit them to a thorough medical examination. In a letter addressed to the researcher Aksakov, he says, after describing his photographic operations:

> "I often came into the cabinet after a materialized form, and *then saw it at the same time as the medium* (Mr. B.). For this reason, I think I have obtained *the best scientific assurance that one can have*, that each of these forms that appeared was an individuality distinct from the material envelope of the medium, for I examined them with the help of various instruments. I have detected in them *the existence of respiration and circulation*; I measured their height, body circumference, *took their weight*, etc."
>
> These apparitions looked noble and graceful both morally and physically; they seem to be *gradually formed at the expense of a nebulous mass*, whereas *their disappearance is instant and absolute* ... Having often had the opportunity (in presence of competent witnesses) to stand between the medium and 'the materialized mind,' to shake hands with it and *talk to it for nearly an hour*, I do not feel inclined to accept fanciful assumptions, such as illusions caused by sight and the crowd, a playfulness of the unconscious, a psychic or nervous force, and the like. The truth regarding questions of *matter* and *spirit* can only be acquired by means of research."

Indeed, without a shadow of a doubt, but already we have enough documents from qualified persons to know, a little better than philosophers or physiologists, the intelligent principle of humans. We are now scientifically certain that it survives the dissolution of the material body and that it carries into the afterlife a spiritual body appropriate to the new environment in which it continues its uninterrupted evolution.

It is not always unknown spirits that show themselves in the seances. Sometimes it is the phantom of a loved one which one of the attendants recognizes with indescribable joy; and then all sophisms of criticism vanish away. Now it is Mr. Livermore, an American banker with a calculating and cold mind, who sees his dear spouse Estelle, and who obtains from the phantom a handwriting identical to that which she possessed during her lifetime. Then we have the case of Dr. Nichols, who kisses his daughter and is able to keep a mold of her hand, as well as drawings and messages written by her. An then there is the case of a niece named Blanche, who speaks French to her aunt at Dr Gibier's, despite the fact that the medium did not know a word of that idiom; and so on.

With Eusapia, which we have become too accustomed to considering as a mere physical effects medium, the illustrious Cesare Lombroso saw his mother; the great Italian writer and journalist Luigi Arnaldo Vassallo, saw his son Arnaldino; Professor Porro, his daughter Elsa; Dr. Venzano, his father and one of his relatives; not to mention the apparitions recognized by Professor E. Bozzano, Prince Ruspoli, and so on and on. These latter witnesses were not very willing to pay for vague apparitions, taking their wishes for realities. If they ended up convinced, it was only after carefully scrutinizing all the circumstances and recognizing that no other hypothesis could explain these splendid manifestations.

Spiritism did not invent anything. All its teachings are based on the knowledge it has acquired by communicating with spirits; and it is for its adherents an unparalleled joy to see how each of the points of Spiritism is confirmed as the investigation, begun in the second half of the 19th century, has extended further and further. Every step forward took by independent investigation inevitably leads to Spiritist teachings. Formerly, there was a total, obstinate and absolute negation of Spiritist manifestations in all their forms: from simple table turning and automatic writing to communications and materializations. Nowadays, there is little more left than backward and ignorant people that still challenge the reality of facts. The vast majority of those who have dealt with this issue accepts them unreservedly, leaving only their origin and their nature to be discussed. Then a second evolution has taken place; among scholars, names such as such as Lodge, F. W. H. Myers, Hodgson, Hyslop, among others, enter the scene, bringing in intellectual proofs obtained by means of trance or mediumistic writing, perfectly convinced that they have been indisputably connected with some of their departed friends or relatives, without telepathy or clairvoyance being able to account for all the facts. It is therefore the practices of ordinary Spiritism, commonplace even, which have triumphed. Then, transcendental manifestations have taken place: tangible apparitions occur, and then we see counterfeits of the perispirit theory appear under the most varied guises. To explain these hands that act at a distance, Ochorowicz will come up with a *dynamic hand* and Charles Richet with the concept of *ectoplasm*, Morselli with the so-called *psychodynamism*, etc. But who does not see that these are not only words, since the splitting of the human being makes one naturally witness the full exteriorization of the fluidic body.

All these testimonies should be well valued as they ought to be, for being rigorously attached to the facts themselves, while there emerges the inanity of all the theories devised to dispense with spirits as their explanation. The psychodynamic and biopsychical hypothesis, the supposed creations or transfigurations of second personalities, are so forced, so artificial, so arbitrary, and they gather so many rational impossibilities, that they will appear absolutely improbable before ten years' time, like Hartmann's theory of collective hallucination, which charmed the majority of superficial critics, and then sank when confronted with spirit photographs, imprints and casting molds.

Logical necessity for the existence of the perispirit

There is no doubt the Spiritist truth will cause a revolution among pure spiritualists who believed that the soul is completely *immaterial*, as well as among physiologists who had become accustomed to counting out of their reasoning. But a FACT has an invincible power for the mere reason that *it exists*, and sooner or later, in spite of all denials, it finally imposes itself sovereignly. It is then that new horizons open up before the researchers. Since the spirit is capable, under certain conditions, of reconstituting its former material body, hence it indisputably possesses in itself the dynamic status which presides over the organization, maintenance and repair of the earthly body. In the same way, it must be admitted that, since the perispirit persists after death, this is a demonstration that it existed before birth, so that it appears to us as a materialization of long duration, while the tangible apparitions have only an ephemeral existence, because they have been produced outside the processes of generation. This interpretation of the facts seems to logically explain how order and harmony are maintained in the formidably intricate phenomena that constitute a living being. If there really exists in humans a second body which is the indefectible model according to which the fleshly one is organized, we understand that, despite the whirlwind of matter passing through us, the individual type is maintained in the midst of incessant mutations resulting of the disintegration and reconstitution of all the parts of one's body, like a house of which, every second, one would change the bricks and mortar of all its parts in. The perispirit is the regulator of functions, the architect who watches over the maintenance of the whole building, because this task could hardly depend on the blind activities of matter.

If one thinks of the diversity of the organs which form the human body; of the variety of tissues which serve to build each organ; of the prodigious number of aggregated cells (several trillions) which form all the tissues, together with the colossal number of molecules of the protoplasm; and finally of the almost infinite quantity of atoms which constitute each organic molecule; then one finds oneself in presence of a veritable universe, so diversified that it exceeds in complexity all that human imagination is able to conceive. The wonder is the perfect order that reigns in these billions of intricate interactions.

Successive groupings of phenomena harmonize in series that lead to total unity, as said by Louis Bourdeau in these inspired lines:[53]

> "Without our being conscious of it, a permanent work of synthesis is taking place, which binds, in the individual phenomenon of life, an immense multitude of elements through actions that are at once mechanical, physical, chemical, plastic and functional. The built-up power of which each group is depositary, and the increasingly complex resultants which their union determines, makes one dizzy for a moment when thinking of these abysmal depths."

Each cell works on its behalf, blindly; the forces of the outside world are themselves unconscious; who then disciplines all these elements to lead them to the ultimate goal, which is the maintenance of life? There is clearly a plan that is maintained and requires a leading plastic force that cannot be caused by a series of accidental events. How can one suppose a continuity of efforts always following the same direction, in a set whose parts perpetually change? If, in the midst of this whirlwind, something remains stable, it is logical to see in it the organizer which matter obeys. Now, this *something* is the perispirit, since its existence can objectively be observed during one's lifetime, and which survives death. When the perispirit becomes better known,

53 L. Bourdeau, *Le Problème de la Vie* (Paris: F. Alcan, 1901).

new and extremely valuable knowledge will result both for physiology and medicine.

What the ancients called the *vis medicatrix naturæ* [the healing power of human nature], is the stable, incorruptible mechanism, always on the alert, which defends the organism against mechanical, physical, chemical, and microbial actions which assail it relentlessly; and which reconstitutes incessantly the integrity of the living being when it is destroyed. In a word, the body is not just a mass of simply juxtaposed or contiguous cells, it is a whole in which each part has a well-defined role, albeit subordinated to the place it occupies in the overall plan. The perispirit is the physical realization of this 'guiding idea' that Claude Bernard points out as being the true characteristic of life; it is also the 'vital pattern' that each of us realizes and preserves for the duration of our lifetime. Here is how the great physiologist expresses himself in his *An Introduction to the Study of Experimental Medicine*[54] and in *La Science Expérimentale*:[55]

> "If I had to define life in a single phrase, ... I should say: life is creation.... So that what distinguishes a living machine is not the nature of its physiochemical properties, ... but rather the creation of the machine ... according to a definite idea ..."

Elsewhere he says that, this grouping is made as a result of the laws which govern the physiochemical properties of matter; but what is essentially in the realm of life, which does not belong to physics or chemistry, is the *guiding idea* of this vital evolution.

He also affirms that, there is something like a *vital pattern* which traces the plan of each being, of each organ, so that, considered in isolation, each phenomenon of the organism is dependent on the general forces of Nature. Taken in their succession and in their ensemble, they seem to reveal a special

---

54 [Trans. note] C. BERNARD, *An Introduction to the Study of Experimental Medicine* (Trans. H. C. Greene. USA: Schuman, 1949), p. 93.

55 [Trans. note] C. BERNARD, *La Science Expérimentale* (Paris: Baillière & Fils, 1878), "Définition de la vie," p. 149 *et seq.*

bond, and seem directed *by some invisible condition*, on the road they follow, in the order that binds them.

Finally, in even more explicit terms:

> "Life is *an idea*; it is the idea of the common result in which all the anatomical elements are associated and disciplined, the idea of the harmony which results from their concert ensemble, from the order which reigns in their action.

The billions of individual lives of cells are governed by a higher organism which ranks them and imposes on them their conditions of existence; it is the perispirit that acts automatically to produce these effects, although we are not at all aware of its incessant action. Strictly speaking, it constitutes the physiological unconscious, just as it is the physical basis of this subconsciousness that exists in each of us for the conservation of memories, and which is even more complex than imagined by psychologists who know only matter, for it contains in itself the residues of our past lives, the result of which is this absolutely individual phenomenon called individual character.

We see, from what precedes, that if the soul carries with it into the spiritual plane an organism as complex as the perispirit, which does not serve it in the hereafter to maintain its life, it is because it is infinitely probable that the soul must return here below, otherwise the mechanism which serves for the maintenance of earthly life would not persist in the spiritual world, for it is a law of nature that the absence of exercise causes atrophy of useless organs and makes them disappear in the long run.

WHERE AND HOW DID THE PERISPIRIT ACQUIRE ITS FUNCTIONAL PROPERTIES?

But where and how could this marvelous mechanism come into being and fix itself indelibly in the fluidic envelope? Having studied this very complex question elsewhere,[56] I can give here only a few summarized and necessarily incomplete indications. Here are the principal points which emerge from the observation of facts and which seem to legitimize the hypothesis of the passage of the human soul through the series of animal species inferior to humanity.

One of the most magnificent discoveries of the 19th century was the demonstration of the unity of composition of all living beings. Plants, like animals or humans, are all formed by cells which, by their variety of forms, their groupings and their properties, have given birth by diversifying to the innumerable multitude of beings that populate the world, in the air, water and earth. The simplest creatures can live in the form of isolated cells like those of blood, or like microbes; but in all of them there is a fundamental substance: the protoplasm, which is their really living part. All beings, whichever they may be, are organized, reproduce, manufacture with heterogeneous materials substance analogous to theirs, in a word, feed and evolve, that is to say, are born, grow and die. They all need water, heat, air and a nutritious environment. All are irritable, that is to say, they react by moving to any external excitation. It may be affirmed that at all stages of life species the operations of respiration and digestion are basically the same; what varies are the instruments intended to produce these results. Reproduction is also identical, being derived from another being by an embryo. Sleep is a necessity for every being. Under these effects we recognize a general unity of action which shows how variety may have sprung from an original uniformity. So there is an

56 G. DELANNE, *Évolution Animique* (Paris: Chamuel, 1897).

undeniable identity in the vital processes of all organisms, and then the idea of universal kinship among all beings results naturally. Since there is no spontaneous generation, all beings, plants or animals, that exist today come directly from ancestors that preceded them since millions of years ago, during different geological periods. Research carried out in old lands has revealed that animals and plants become simpler as we go back in the past. How did this evolution occur? This is what we shall see further on.

It is more than probable that all theories conceived to explain evolution each contain a part of truth; but we do not need to subscribe to one over the other. It suffices to note that every being which is born replicates during fetal life all the simpler forms which have preceded it in its ancestors. Humans themselves, in the maternal womb, are at first only a simple cell which, once fertilized, diversifies itself and presents, in abbreviated form, a picture of all the organisms which took millions of years to evolve into its current build. The embryo is an irrefutable evidence of our origins. As Claude Bernard puts it:

> "We see in the evolution [of the embryo] a simple sketch of being before any organization. The contours of the body and organs first are quite simply arrested, starting with the temporary organic framework which will serve as functional and temporary devices of the fetus. No tissue is distinct yet. The whole mass is then constituted only by plasma and embryonic cells. But in this vital canvas is *drawn the ideal design* of an organism still invisible to us, which has assigned to each part and each element its place, its structure and its properties. Where there must be blood vessels, nerves, muscles, bones, etc., the embryonic cells are changed into blood-corpuscles, arterial, venous, muscular, nervous, and bone tissues."[57]

---

57 [Trans. note] Claude BERNARD, "Le problème de la physiologie générale" in *Revue des Deux Mondes*, 2e période, tome 72, 1867, p. 887.

Since it is the perispirit that organizes matter, as it resurrects extinct forms, it seems logical to conclude that it contains traces of this past, because heredity, as we shall see later, is powerless to make us understand what is actually happening. It seems legitimate to assume that the perispirit has itself evolved through these lower stages before reaching the highest point of its evolution.

The intelligent principle would have slowly climbed the ladder of the immense series of animal beings before moving on to humanity. The animals present an undeniable gradation in intellectual manifestations, from the most rudimentary to the human ones, in such a way that the hypothesis of reincarnation of the same being rising, by its own efforts, to an ever greater degree, would allow it to reach us without interruption.

But what we see realized before our eyes, that is, the continuity of forms that are connected to one another like the rings of a gigantic chain, has also occurred in the past. Hence, it is conceivable that progress is due, no longer to exclusively external causes, but also at the same time, to the intelligent psyche striving to break the waste slag of matter, and making uninterrupted efforts to soften it, thus allowing its faculties to enter into an increasingly intimate relation with the external nature. Therefore, the creation of the senses, and then of increasingly perfected organs, would be the result of an intentional effort, and not the products of fortunate chance, as materialists want.

Animal reincarnation is not a mere hypothesis; it can already rely on some facts that the future will multiply considerably. Then we will understand the role of animals here below and the purely materialistic theory of a physical evolution will be replaced by the tenet of the intelligent principle going through the chain of lower realms so as to reach human level and later rise itself to other destinies, when it will be released from all earthly hindrances.

No doubt, there are still a great deal of obscurities as to how such an evolution takes place. It will require persevering studies to justify each of the points of this theory, but as such, it offers to the human spirit a rational picture of our origins; and it is reconciled with scientific discoveries as well as with Spiritist experimentation, which despite being still so little developed, has already allowed us to ascertain certain facts.

Now we can understand the major theoretical and practical scope of materialization seances because, first, they prove the immortality of the soul, and then, by revealing the existence of the perispirit, open before us new perspectives whose immense range can only be suspected today.

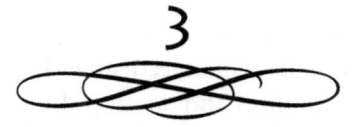

THE ANIMAL SOUL, AN ESSAY ON THE UNITY OF THE LAWS OF LIFE THROUGHOUT THE ORGANIC SCALE

THE ASSUMPTION OF THE PASSAGE OF THE SOUL THROUGH THE ANIMAL SCALE IS ACCEPTED BY ALLAN KARDEC · THEORIES OF EVOLUTION: FROM LAMARCK TO DARWIN · QUINTON AND DE VRIES · FORMATION AND GRADUAL DEVELOPMENT OF THE SPIRIT · PASSAGE OF THE INTELLIGENT PRINCIPLE THROUGH THE ANIMAL KINGDOM · THERE ARE NO ABSOLUTE DIFFERENCES BETWEEN THE ANIMAL SOUL AND OURS

NECESSITY FOR EARTHLY INCARNATIONS

WHEN ACCEPTING that the spiritual principle of humans passed through the animal chain until it gradually reached humanity, I am not distancing myself from the Spiritist tradition, since Allan Kardec, in his book *Genesis*, fully admits this possibility, and justifies it by showing that it is a logical explanation for the existence of animals and the role they play here below. Indeed, he expresses himself in the following terms:[58]

> "Taking humankind at its lowest degree of the intellectual scale, such as the least evolved humans, one questions if that is the starting point for the human soul.

---

58 Allan KARDEC, *Genesis* (Trans. D. W. Kimble, I. Reis. Brasilia: International Spiritist Council, 2011), part one, ch. XI, section 23.

According to the opinion of certain spiritualist philosophers, the intelligent principle, distinct from the material principle, individualizes and develops by passing through the many degrees of animality. This is the time when the soul rehearses for life and develops its first skills through practice. One might say that this is its incubation period. Having arrived at the degree of development that the human state requires, it receives the special characteristics that comprise the human soul. Hence, there would be a spiritual filiation from animal to human being, just as there is a corporeal filiation.

Founded on the great law of unity that presides over creation, one must agree that this theory is in keeping with the justice and goodness of the Creator. It gives a reason, an objective and a destiny to animals, which are no longer disinherited beings, but which find in the future reserved for them a compensation for their sufferings. What constitutes the spiritual human being is not its origin, but the special attributes it is endowed with upon entering humanity, attributes that transform it and make it into a distinct being, just as the tasty fruit is distinct from the bitter root that produced it. By having passed through the lineage of animality, the human being would not be any less human; it would not be any more an animal than the fruit is the root, just as a learned person is not the shapeless fetus through which he or she debuted in the world."

Some spiritualistic philosophers, and even some Spiritists, have supposed that the soul incarnates only once in each of the worlds that dot the infinite space. This way of conceiving evolution seems to me all the more inaccurate, for the properties of the perispirit can only have been acquired by a long series of incarnations on Earth, since the perispirit organizes its physical body according to the laws which are peculiar to our planet. The other inhabited worlds of our solar system, by the mere fact that they are at different distances from the central star, necessarily have habitability conditions which are dissimilar to ours. It is infinitely probable, indeed, that the first organized forms being dependent on the biological and physiochemical laws peculiar to each of these worlds, were inevitably different on these planets; seeing that gravity, heat, light, electric potential, and the gases composing the atmosphere – besides their different pressure the other factors that contribute to the maintenance and organization of life – are entirely different on each of these worlds.

To these reasons, in a sort of physiopsychological order, Allan Kardec adds the following, which are equally important. This is what he says:[59]

> "Some persons believe that the soul's various existences are accomplished by going from world to world, and not on one and the same globe, where each spirit would appear only once.
> This doctrine would be acceptable if all earth's inhabitants were at the same intellectual and moral level. In that case, they could not progress except by going from one world to another, and their reincarnation on earth would be pointless. God, however, does nothing pointless. On earth we find all degrees of intelligence and morality, from primitivism bordering on animality to the most advanced civilization; hence it offers a vast field for progress. It would bear asking why primitives would be obligated to seek the next evolutionary level elsewhere when it and successive levels lie right next them where they now are; why advanced humans could take their first steps only on less evolved worlds when beings analogous to all such worlds are all around them; and why there are different degrees of advancement, not only from culture to culture, but within the same culture and the same family. If such were the case, God would have done something useless in placing ignorance and wisdom, barbarism and civilization, good and evil side by side, when in reality it is precisely such contact that enables stragglers to progress.
> There is therefore no more need for humans to change worlds at each step than there is for a student to change schools at each grade. Far from being an advantage for

---

59 *Op. cit.*, *ibid.*, ch. xi, section 34.

progress it would be a hindrance, because the spirit would be deprived of the example of seeing the higher degrees, and of the possibility of correcting its errors within the same environment and in the presence of those whom it had offended, a possibility that represents for it the most powerful means of moral progress. After a short cohabitation, spirits would disperse and become strangers to one another, and the bonds of family and friendship, without time to consolidate, would be broken.

Furthermore, to a moral unsuitability, a material unsuitability would be added. The nature of the elements, the organic laws and the conditions for life vary from world to world; in this regard, there are no two that are perfectly identical. Our treatises on physics, chemistry, anatomy, medicine, botany, etc. might be of no use on other worlds. Whatever is learned on other worlds is not lost, however; not only does it develop the intelligence, but it also helps to develop ideas previously acquired on them. If the spirit made but one appearance – often of brief duration – on the same world, at each migration it would find itself in entirely different conditions. Each time, it would operate on new elements with powers and according to laws unfamiliar to it before having had time to work with known elements, to study them, and to apply them. Each time, it would be a new apprenticeship, and these incessant changes would be an obstacle to progress. The spirit must therefore remain on the same world until it has acquired the sum of knowledge and degree of perfection that such world renders possible. Thus it is and thus it must be that spirits depart for a more advanced world, leaving behind the old one on which there is nothing else to acquire – such is the principle. If there are some who leave before that time, it is obviously due to individual causes that God has weighed in the divine wisdom."

Let us study then, in the light of contemporary scientific discoveries, the connection among them, not only currently living beings, but all those which have preceded them on Earth. This will allow us to unfold the majestic panorama of life from its origins to current times.

Animal evolution

In a certain way, science shows us that evolution has brought out multiplicity of original unity. The nebulae gave birth to the suns, these to the planets. The aspects of matter multiplied and life appeared in rudimentary forms before blossoming into the marvelous complexity of animal and vegetable beings that inhabit today not only the surface of the globe, but the waters, the atmosphere and inside the earth. We can see that the manifestations of intelligence are, in a general way, correlative to the complexity of organisms. As curious as the dwellings of ants, bees, or beavers, may be; and notwithstanding the ingenuity revealed by certain nests' dispositions; all these constructions cannot compare to ours, and such difference precisely indicates the degree of evolution which separates us from them.

Animals do not know tools; they only have their limbs to carry out all their labors. The great conquest of humans was to make tools they lacked, and artificially increase the range of their senses.

In this hugely prodigious multiplicity of living beings, all degrees are observed; the manifestations of intelligence can almost be confused in the lower realms with purely physiochemical reactions determining those mechanical movements to which physiologists have given the name of *tropism*.[60] When one ascends the ladder of beings, all uncertainty disappears, and a true psychism (i.e., psychic or mental activity) manifests itself. Not only do instincts become more complex, but intelligence is translated by acts comparable to our own as humans; since the elephant, the dog or the monkey all show that there is not a difference of nature between some of their actions and those which we accomplish as a result of reasoned deliberation.

---

60 [Trans. note] Involuntary orienting response to an external stimulus

The hypothesis proposed by Descartes, that animals are only automatons reacting mechanically to the excitations of the external or internal environment, seems to me untenable from whatever standpoint it may be viewed. If we accept, with the materialists, that intelligence is a function of the brain, as there exists in the higher vertebrates a very complex nervous system; and that it presents with ours an analogy of constitution, disposition, and reaction; then what takes place with humans must necessarily take place with them. The brain of a monkey or even a dog differs from the human brain only in their greater simplicity, but the topography is about the same, the neurons alike. Therefore, it must logically be admitted that the external manifestations which we describe as intelligent in our realm must bear the same name if we observe them in animals.

It is not only anatomy and physiology that demonstrate an analogy of constitution and vital functions between animal and human tissues. Now it is also experience.

To put it like Mr. Le Dantec would have done, we can say that "dog essence" can live in the " human essence" and adapt to it perfectly. Better still, and here we are back to the notion of perispirit, it is the location in the body of the animal that gives living tissues their specificity. An artery can be grafted into another body and play the role of a vein, or vice versa when it replaces a sick part of it. Thus there is an organic plan, and living matter obeys it so much that it changes its function if it is forced to live in a place other than that for which it was originally conceived. I am not inventing anything. Experiments carried by the surgeon Alexis Carrel have established it categorically. Here is what he found:[61]

> "Thanks to his technique, Dr. Carrel was able to *patch* several inches of *abdominal aorta* with a piece of *peritoneum* – something unheard of. And it held in place! And the piece of peritoneum soon turned into a vascular wall! What

---

[61] *Journal des Accoucheurs* [*Journal of the Obstetricians*], Aug. 1 [year?], p. 8.

future holds for the radical cure of aneurysms! Instead of the peritoneum, a vein can be used; for example, a piece of femoral vein instead of a carotid fragment. And blood circulation is done as well! *with the vein transforming itself into an artery!*"

"For the past two years, Dr. Carrel's laboratory she-dog has housed in its body, instead of an abdominal artery, a piece of popliteal artery taken from *a young man* whose leg had just been amputated – and this *human artery* works admirably well *in the animal*."

"Unexpectedly, Dr. Carrel can keep fragments of vessels, veins or arteries, and even other tissues, in specially arranged tubes, without the vitality of the latter being affected. They are transplanted and then they blend themselves. Normal blood circulation is restored in these vessels which were kept empty so long. *Once revived, they immediately adapt to the new functions imposed on them ...*"

"Finally, a fact that exceeds all expectations and that one would not believe had Professor Pozzi not seen it with his own eyes, Dr. Carrel is able to *replace limbs*. There is a white dog and a black dog of the same size in his laboratory, each of them wearing the right hind leg of the other. Neither of them seems to suspect it, and the white dog's black leg and the black dog's white leg are as strong, as vigorous, and as free from functional constraints as they were when they still belonged to their former owners ..."

So we can see that my assertion about the resemblance between living human and animal tissues is seriously founded; and that since the higher vertebrates have a similar nervous system, analogous to ours in constitution and disposition, it is not philosophically correct to deny them the faculty of thinking, when we admit that it is attached to the functioning of the cervical cell.

As Spiritists, since we have the proof of the independent existence of the animistic[62] principle, we can hardly refuse to admit that it exists in animals; for we know, apart from the

---

62 [Trans. note] See footnote 31 above.

logical reasons which lead us to admit it, a number of facts that are demonstrative. It has been possible sometimes to observe in materialization seances – as we shall see further below – that dead animals have reappeared with their former physical semblance, just as the fluidic duplication of certain other animals has sometimes been observed. Should these facts be real, the result would be that there exists from a spiritual standpoint the same general unity as that revealed by science regarding living beings. These are formed of cells; they always come from a being just like them, they develop and die by the same processes; they have identical requirements to maintain their lives. Since the beginning of time, the incalculable myriads of beings that have passed through our globe in uninterrupted formation have changed in such a prodigious way, that when we discover fossils, they look like apocalyptic creations, though the organs and functions were everywhere the same. However, it is their succession that has brought us to where we are now, since spontaneous procreation does not exist.

Science has formulated a number of hypotheses to explain the transformation of beings. Lamarck and Darwin have devised seductive theories, completed by those of Quinton and De Vries to a certain extent. But the true cause of evolution must be sought, according to my own view, in the efforts that the intelligent principle has made to disengage itself more and more from the swaddling clothes of matter. Lamarck has shown very well the force of the influence of the environment for modifying organisms; Darwin made us understand how the struggle for life brought the survival of the fittest, of those who knew best how to adapt themselves. Spontaneous variations only highlight the latent work done within organisms, and the law of constancy of the organic environment, discovered by Quinton, indicates the effort that living beings perform to maintain the essential conditions of vital functioning, despite the changes of the outside world. All these causes have been ancillary in polishing the spiritual being, to cause it to bring forth the potentialities that were dormant in it, so that it became more and more capable of getting acquainted with itself and with Nature.

Today, there are still representatives of all possible frames of mind. From plants to humans, through the whole animal kingdom, it is a gradual and continuous series that starts from almost total unconsciousness to the full light of reason that enlightens higher human beings. Instead of seeing in this great hierarchy only separate units, each of which would be an ephemeral spark, the theory of successive lives compels us to think that every being at the summit has passed through lower phases and that its development is not due to the whim of a Creator who would have privileged it, but instead owed entirely to its own effort. Thus suddenly, order, justice, and harmony are introduced into the explanation of Nature; evolution is no longer a succession of fortunate chances, but the development of a logical plan to bring the triumph of the spirit over matter.

FORMATION AND GRADUAL DEVELOPMENT OF THE SPIRIT

Although the inner nature of the thinking principle is still unknown to us, we ought to look for its origins in all living beings, as minute as they may seem to us. Doubtless, the individuality of this principle is not apparent in the lower forms of life, but it is a logical necessity to see in all vital manifestations an action of this spiritual principle, even if it is still undifferentiated in the beings that are at the bottom of the organic ladder, as I said in a memoir presented at the International Spiritual Congress of 1898 in London.

We are therefore logically constrained to seek in the vegetable kingdom the beginnings of the animal evolution, because the form that plants take and preserve during their lifetime implies the existence of a perispiritual[63] double

---

63 [Trans. note] The terms *perispirit*, perispiritual, perispiritic and perispiritually are all Spiritist neologisms originated with Allan Kardec,

presiding over their exchanges and maintaining their fixed type as plants. French physician and neurologist Alfred Vulpian once wrote:[64]

> "Nature has not established a definite line of demarcation between the vegetable and animal kingdoms. Animals and plants proceed from one another in imperceptible progression, and they are rightly brought together under the common name of organic kingdom."

The analogy of the role played by the perispirit to a multipole electromagnet,[65] whose lines of force would draw not only the external form of the individual, but also all of the organic systems, seems to have passed from the hypothetical domain to that of scientific observation. According to an announcement made at the Académie des Sciences on May 12, 1898, by G. M. Stanoiewitch, drawings taken from nature show that the tissues are formed according to clearly visible lines of force.

One of those drawings reproduces the appearance of a branch of fir with two knots which play the same role and produce the same disturbances in the parts where they are found as an electric or magnetic pole would do if introduced into a field of the same nature. The other demonstrates that differentiation has occurred along the lines of force; a third represents the cross section of an oak branch a few centimeters above a branch. We see, down to the smallest details, the same appearance of an electromagnetic field formed by two rectilinear streams, crossed, of the same direction, and of substantially the same intensity.

These observations seem to establish the existence of a fluidic double of the plant, analogous to that observed in humans.

---

which refer to a fluidic double or spiritual body.
64 A. VULPIAN, *Leçons sur la Physiologie ... du Système Nerveux* (Paris: G. Baillière, 1866), p. 39.
65 G. DELANNE, *Évolution Animique* (Paris: Chamuel, 1897), p. 68.

There is indeed something in living beings which is not explicable by physical, chemical or mechanical laws. This something is the form allocated to them. Not only natural laws cannot explain the forms of individuals, but all the observations make us think that the plastic force that builds the structural framework and the functional type of these beings cannot possibly reside in this mobile, fluctuating set in perpetual instability, which is the physical body.

Whatever the value of these observations regarding the beginnings of the thinking being, the animal series will show us the continuous progress of all the animistic[66] manifestations.

Passage of the intelligent principle throughout the animal series

Among the innumerable multitude of lower organisms, the animistic principle exists only in an impersonal, diffuse state, because the nervous system has not yet differentiated itself. Such beings are deaf, blind, and dumb; they are zoophytes. But as soon as it appears in the annulated species, it begins to specify its common properties, and differentiations occur by the formation of sensory organs.

As the nervous system acquires more importance, instinctive manifestations, which are limited to the search for food, are diversified and present an ever greater complexity. Here is how French anatomist and psychiatrist François Leuret describe this progression:

1st) In animals that seem to establish a transition to the lower class, one can observe instincts exclusively limited to the search for food (annelids: leeches).

2nd) More extensive and more numerous sensations, extreme passion for procreation, voracity, blind cruelty (crustaceans: crayfish).

66 [Trans. note] See footnote 31 above.

3rd) After that, even more extensive sensations, building of a nest, voracity, cunning, deception (arachnids: spiders).

4th) Finally very extensive sensations, building of a nest, relational life, sociability (insects: ants, bees).

In vertebrates; if we always take as a basis the development of the nervous system, and more particularly of the brain as the criterion of intelligence; one sees, according to Leuret, that the encephalon size taken as a unit is, in proportion to the weight of the body:

1. In fish	size ratio of 1 to ...	5668
2. In reptiles	size ratio of 1 to ...	1321
3. In birds	size ratio of 1 to ...	212
4. In mammals	size ratio of 1 to ...	186

Therefore there is a continuous progression of the encephalon, passing from one phylum to the next which is immediately superior to it; but on the condition that the weighings refer to each group taken as a whole, and not to this or that species taken separately.

For it is a well-proven fact today that progress in the animal series takes place, not in a straight line or in a single line, but in unequal parallel lines.

It has been said that the human brain is so developed, that no being, because of the dimensions and weight of their encephala, can be compared to us, even remotely. This is certainly true; however this difference is not such that it suffices to constitute a new realm. The brain of a monkey or a dog, or a cat, represents pretty much, as a whole, the general pattern of the human brain. Comparative anatomy has perfectly demonstrated the analogy among the different parts. Without going into details, it is enough to point out that any anatomist who has studied the brain of a monkey has a fairly exact knowledge of the anatomy of the human brain.

The number of convolutions in the structure of the cerebral apparatus, says Charles Richet, is the element which has taken the most importance in the human brain. It is especially by its convolutions that the human brain differs from the brain of other vertebrates. On the encephalon of the dog, however, we can distinguish the primitive plan and the outline of the deep and complicated convolutions found in an adult human being. In passing from animal to human, the brain has perfected itself, grew larger, diversified, but basically remained the same organ.

Therefore we should not be surprised to discover in vertebrates the outline of what will later become the human soul. We must not expect to find in animals an intelligence or sentiments comparable in intensity to what we observe in humans, but what we must find there, if animal evolution is a fact, is the initial germ of all these faculties. This is precisely what experiments have confirmed. Numerous data collections devoted to the study of animal faculties have established that we observe among them, from an intellectual standpoint: attention, judgment, memory, imagination, abstraction, reasoning; an action language and a voice language.

Passionate feelings are affirmed by conjugal love, maternal love, sometimes love of neighbor. There is also sympathy, hatred, the desire for revenge, sensitivity to mockery. Moral feelings, very little developed, can sometimes be observed in manifestations of notions of justice and injustice, and remorse. Finally, social sentiments are evident among those that live in groups through actions of mutual service, solidarity and even true loving fellowship.

> "When animals fight with one another, when they associate for a common purpose, when they warn one another in danger, when they come to the rescue of one another, when they display pain or joy, they manifest impulses of the same kind as are considered among the moral attributes of man.... The gradations of the moral faculties among the higher animals and man are moreover so imperceptible,

that, to deny to the first a certain sense of responsibility and consciousness, would certainly be an exaggeration of the differences which distinguish animals and man."[67]

Those were words of Louis Agassiz. The next chapter will show us the accuracy of this Swiss-American scientist's assessments.

---

[67] L. AGASSIZ, *An Essay on Classification* (London: Trubner & Co., 1859), pp. 96–97.

4

ANIMAL INTELLIGENCE

Observations that seem to favor the hypothesis of the evolution of the soul · The horses of Elberfeld · The dog Rolf · The she-dog Lola · Zou

To support the assertions of naturalists who have admitted that animal intelligence exists, experiments of the highest interest have been pursued for several years, mainly in Germany, on horses and on dogs. They tend to show that our lower fellow beings are not as far removed from us intellectually as we would usually imagine. I will briefly summarize the published observations about the Elberfeld[68] horses, and the dogs Rolf and Lola.

The calculating horses

In 1912, the Paris press made a big fuss about the publication[69] of experiments by a certain Mr. Krall, a rich merchant from Elberfeld, with his horses Muhamed and Zarif. These intelligent quadrupeds, by means of a conventional alphabet, could converse with their master, make complicated calculations, even going as far as the extraction of square and cubic roots. It is understandable that such claims were met with general disbelief. However, several renowned psychologists having studied the case of these remarkable animals, found that there was really a new field of investigation of animal psychology; and many reports were published in the *Annales des Sciences Psychiques* of the years 1912 and 1913,

---

68 [Trans. note] Named after the German city of Elberfeld, later merged into Wuppertal, where the horses were trained.
69 For Wilhelm von Hosten's training method, see the *Annales des Sciences Psychiques*, January 1913, p. 1.

in the *Archives de Psychologie de la Suisse Romande* and in the Italian journal *Psyche*. I will freely quote some passages borrowed from these different sources. They should establish the certainty of the remarkable faculties of these animals.

Mr. Krall was not the first to study the intelligence of horses; the honor goes to a precursor named Wilhelm von Osten, who in 1890 thought he noticed in the horse Clever Hans, a Russian stallion, signs of an intelligence that he decided to cultivate. With tireless patience, he tried to make himself understood by Hans, who was able not only to count, that is to say, to tap on a springboard placed in front of it with his right hoof the number of the units and with its left hoof that of the tens, but also to make real calculations, to solve small problems. He learned to read and indicated the date of each day of the current week, and so on.

The buzz around these sensational results caused violent controversy. A commission was appointed in 1904, composed of Misters Stumpf and Nagel, professors of psychology and physiology at the University of Berlin; the director of the local zoo; a circus director; veterinarians; and cavalry officers. The result of this investigation was that there were no tricks or deception, since the horse was calculating with exactitude, even in the absence of its owner. It was then that Mr. Oskar Pfungst, a student of the Psychology Laboratory of Berlin, after a careful study of Clever Hans, thought he could assert that the horse must have figured out exact answers by observing unconscious movements of the head or eyes of the experimenter. From then on, the question of animal intelligence appeared to be buried and, in 1909, the precursor, Von Osten, died in despair.

But then, one of his admirers and pupil, Mr. Krall, unconvinced of the reality of the explanations given by Mr. Pfungst, and well versed in the study of animal psychology, having inherited the horse Clever Hans, studied it methodically and made known the results of his work in a large volume which again drew attention to this fascinating issue. In fact, Mr. Krall asserted that Hans was able to operate in complete darkness, and also when blinders were put over its eyes, preventing it from seeing the participants. Finally, the horse was able to give exact answers, contrary to what Mr Pfungst had said, even when the questions were asked more than 15 feet away behind it.

There was no longer any doubt: Clever Hans did not obey any visible signals, and the exact answers were the product of the horse's own psyche.

Mr. Krall discovered in a series of experiments that the visual acuity of the horse is extremely fine and very large, and that it is not subject to the optical illusions that one might try to provoke in it. Finally Clever Hans perfectly understood the German language and became able to express ideas by means of a conventional alphabet hit with its hoof.[70]

As a result of this last research, Clever Hans, now old and tired, gave only uncertain answers, which led Mr. Krall to acquire two Arab stallions, Muhamed and Zarif, which he started training, thus obtaining the brightest results in no time. Thirteen days after the first lesson, Muhamed could solve small additions and subtractions. Remarkably, Mr. Krall never taught his horses how we humans do these mathematical operations, but only what they entail.

The following year, in the month of May, Muhamed could understand French and German, and extract square and cubic roots, performing small calculations such as the following:

$$\frac{(3 \times 4) + \sqrt{36}}{3} \qquad \frac{\sqrt{36} \times \sqrt{64}}{4}$$

On the other hand, Zarif learned to spell on its own words that were pronounced before it and that it had never seen written before. It is understandable that such results aroused general astonishment, for, as Professor Edouard Claparède wrote, that was the greatest event ever to have occurred in general psychology. Scientists came from all corners, who, at first skeptical, returned convinced of the

---

[70] For details please refer to Dr. Assagioli's report published in the *Annales des Sciences Psychiques*, no. 1, January 1913.

reality of Mr. Krall's stories. Among the renowned men of science who passed judgment on the horses of Elberfeld, first and foremost I would like to quote the illustrious Ernst Haeckel, who wrote to Mr. Krall:

> "Your careful and critical research shows convincingly the existence of reasoning in animals, which for me has never been in doubt."

The famous naturalist evidently saw in this similarity between animals and humans a confirmation of his materialistic theories. Next is Dr. Edinger, an eminent neurologist at Frankfurt; Professors Dr. H. Kraemer and Dr. H. E. Ziegler, both of Stuttgart; Dr. Paul Sarazin from Basel; Professor Ostwald of Berlin; Prof. Dr. A. Beredka, of the Institut Pasteur, Paris; Dr. Claparède, from the University of Geneva; Professor Scheeller; the physician Professor Gehrke, from Berlin; Professor Goldstein, from Darmstadt; Professor Dr. von Buttel-Reopen, of Oldenburg; Professor William Mackenzie of Genoa; Prof. Dr. R. Assagioli, Editor-in-Chief of the journal *Psyche*, in Florence; Dr. Hartkopf, of Cologne; Dr. Freudenberg, of Brussels, who came to Elberfeld to check the unexpected faculties which were revealed among the horses of Mr. Krall; Dr. Ferrari, professor of neurology at the University of Bologna, who, after having published in the Italian *Rivista de Psicologia* and the French *Annales des Sciences Psychiques*, an article contrary to the thesis of Mr. Krall, then declared himself convinced of the reality of horse intelligence after a more thorough examination of the issue.

Enumerating all the prestigious endorsements above is essential in order to make us accept the reality of intelligence in horses, since most of us are usually inclined to see our domestic animals only as mere machines.

However, as Alfred Russel Wallace puts it, "facts are stubborn things," and we must bow to them when they are irrefutably established, which is the case here. Actually, how else can one explain results like this as an animal's own work? One day Mr. Mackenzie and other participants wrote the following fourth root problem on the blackboard: $\sqrt[4]{(1874161)}$. Then the exactly correct answer, 37, was given by the horse Muhamed, while the participants were all in the outside yard, watching what was happening in the stable through a small opening. Another time, the problem was posed by telephone and Muhamed's solution, although ignored by the person who was writing it on the board, was given exactly by the intelligent quadruped.

Better still, questions enclosed in sealed envelopes, of which none of the participants knew the solutions, were sent by Dr. Hartkopf from Cologne. Muhamed answered all of them exactly. On the other hand, the Belgian playwright, poet, and essayist Maurice Maeterlinck, in his book *The Unknown Guest*,[71] reports that, having gone to Elberfeld, he asked Muhamed and Zarif some small mathematical problems to which he did not know the solution, having not looked at the numbers that were presented to be added up; however, in all instances, the answers were always correct.

So it seems that this is not a transmission of thought or even a telepathic action coming from anyone. As the issue is of the utmost importance, I will cite a report made by Professor G. Grabow against the hypothesis of the transmission of thought as an explanation for all cases. He was experimenting with horse Clever Hans. He wrote as follows:

> "I stuck playing cards on white paper and put on each of them numbers for small operations, for example: 2+3; 4+2; 7–2; 12–5; 5×2, etc ... As we had agreed, Mr. von Osten had to stand in the left corner of the courtyard, while I was standing in the right corner; then he had to send me Hans. This was done. Hans came in front of me and I said to it: 'Hans, I'll show you a card on which there is a calculation to make: go to the gentleman opposite, and if you give the

---

71 [Trans. note] M. MAETERLINCK, *The Unknown Guest* (Trans. A. Teixeira de Mattos. London: Methuen & Co., 1914), ch. IV, "The Elberfeld Horses," p. 181 *et seq*.

right answer, you will have sugar. Do you want it?' Hans replied in the affirmative, lowering its head.

I pulled the cards out of my pocket and shuffled them so that I did not know what was the card below, and then showed it to Hans. I asked it, 'Did you understand?' It answered 'yes' again. 'Then go to the gentleman opposite and give him the answer. Hans went to Von Osten, who asked him, 'So what's the solution?' Hans stomped five times. What is the first digit? Answer: 2. What is the second digit? Answer: 3. Only then did I look at the card below the deck. Indeed, on this card there were 2+3, which Hans had read, understood, and calculated correctly. All this without anyone having been able to help the horse, let alone being helped by an unconscious suggestion which, in this case, was impossible. As for me, I did not know the numbers, and Von Osten could not have seen them on the other side of the court.

This experience was repeated in the same way and Hans answered its master: 7. Which number is the first? Answer: 12. So Hans understood the minus sign and solved the problem 12–5 quite correctly and without any help.

Signed: Dr, Grabow
Member of the Council of Higher Education of Prussia"

The two following examples are all the more interesting for showing a truly intelligent initiative:

(Mr. Krall, speaking of his horse Zarif, told Maeterlinck the following two anecdotes which demonstrate the spontaneity of the intelligence of these remarkable solipeds.)

"One morning, for instance, I came to the stable and was preparing to give him his lesson in arithmetic. He was no sooner in front of the spring-board than he began to stamp with his foot. I left him alone and was astounded to hear a whole sentence, an absolutely human sentence, come letter by letter from his hoof: 'Albert has beaten Hänschen,' was what he said to me that day. Another time, I wrote down from his dictation, 'Hänschen has bitten Kama.' Like a child seeing its father after an absence, he felt the need to inform

Figure 1. CLEVER HANS WITH WILHELM VON OSTEN

me of the little doings of the stable ; he provided me with the artless chronicle of a humble and uneventful life...."[72]

This was a truly spontaneous initiative by an animal.

In another circumstance, Zarif spelled out "me tired," and instead of solving a problem proposed to it, it gave the name of Mr. Claparède, omitting the vowels as it was customary with these horses.

Mr. Krall bought a handsome blind horse named Berto and taught it calculation by touch, pointing out the numbers with a finger on the skin of the animal. The attempt was a complete success, says Dr. Assagioli, since, in a very short time, Berto learned to hit the number of blows corresponding to the figures drawn on its skin. It was able to give the exact result of several simple additions spoken aloud like 65+11; 65+12, etc.; and a few days earlier, it had answered correctly to questions such as 9–4, 8–2, 3×3, and so on.

Finally a little Shetland pony named Haenschen also learned calculation. Here, then, are different horses, whether in race or age, which testify to their intelligence by answering exactly the little problems that are posed to them. No doubt, like humans elsewhere, they are not always well disposed; they happen to make mistakes and, oddly enough, it seems that sometimes the personality of the one who examines them influences their mentality; to the point that with some people they reply quickly and well, whereas they show repugnance and bad will toward those disliked by them.

All these facts seem to establish that, contrary to popular opinion, the horse is really intelligent, that it is capable of reasoning, and that it is closer to humanity than one was tempted to suppose if looking only at its place on the zoological scale.

Now the following are the cases of other pets that have proved to be even more extraordinary than the horses of Mr. Krall.

---

72 *Op. cit.*, ibid., p. 218.

A DOG NAMED ROLF

The facts that I will now narrate are partly drawn from a lecture given by Mr. Edmond Duchâtel, a member of the Société Psychique of Paris,[73] and a work of Dr. Mackenzie, published in the *Annales des Sciences Psychiques*.[74]

It was through an article published in the French newspaper *Le Malin* that Mr. Duchâtel was informed of the actions and gestures of the dog Rolf, which made him decide to check for himself the reality of such strange stories. He went to see Mrs. Moekel, the wife of a lawyer who lived in Mannheim, Germany. The following are some of the experiments he conducted. Let me say right away that Rolf was a three-year-old Scottish Airedale terrier with red hair, and about 23 inches tall.

To begin with, Mr. Duchâtel posed to the little animal the following problem, $(96-10) \div 9$. Few elementary school children would be able to solve this little math problem; however, Rolf answered immediately 9. Asked if there was a remainder, he gave the number 5. He still solved exactly these two questions: 10+3=13; and 6−2=4. Here is an important observation: the dog, intrigued by the presence of a stranger, asked Mrs. Moekel, using her conventional alphabet: "Who is this gentleman?" Mrs. Moekel having shown him the signature in Mr. Duchâtel's letter, the dog struck the approximation *"Duhadl"* (pronounced "Duchâtel"), a truly extraordinary result. There was a spontaneous intervention on the part of the dog because it had never been taught to ask this question. Here are the details furnished by M. Duchâtel on the manner in which Madame Moekel's little favorite expressed itself:

"The alphabet of Rolf consists of:

---

73 See the *Annales des Sciences Psychiques*, October 1913, p. 290 et seq.
74 See the *Annales des Sciences Psychiques*, January–February 1914; and the *Archives de la Suisse Romande*.

1st. Of 24 struck signs corresponding to 24 letters (this is the proper alphabetical part);

2nd. Of 5 conventional signs corresponding to 5 [German] words which are: *Ia* (yes), 2 strokes; *Nein* (no), 3 strokes; *Müde* (tired), 4 strokes; *Gasse* (street, go to the street), 5 strokes; *Bett* (bed, go to bed), 7 strokes.

Note that the 24 letters are borrowed from the first 25 digits and not the first 24 digits.

Is it because the number 4 would have duplicated the answer Yes repeated twice, or mixed up with the sign for the word Tired?"

Or should we rather attribute this gap in the choice of signs to the manner so original that one may find it unlikely that the letters were chosen, according to the work that Ms. Moekel had so kindly had of confiding about Rolf's life to me.

Moreover, in the same work reserved for the journal *Tierseele* (*Animal Soul*), in a report which will soon appear in Bonn [Germany], one can read that Rolf never uses the German letters Q, X, and V which is roughly pronounced as F.

But we should add that Rolf's simplifications do not end there. The dog seems to be a resolute partisan of phonetic spelling, it removes as many letters as possible – most often the vowels disappear, especially if they are weakly pronounced – and although the German language already has a very simple spelling, Rolf finds a way to halve the length of words.

For example, the name of his homeland Mannheim, which usually is spelled with 8 letters, he writes it in 4 letters: Mann. Rolf is able to distinguish and perfectly name all the objects that surround it, and also to realize what a drawing depicts. Mr. Duchâtel having shown it the cover of an illustrated magazine brought in at that very moment by one of Mrs. Moekel's children, showing a blanket representing a vase with flowers, the dog answered immediately: 'Glass with little flowers.'"

Rolf showed great affection to Mrs. Moekel because she had taken good care of it following a serious accident that the dog had suffered. So it made every effort to satisfy it. Almost never leaving her, it attended the lessons given by Mrs. Moekel to her youngest daughter. It was then that the most astonishing thing happened, something that no one could ever have imagined: the dog seemed to understand the calculation lessons without it ever having been directly taught to it. The story is so remarkable that I think Mrs. Moekel's testimony should be quoted in full:[75]

> One day at noon I was sitting with the children and doing the thankless job of helping them with their homework. Our little Frieda, so kind and lively, but a little dazed, obstinately resisted to obtain the solution for the 122+2 problem, when, in a bad mood, I gave her a slight reprimand. At this moment the dog, lying under the desk, was looking at us so wide-eyed that I exclaimed: 'Rolf, what's the matter with you? Do you know what 2 plus 2 is?'
> Then, to my complete astonishment, the dog patted 4 times on my arm. My elder daughter suggested that I ask the dog how much 5 plus 5 is. The answer promptly followed with 10 paw strokes. The same evening, continuing our trials, we saw that the animal was resolving without fail all simple problems of addition, subtraction and multiplication posed to it."

Note that, to learn the alphabet strokes, it was this prodigious animal which indicated the number of paw strokes that corresponded to each letter. This is how Ms. Moekel recounts the dog's training:[76]

> "What do you give me for an A? It immediately answered with 4 paw strokes. Then for a B, answer 7 paw strokes, and so on. I carefully noted the numbers given by Rolf, and the next day I was able to establish, to my astonishment, that the animal had fixed these numbers in its memory. We took about five letters each day, but I do not think Rolf would have needed that kind of caution, and that it would have

---

75 [Trans. note] Paula MOEKEL, *Mein Hund Rolf* (Stuttgart: R. Lutz, 1919), pp. 21–22.
76 [Trans. note] *Op. cit.*, p. 29.

remembered all the letters at once. I had inserted the letters Q, X and V, but Rolf has never used them yet.
So I made Rolf get easy words, I dictated letters of the alphabet that I wrote and displayed to it when the word was complete.
Rolf understood very easily and seemed to have great joy in learning."

It is undeniable that we are in presence of intellectual manifestations of the dog and, a remarkable fact, that it itself chose the numbers corresponding to the letters of the alphabet, just as, spontaneously, he had been able to hit with its paw the number of strokes needed to solve that first problem posed to it, of 2+2. Therefore the dog itself took the initiative of using this mode of response, and this fact alone already denotes more thought on its part than we could have expected from an animal that had never been trained to use paw strokes to express its ideas. Sometimes Rolf was mischievous. Once, as it heard talking about people that were hostile to it, Rolf immediately patted out: "They are jackasses." Rolf was reprimanded, and told that it too was sometimes a jackass. Rolf answered "no." Then what are you? "Mommy's Lol"[77] (Lol is the diminutive of Rolf.)

Rolf's mentality is manifested through associations of ideas which are peculiar to it. Thus during a reading, the word 'autumn' having appeared, Rolf was asked what autumn meant. Instead of the word 'season,' which was expected, Rolf replied, "The time when there are apples." That was simply because at that time of the year the Moekels used to make Rolf eat them baked in the oven.

Another remark by remarkable Rolf: Mr. and Mrs. Moekel received the announcement of the engagement of one of their friends with Miss Daisy Falham Chester. The family was involved in this event when Rolf intervened: "Doctor gave young lady same name as our cat." Daisy was the name of

---

77 [Trans. note] *Op. cit.*, p. 128.

Figure 2. ROLF WITH PAULA MOEKEL

the house cat, and this coincidence seems to have enlivened Rolf's mischievous soul.

About this cat, it is useful to point out that it also knew how to make small calculations.

That is why one day, when Rolf felt tired, instead of answering the question he requested, "Let Barbara take Lol away and bring in Daisy."

After all these examples, we can say with French psychiatrist Edgar Bérillon:[78]

> "The animals whose nervous system presents so much analogy to the structure and morphology of the human one are not automatons devoid of consciousness, intelligence and reasoning, such as good persons are pleased to represent them. Education and training efforts identical to those used for the upbringing of a child would in the long run lead to unexpected results."

This is precisely what all the people who are fond of animals and have the patience necessary to educate them have verified, as we shall see a little further on.

In Dr. Mackenzie's report we find the story of a touching little scene:

> "Mrs. Moekel having separated from her little daughter Frieda to send her to a boarding school, cried, when Rolf, without being invited, patted out: "Mommy, do not cry, it hurts Lol."

Rolf had a companion, the dog Jela, who also knew arithmetic, but was less skilled than her partner.

We have seen that the cat Daisy was able to do some small calculations too. This was the case with Dr. Mackenzie and Dr. Wilser who posed the following problems:

17+4 divided by 7, minus 1, she answered: there are 2 left.

3×3−5, she answered: there are 4 left.

---

[78] E. Bérillon, "Les Mémoires topographiques et la capacité calculatrice chez les animaux" in *Revue de Psychothérapie et de Psychologie Appliquée*, Paris, 1912.

This is definitely the best demonstration of Mrs. Moekel's prowess at training and education.

It should not be assumed, however, that these animals had no difficulty in performing this mental work; sometimes the solution of arithmetic problems would cause enormous strain to them. Dr. Mackenzie once remarked:

> "One is stunned at the dog's very visible mental effort, which results in sighing, gasping or yawning, and can even produce nasal bleeding after long, tiring sessions."

Therefore it is the animal itself which indisputably makes those intellectual efforts without any extraneous intervention.

Despite Rolf's intelligence, the dog is still an animal for which physical satisfaction takes precedence over all other things. To the question asked by Dr. Mackenzie, "Tell me what you love more than anything?" Rolf answered without hesitation, "Eat smoked salmon." To completely exclude the hypotheses of unconscious signs that the animal would perceive, or of a perception of thought, Dr. Mackenzie resumed, by varying it a little, the same experiment of Dr. Grabow with the horse Hans. Because of its importance, I will quote Dr. Mackenzie's report verbatim:[79]

> "So I decide to prepare four small cardboard cards which I brought with me. I asked Mrs. Moekel to draw a canary or other bird in ink, and to write on the other one with her usual handwriting, for the dog, the name of the little girl Karla whom the dog really liked.
> In the meantime, I drew on one of the two remaining small cards a big star and filled it with color using a blue pencil, and, on the other, two contiguous squares, one blue, the other red, they too filled with color.
> Throughout these preparations, Rolf remained away outside; when it returned, the boxes were already enclosed in envelopes also brought by me. Then I asked little Karla to go to another room and mix the envelopes as best she

---

[79] *Annales des Sciences Psychiques*, February 1914, pp. 40–41.

could, so that I would not know their contents, and bring them back to me. That was what she did.

All the participants, myself included, stood behind Ms. Moekel. I also excluded, after a careful surveillance, the slightest possibility of any tricks involving mirrors.

The flash cards were all with their drawn part on the same side, that is to say, toward the face of their respective envelopes. This way I could easily take any of them out of its envelope without ever seeing the drawing on it. I made this maneuver behind Mrs. Moekel's head, lifting the card, ignored by me, above her head, and holding it up and down, always with the drawn side facing toward the dog only.

She takes the card as I hold it; shows it for a moment to the dog, prompting it to say what it saw – so I always take the card back the same way, and I put it back in the envelope, which then I insert in my pocket. I am absolutely sure that no other but the dog could see the drawing. However, Rolf does not want to hear about answering: it pats out 4 ('tired'), lies on the ground and wants to leave.

Ms. Moekel, very worried about the outcome of the experiment, begs, pleads, then threatens Rolf.

In my turn I instigate and encourage the dog as much I can, and promise that if it replies well I will show it several images that I brought for it. This seems to change its resolve, and finally, without the slightest hesitation, Rolf pats out: 'red and blue square.'

So, luckily, it was a drawing made by myself that had been picked out earlier, thus eliminating any suspicion whatsoever about the validity of this experiment, which can be said to haven been a complete success after all."

Rolf knows exactly what differentiates itself from its fellow dogs. Dr. Mackenzie, having shown it an engraving representing a basset dog, Rolf replies, "Dog." Then the doctor asked, "How is it different from you?" Immediately Rolf patted out, "Other paws." It was impossible to better specify the difference.

It is therefore quite obvious that it was Rolf itself which, without any extraneous intervention, knew how to recognize and describe Dr. Mackenzie's drawing, while at the same time finding the exact words to express its thought. These are truly intelligent phenomena which show that the animal psyche is closer to ours than one could ever have imagined.

An interesting question is how animals come to understand each other without articulated language. In the correspondence exchanged between Mrs. Moekel and Dr. Mackenzie, here is what we find about it. When Ms. Moekel was quizzing Rolf, she asked:

> "'How do you get along with other dogs? That is, how do you make sense of them and how do they understand you?' Rolf kept silent.
> 'Did you understand my question?' Answer: 'Yes.' 'So?' Answer: *'Bellen, welden, auch* [or *aug*]* *sehen klappen mit mund'*[80] ('Barking, wagging tail, also see the movements with the mouth').
> (*) The word *aug* could mean *Auge* (eye). In that case, the answer would have been even more accurate and complete."

The day when official, mainstream science decides to engage in the path opened by Mr. von Osten, Mr. Krall and Mrs. Moekel, the veil that still covers the process of development of intelligence throughout the animal series will be torn apart and we will eventually understand how this progression of the mind takes place; which, from the lowest levels of the zoological scale, reaches the magnificent development that is observed among the most illustrious representatives of the human race.

---

[80] Keep in mind that Rolf used an abbreviated, made-up orthography when patting out its answers (always in German).

Lola

It seems that the study of the intellectual faculties of our domestic animals will now go on everywhere, and especially beyond the Rhine (Germany), because Miss Henny Kindermann published in 1919 a book[81] in which she tells how she taught her dog Lola[82] to read and write. Lola was an offspring of the dog Rolf and seemed as intellectually developed as her father. She learned, indeed, very quickly to do the four arithmetic operations and to solve small problems. She was also able to express her thoughts by means of paw strokes on a conventional alphabet. I deem it interesting to point out certain peculiarities of the dog Lola which established that, if at times she could get acquainted telepathically (which brings the animal closer to the human being) with the thoughts of her mistress, in other circumstances the dog demonstrated a personal will that demonstrated the autonomy of its intelligence. Interestingly, Lola claims to be able to discover through smell the state of mind of her interlocutors. In fact, she could easily detect anxiety, sadness, or fatigue. Moreover, when questioned by Miss Kindermann one day on her impressions of the moment, Lola gave only meaningless answers and seemed visibly embarrassed. Pressed with questions, she answered indistinctly "tell lies." Her interlocutor reassures her:

> "'Lola! I won't be angry; do I smell of lies?' 'Yes.' 'Here at home?' '*Minchen*.' (*Minchen* = Munich.) And then it suddenly dawned on me; an hour earlier I had told the dog that I was going to Munich and that perhaps she might go with me. Yet at the same time I was by no means so sure that

---

81 H. Kindermann, *Lola or The Thought and Speech of Animals*, with a chapter on "Thinking Animals" by Dr. W. Mackenzie (Trans. A. Blake. London: Methuen & Co., 1922).

82 Those wishing to know how she went about it should be able to consult the journal *Psychica*, March 1922, p. 10 and 12; the article is signed by Mr. Maillard.

this could be managed, and thought therefore of taking her to Stuttgart."[83]

This last line might suggest that it was not an exercise in smell, but a thought reading. And, of course, this interpretation which most critics hasten to apply to all manifestations of animal intelligence, has been the subject of careful research by Miss Kindermann. I cannot do better than reproduce below her own conclusions on this subject.

(One day the dog, questioned about the name of a person who was heard to arrive but who had not yet been sighted, designated not the expected entrant, but another lady that Miss Kindermann was waiting for at that moment. Miss Kindermann then asked the dog:)

> "'Why did you give me a wrong answer, saying Frieda when it was Guste?' and Lola responded with, 'You think!' 'What?' said I, 'Did you feel what I was thinking?' 'Yes.' 'And do you always feel what I think?' 'Yes.'
> This was something quite new, but I explained it to myself, and my view has proved to be correct in all subsequent tests undertaken by me. It is this: Dogs are susceptible to thought-transference — also, that they are more particularly open to this when tired and when lazy. Further — they are open to such thought-transference even when not actually aware of the question ..., for here Lola had been able to 'tap' my thoughts with respect to what was familiar to her — (i.e. the name of the other maid) but (and this is the most important point) — a dog cannot receive impressions in respect of matters of which it has no knowledge!
> It has constantly happened that Lola has held out against me in the matter of some figure in her sums and that — later on — I have found myself to have been at fault, this showing that the numerals 'pictured' in my mind can have made no impression on hers; yet, on the other hand, it has also happened that she has accepted my inaccuracies — simply because she was tired, and did not want the trouble of 'thinking for herself.' Indeed, I could see as much in her

---

83 H. KINDERMANN, *Lola* ..., pp. 77–78.

eyes — there would be a sense of inertia about her, which indicated that she was only waiting to 'guess' by means of feeling — a willing receptacle, as it were, ready to receive my thoughts. I have often made the attempt at 'thinking' new things into her head — but have found this quite impossible."[84]

These remarks are very important; thought-reading, a convenient means of explaining certain embarrassing phenomena, cannot play a constant and universal role, and it is interesting to try to specify its limits. It is obvious, both by the example of the dog Lola and by the information on animal psychology currently in our possession, that the subjects observed give undoubted proof of spontaneity and autonomy, since they are sometimes even in complete contradiction with their interrogators.

Here are some examples cited by Miss Kindermann:

"27 July [1916]: Today I invited her to tell me something she might be thinking about, adding: 'Will you say something?' *Ja, esen* [eat].' 'Oh, Lola!' I said in desperation, 'Why all this talk about eating! about food! don't I hear enough of it from senseless laborers and maids? and now you begin too! It can't be otherwise, at present: say something else!' '*Ich am esen*'... 'What? again! well go on.' '... *zu wenig narung. Ich am essen zu wenig nahrung*' (= I from my food (derive) too little nourishment)....[85]

"Now, on the 18 May I said to her : 'Lola, you must write to my father and thank him for the biscuits, he will then send you some more. This is the way to write a letter, one begins — 'dear Father', or just 'dear', and then one tells what one is thinking about, you must, therefore, thank him — and when the letter is finished — you must put 'love from Lola'... Lola started rapping out without further delay, and continued rapidly and 'fluently' — so to speak — her letter running as follows: '*lib, nach uns kom, ich una ..*' (here I interrupted her, believing her about to say '*ich*

---

84 *Op. cit.*, p. 100.
85 *Op. cit.*, p. 188.

und Henny') and asked 'is this right?' She said it was: 'but, Lola,' I urged, 'be sure you are careful! ought this not to be a 'd'?' 'No!' she said. I was at a loss to make out where this 'a' came in, but told her to go on — and Lola rapped; '... *artig eben, oft we, kus ich!*' So the '*una*' had been part of '*unartig*' [naughty]! (= 'dear, come to us, I have just been naughty, often pains,[86] kiss (you) I.') ... This letter seems a brilliant proof of independent thinking."[87]

From these examples we can conclude without fear of rashness that animals are capable of thinking for themselves and have no need to draw from others the elements of their ideas. Humans can no longer be considered Nature's only thinking reeds,[88] since they really differ from certain beings that surround them only by the more considerable extent of their intelligence, but not by the very nature of their faculties of reasoning.

Zou

Mrs. Borderieux, the active director of the periodical *Psychica*, who has long been known for her concern for animals, has recently begun to educate her dog Zou and has already obtained some interesting results with regard to calculation. We can predict that this Parisian animal will follow in the footsteps of its German predecessors. Readers who wish to keep abreast of its progress may do so in the above-mentioned journal, which from time to time publishes interesting accounts of Zou's education and progress.

---

86 The word "naughty" alluded to a reprimand that the dog had just received for going alone hunting, and the expression "often pains" applies to headaches and fatigue which she complains about repeatedly in her communications.

87 H. Kindermann, *Lola* ..., pp. 97–98

88 [Trans. note] G. Delanne's allusion to Blaise Pascal's saying, "Man is a thinking reed."

5

SUPERNORMAL FACULTIES IN ANIMALS AND THEIR INDIVIDUAL PRINCIPLE

ANALOGIES BETWEEN ANIMAL AND HUMAN FACULTIES · TELEPATHY · COLLECTIVE HEARING CASES THAT SEEM TO SHOW THE EXISTENCE OF AN ANIMAL GHOST · A DOG'S PRESENTIMENT · VISION OF AN INVISIBLE FORM BY A DOG · PHANTOM OF A DOG SEEN BY A CAT · PHANTOMS PERCEIVED COLLECTIVELY BY HUMANS AND ANIMALS · PRECEDENCE OF ANIMAL VISION OVER THAT BY HUMANS · PHANTOM VISIBLE TO TWO PERSONS AND A DOG · PLACES HAUNTED BY ANIMALS · THE CASE OF MADAME D'ESPÉRANCE · SEVERAL EXAMPLES OF VISIONS OF DEAD ANIMALS · THE CASE OF MRS. HUMPHRIES · THE LAUGHING DOG · THE CASE OF MR. TWEEDALE, THE PHANTOM OF THE DOG, VISIBLE IN BROAD DAYLIGHT TO SEVERAL PEOPLE · CASES CITED BY DASSIER · PHANTOMS OF ANIMALS IN MATERIALIZATION SEANCES · PITHECANTHROPUS IN SEANCES WITH THE MEDIUM KLUSKI · NEVI · SUMMARY

THE CLEAR ANALOGY which exists between the intellectual manifestations of higher animals and those of humans leads us to ask ourselves whether the supernormal faculties which we observe among us could not exist to any degree in those which we have so rightly classed as our lower fellow beings.

It is obvious that this is an issue that can only be solved through observation. On this subject, however, there are already a number of accounts which have been collected by the great Italian psychologist, Mr. Bozzano. He published them in the French *Annales des Sciences Psychiques* of August 1905. Unfortunately, I cannot, to my great regret, because of the smallness of this volume, reproduce them integrally. Therefore I will only borrow a few cases that seem to seriously support the hypothesis of a transmission of thought between animals and humans, with the initiative of the first. If these observations multiply, the fundamental identity of the intelligent principle in all the higher animals will thus be established so as to leave no doubt. Here is one very interesting first example where it seems that there was not only a psychical action exerted by the animal, but also a kind of temporary possession. The phenomenon having occurred during a dream, it is necessary to make some reservations when it comes the interpretation of the impressions felt by Mr. Rider Haggard as being due to a real possession. One can rather see in them more exactly a case of autosuggestion on the part of the dreamer, which gave him impressions similar to those produced in suffocation by immersion. Be that as it may, here is the story that has been authenticated by the British Society for Psychical Research (SPR):[89]

> "On the night of Saturday, July 9, I went to bed about 12:30, and suffered from what I took to be a nightmare. I was awakened by my wife's voice calling to me from her own bed upon the other aide of the room. As I awoke, the nightmare itself, which had been long and vivid, faded from my brain. All I could remember of it was a sense of awful oppression and of desperate and terrified struggling for life such as the act of drowning would probably involve. But between the time that I heard my wife's voice and the time that my consciousness answered to it, or so it seemed to me, I had another dream. I dreamed that a black retriever dog, a most amiable and intelligent beast named Bob, which was the property of my eldest daughter, was lying on its side among brushwood, or rough growth of some sort, by water. My own personality in some mysterious way seemed to me to be arising from the body of the dog, which I knew quite surely to be Bob and no other ... In my vision the dog was trying to speak to me in words, and, failing, transmitted to my mind in an undefined fashion the knowledge that it was

---

[89] *Journal of the SPR*, no. CCXII, vol. XI, October 1905, p. 278 *et seq*. See also the Italian *Luce e Ombra*, October 1922, etc.; and the French *Revue Psychique*, August 1905.

dying.... I woke to hear my wife asking me why on earth I was making those horrible and weird noises ... and shortly afterwards I went to sleep again and was disturbed no more. On the Sunday morning Mrs. Rider Haggard told the tale at breakfast, and I repeated my story in a few words.

Thinking that the whole thing was nothing more than a disagreeable dream, I made no inquiries about the dog and never learned even that it was missing until that Sunday night, when my little girl, who was in the habit of feeding it, told me so. At breakfast time, I may add, nobody knew that it was gone, as it had been seen late on the previous evening. Then I remembered my dream, and the following day inquiries were set on foot.

To be brief, on the morning of Thursday, the 14th, my servant ... and I discovered the body of the dog floating in the Waveney against a weir about a mile and a quarter away.... In the course of his duties Harry Alger was on the bridge, where he found a dog's collar torn off and broken by the engine, coagulated blood, and bits of flesh, of which remnants he cleaned the rails.... It would seem that the animal must have been killed by an excursion train ..."

"The veterinary surgeon who examined the body of the dog wrote to Mr. Rider Haggard as follows: Cause of Death — Fracture of skull in three places, the skull being smashed almost to a pulp by some heavy, blunt instrument ..."

In discussing this fact, Mr. Bozzano points out that among the causes that could be invoked to explain this dream, a telepathic action of the animal is most likely, since no human person was likely to have witnessed the tragic event. Pure clairvoyance by telesthesia itself would have required an external cause, and the thought of the animal is also the only cause that can be invoked in this case. Let us see other examples where this action also seems to have been at play. We know that sometimes the one who feels a telepathic impression feels an urge to move. It seems likely that in the next story something similar happened. Here it is:

"I own a rough terrier, about 5 years old, which I have brought up from a pup. I have always been a great lover of animals, dogs especially. This dog returns my affection so much that I never go anywhere, not even leave the room, but he must follow me. He is death on rats, and the scullery being visited occasionally by these rodents, I have a comfortable bed for Fido to sleep on. In this room there is a fireplace with an oven suitable for baking, and a boiler for washing, with a flue running back into the chimney.... It was my custom to take him to his bed the last thing before retiring for the night. I had undressed and was about getting into bed, when an unaccountable feeling came over me of impending danger. I could think of nothing possible but Fire, and the impression was so strong that I yielded to it and actually dressed again, and went downstairs and examined each room to satisfy myself that all was right. When I got to the scullery I missed Fido, and thinking he had slipped by me unobserved to go upstairs, I immediately began to call him, but getting no response, I called to my sister-in-law to know if she had heard him, and getting an answer in the negative, I began to feel excited, and rushed back to the scullery again, and called repeatedly, but not a sound could be heard. What to do I did not know. It then occurred to me that if anything will get him to respond it will be the sentence, 'Come for a walk, Fido,' which always gave him delight. As soon as I had repeated this sentence, I heard a faint cry, muffled as if distant ; calling again, the cry of a dog in distress came plainly.... Hearing the noise my sister-in-law came to the scene. We found a rat-hole in the fireplace which led to the flue. Fido had evidently chased the rat into the flue and could not turn or retreat.... This occurred a few months ago and was reported at the time in our local paper, but I never thought of sending it to you until I read the Rider Haggard story.

[Signed:] J. R. Young"[90]

---

90 *Op. cit., ibid.*, p. 323.

I repeat that there are many other examples of such telepathic action that had to be excluded here for lack of room; therefore I feel obliged to refer the reader to the work of Mr. Bozzano.

I now come to a case where the telepathic action was felt by two people at the same time, which excludes the hypothesis of a hallucination between the animal soul and the human soul, since it seems that here we have to deal with an animal double producing a physical noise (i.e., a collective auditory case) at the Beauchamps.

> "Last night—Megatherium [a small Indian dog] sleeping with [my daughter]—I woke, hearing him run round my bedroom. I know his step so well. [My husband] woke too. I said 'Listen.' He said, 'It is Meg.' We lighted a candle, looked well, there was nothing and the door was shut. Then I had a feeling something was wrong with the dog—it came into my head he had died at this minute, and I looked for my watch to see the time, and then I thought I must go up and see about him. It was so cold, and it seemed so silly, and while I was thinking I fell asleep. It must have been some little time after, someone knocked at the door, and it was [my daughter] in agony. 'Oh! mamma, Meg is dying.' We flew upstairs. He was lying on his side like dead—his legs stretched straight out like a dead thing's. [My husband] picked him up, and for a while couldn't see what was wrong, for he was not dead. Then we found he had nearly strangled himself—got the strap of his coat somewhat from under his stomach and round his neck. He soon revived and recovered when we got it off, and he could breathe freely."[91]

One might perhaps suppose that in this case it was the anxiety felt by Miss Beauchamp that was transmitted to her mother. But then it is quite improbable that the supposed hallucination would be translated for the two percipients in the form of sounds reminiscent of Meg's jumps. I believe

---

91 *Proceedings of the SPR*, vol. XXXIII, year 1923, part LXXXVI, p. 342.

that here the hypothesis of an animal double is the most probable.

A very curious observation reported by the famous Danish writer Hans Christian Andersen seems to establish that there can exist sympathetic relations at great distances between humans and animals, and that this action is capable of being translated in the form of presentiments, exactly like those which take place between humans. This curious story is reproduced below:[92]

> "The Danish storyteller Andersen had a friend, a professor named Linden, who was suffering from pulmonary consumption. The Administration granted him subsidies for a trip to Italy. Linden had a dog named Love, a white poodle he loved very much and gave to Andersen for the duration of his absence. Andersen accepted this charge and ensured the dog's sustenance without otherwise taking care of it. He laughed heartily one day, when the maid said to him: 'Love can feel what is happening to its master. It is either joyful or sad, depending on whether its master is doing well or badly.' – 'What do you mean?' said Andersen. – 'Oh? but that is easy to see in its way of being. Why does it accept or refuse food without being ill? Why does it let its head hang down several days before you get bad news from Mr. Linden? The dog knows exactly what its master does in Italy, and it sees it, for its eyes sometimes have a singular expression.' From that moment on, despite his skepticism, Andersen watched the dog more closely. One night he felt something cold in his hand and, opening his eyes, he saw the dog beside his bed, licking his hand. He shivered. He stroked the animal to calm it, but then Love uttered a plaintive howl and threw itself on the ground, with its four legs stretched. At that moment, Andersen told later, I knew very exactly that my friend was dead. I was so sure that the next day I replaced my brown garment with a black one. In the morning, I met with a person of my acquaintance who asked my reason for

---

92 [Trans. note] Although duly translated from its French version, no original is given by G. Delanne, nor could it be located.

mourning. I told him: 'At 11:30 minus three minutes last night, Olof Linden died.' As I learned later, that was indeed the exact moment of his death."

In the example below, the witnesses describe objects moving without apparent contact in a haunted house, while a dog appears to have been aware of the intelligent but invisible character who was behind the phenomena.

A LIKELY CASE OF CLAIRVOYANCE[93]

About a haunted house in Versailles, France, in a letter addressed to Dr. Darieux, Mr. H. de V. says: "After about ten minutes, as the servant told us her troubles, an old wheelchair, placed in a corner on the left, started to move, and, describing a broken path, passed between Mr. Sherwood and me, then turned around itself about a meter behind us, striking the floor with its hind feet two or three times, and then returning in a straight line back to its corner. This happened in broad daylight and we were able to make sure there was no trickery or anything of the sort. The same chair resumed its course three different times, being cautious, strange thing, not to hurt anyone. At the same time violent blows were heard at the other corner of the neighboring room, which was wide open and completely deserted. The friend who had driven us there threw his dog to the corner of the room; the animal came back squealing, obviously in deep terror. Our friend was obliged to hold the dog in his arms for as long as we remained in the house.

Here is another example where the clairvoyance of a sensitive is confirmed by that of an animal.[94]

---

93 Case borrowed from German journal *Psychische Studien*, Nov. 1905.
94 *Psychische Studien*, July 1908. [Trans note: See also footnote 20 above.]

Phantom of a dog seen by a cat

Mr. Carrington reports the following, very peculiar, fact: A gentleman and two ladies were walking in the countryside, when one of the ladies, who is a seeing medium, declared that she could see a dog walking in front of them. She described it meticulously to the other two people, who saw nothing. As they talked about it, a cat came out of a neighboring house and approached very quietly the spot where the lady accused the presence of a dog. When the cat got there, it stopped abruptly, arched its back high, hissed angrily, and clawed at the phantom, then suddenly turned around and ran back to its house.

Phantoms collectively perceived by humans and animals

Collections of psychical observations contain a large number of narratives of which I would like to call attention to this fact of the highest interest, namely, that apparitions have been seen simultaneously by those present and by animals. Assuming that the vision has been subjective, it demonstrates that animals possess, like humans, an indisputable faculty of clairvoyance. Conversely, if one would conjecture that the vision was objective, then it must be deduced that the phantom was real, since the dog perceived it at the same time as the people.

Here are two examples where the phantom was first seen by the animal. It seems from this story that often dogs perceive by clairvoyance beings that are invisible to those present, which brings the case closer to the one reported about the haunted house of Versailles.

Visions of Human Phantoms Not Relatable to Any Telepathic Coincidence and Perceived Collectively by Humans and Animals

"From Mr. H. E. S.

August 8th, 1892.

[When aged about 18] about the year 1874, in my father's house, I got up one summer morning about five o'clock, and lighted a fire to get myself some tea. A large bull-terrier dog used to follow me about everywhere, so of course he had to be near me when I was getting the fire to light. He gave a short growl and looked towards the door; this caused me to look round, and to my great terror I saw a tall, dark figure with flashing bright eyes coming into the kitchen towards me. I screamed for help and fell to the floor. My father and brothers ran down from their bedrooms thinking that thieves were in the house. I told them what I had seen, but they said it was an imagination caused by a recent illness. But why should the dog have seen something as well as myself? This dog often used to see things invisible to me. He would start and snap at them, and then turn to me a look with his big eyes, as much as to say : 'Did you see that ?'"[95]

Vision First Perceived by an Animal Instead of a Human

"'It was during the winter of 18— that one evening I happened to be sitting by the side of a cheerful fire in my bedroom, busily engaged in caressing a favorite cat – the illustrious Lady Catherine, now, alas! no more. She lay in a pensive attitude and a winking state of drowsiness in my lap. Although my room might be without candles it was perfectly illuminated by the light of the fire. There were two doors

---

95 *Proceedings of the SPR*, vol. x, p. 327.

– one behind me leading into an apartment which had been locked up for the winter, and another on the opposite aide of the room, which communicated with the passage. Mamma had not left me many minutes, and the high-backed, old-fashioned armchair which she had occupied remained vacant at the opposite comer of the fire-place. Puss, who lay with her head upon my arm, became more and more sleepy, and I pondered on the propriety of preparing for bed. Of a sudden I became aware that something had affected my pet's equanimity. The purring ceased, and she exhibited rapidly increasing symptoms of uneasiness. I bent down and endeavored to coax her into quietness, but she instantly struggled to her feet in my lap, and spitting vehemently, with back arched and tail swollen, she assumed a mingled attitude of terror and defiance.

The change in her position obliged me to raise my head, and on looking up, to my inexpressible horror, I then perceived a little, hideous, wrinkled old bag occupied mamma's chair. Her hands were resting on her knees and her body was stooped forward so as to bring her face into close proximity with mine. Her eyes, piercingly fierce and shining with an overpowering luster, were steadfastly fixed on me. It was as if a fiend were glaring at me through them. Her dress and general appearance denoted her to belong to the French *bourgeoisie*; but those eyes, so wonderfully large, and in their expression so intensely wicked, entirely absorbed my senses and precluded any attention to detail. I should have screamed, but my breath was gone while that terrible gaze so horribly fascinated me. I could neither withdraw my eyes nor rise from my seat.

I had meanwhile been trying to keep a tight hold on the cat, but she seemed resolutely determined not to stay in such ugly neighborhood, and after some most desperate efforts, at length succeeded in escaping from my grasp. Leaping over chairs and tables and all that came in her way, she repeatedly threw herself with frightful violence against the top panel of the door which communicated with the disused room. Then, returning in the same frantic manner, she furiously dashed against the door on the opposite side. My terror was now divided, and I looked by turns, now at the old woman whose great staring eyes were constantly fixed on me, and now at the cat, who was becoming every instant more frantic. At last the dreadful idea that the animal had gone mad had the effect of restoring my breath, and I screamed loudly.

Mamma ran in immediately, and the cat, on the door opening, literally sprang over my head, and for upwards of half-an-hour ran up and down stairs as if pursued. I turned to point out the object of my terror: it was gone.

Under such circumstances the lapse of time is difficult to appreciate, but I should think that the apparition lasted about four or five minutes..

Some time afterward it transpired that a former proprietor of the house, a woman, had hanged herself in that very room. — [Signed:] Miss K.'

General K., brother of the percipient, confirms the above account. (For further details concerning this case, see the *Journal of the SPR*, Vol. III, pp. 268–271.)"[96]

The impression produced on the cat was so profound that for half an hour it remained frantic. In this case, it is more likely that the apparition was real. Let us see one last story: a ghost that manifests itself to two people is also visible to a dog.

The apparition of Palladia
visual, auditory, collective

(*Palladia was a girl who died at the age of 15 and appeared on different occasions and to several people.*)

"In 1885 I was living with my parents at a country house in the province of Poltava. A lady of our acquaintance had come to spend a few days with us, along with her two daughters. Some time after their arrival, having awoke at daybreak,

---

[96] E. Bozzano, "Animals and Psychic Perceptions" in *The Annals of Psychical Science*, vol. II, London, July–December 1905, pp. 105–106.

I saw Palladia ... She stood before me, at about five paces away, and looked at me with a joyful smile. Approaching me, she spoke these few words: 'I have been, I have seen,' and disappeared, still smiling. What these words meant, I could not understand. My setter slept in the room with me. From the time when I perceived Palladia, my dog bristled up its hair, and jumped yelping on to my bed; pressing up against me, he looked in the direction in which I saw Palladia. The dog did not bark, whereas ordinarily he did not let anyone come into the room without barking and growling. And every time that my dog saw Palladia, he pressed close up to me, as though seeking refuge. When Palladia disappeared, and I went into the main part of the house, I said nothing to anyone about this incident. In the evening of the same day, the eldest daughter of the lady who was with us told me that a strange thing had happened to her that morning. 'Having woke early,' she said, 'I felt as though there was someone at the head of my bed, and I distinctly heard a voice saying to me: 'Do not be afraid of me, I am good and loving.' I turned my head, but saw nothing; my mother and sister were sleeping quietly; I was greatly astonished, for nothing of the sort has happened to me before.' Upon which I replied that many inexplicable things happen to us; but I did not tell her anything of what I had seen that morning. Not until a year later, when I was already her fiancé, did I inform her of the apparition and the words of Palladia on that same morning. Was it not that she had come to see her also? I ought to add that I had not seen the young lady before she paid us this visit, and that I never thought that I was destined to marry her."[97]

Haunted places

In all countries one finds stories according to which certain places or localities seem to be haunted. Abnormal phenomena occur there, such as inexplicable noises,

---

97 *Op. cit., ibid.*, p. 99.

displacements of objects without known cause, and even apparitions. Here are two rather peculiar cases where animals have experienced real terror. The first is reported in the book written by British researchers F. W. H. Myers, Gurney and Podmore, *The Phantasms of the Living*, Vol. II, page 197:

[A collective case]

"The following daylight example is from the Misses Montgomery, of Beaulieu, Drogheda.

"March 2nd, 1884.

'About the year 1875, 1 and my sister (we were about 13 years old then) were driving home in the tax-cart one summer afternoon about 4 o'clock, when there suddenly appeared, floating over the hedge, a female figure moving noiselessly across the road; the figure was in white, and the body in a slanting position, some 1 feet above the ground. The horse suddenly stopped and shook with fright, so much so that we could not get it on. I called out to my sister: 'Did you see that?' and she said she had, and so did the boy Caffrey, who was in the cart. The figure went over the hedge, on the other side of the road, and passed over a field, till we lost sight of it in a plantation beyond. Altogether, I suppose, we watched it for a couple of minutes. It never touched the ground at all, but floated calmly along. On reaching home we told our mother of what we had seen, and we were perfectly certain it was not a mere delusion or illusion, nor an owl, or anything of the kind.'

'I have never seen anything like this nor any apparition before or since. We were all in good health at the time, and no one had suggested any grounds for the apparition beforehand; but we afterwards heard that the road was supposed to be haunted, and a figure had been seen by some of the country folks.'

Violet Montgomery.
Sidney Montgomery."

The second case is even more significant, because many animals that were influenced by this haunted place died as a result of the terror they had felt.

"In the immediate vicinity of Ahrensburg, the only town in the island of Oesel, is the public cemetery ... Several persons, who had attached their horses in front of the same chapel reported that they found them covered with sweat, trembling; and in the utmost terror ... One day in the course of the next month (July) it happened that eleven horses were fastened close to the columns of the chapel ... When the owners reached the spot they found the poor animals in a pitiable condition. Several of them, in their frantic efforts to escape, had thrown themselves on the ground, and lay struggling there; others were scarcely able to walk or stand; and all were violently affected ... In the case of three or four of them these means proved unavailing. They died within a day or two ... An official report setting forth the state of the vault and of the chapel at the time when the commission set seals upon the doors, verifying the fact that the seals were afterward found unbroken ..."[98]

The few examples that I have reported here were taken from a vast number of others that the lack of room does not allow me to reproduce.

They present a variety of manifestations that bring them closer to those found in humans.

We have seen, indeed, that a telepathic action is the most probable explanation for the case of Rider Haggard and Mr. Young. However, we found that a double of the dog Megatherium would be the most likely hypothesis to explain the sounds perceived by Mr. and Mrs. Beauchamp.

It is not just presentiments that are not exclusively found in dogs, but clairvoyance (spirit sight) reported in haunted houses, so that all that we have agreed to call supernormal faculties thus demonstrates to also belong to the animal psyche, which definitely resembles the human soul.

To answer the objection that we cannot attach much importance to anecdotes of this nature, which can be invented

---

[98] R. D. OWEN, *Footfalls on the Boundary of Another World* (Philadelphia: J. B. Lippincott & Co., 1860), pp. 260, 262, 263, 268.

from scratch or distorted by the imagination of the narrators, I should recall that these stories are borrowed for the most part from the reputed Society for Psychical Research in Britain, which instituted careful inquiries of each of the cases we have highlighted here, retaining only those which have been deemed indisputably authentic.

I will now come to another aspect of the issue, which is to establish the survival of the thinking principle in animals. I will do so by quoting examples of visions of posthumous animals and some facts which seem to establish that the thinking individuality of our lower fellow beings is also attached to an indestructible form which is their spiritual body.

Thus, there is indeed perfect continuity in all the manifestations of an incarnate or disincarnate intelligence at all stages of the life scale.

Let us begin this study with the vision of deceased animals which mediums and those with clairvoyance accurately describe without having ever known them or, if they knew them at all, without being informed of their deaths.

Here is a first example related by the famous medium Madame d'Espérance. I borrowed the following story from an interesting article written by her, published in the British periodical *Light*, on October 22, 1904, p. 511:

> "On one occasion have I had any personal experience of the spiritual existence of an animal whom I had known well in life. It was a small terrier, a great favorite and friend of the family, who, in consequence of her master leaving the country, had been given to an admirer dwelling a hundred miles or so away.
> One morning, a year or more later, on entering the dining room, 1 saw, to my astonishment, 'Morna' scurrying round the room in a perfect frenzy of delight, round and round, under tables and chairs, as she was wont to do in moments of excitement or joy after an absence from home. Naturally I concluded that 'Morna's' new owner had brought her, or

that she had found her way home again herself, and I went to make inquiries of the other members of the family. No one, however, knew anything of the dog's return, and search or call as we would, 'Morna' did not show herself again. I was told I must have dreamed I saw the dog, or had been deceived by a shadow, and the incident was forgotten. Months, or perhaps a year, passed before we met 'Morna's' new owner, and asked after her welfare. He then told us that 'Morna' was dead, had been engaged in battle with an enemy and had died from the wounds she received. As far as I could ascertain, this had happened about the time, or a little while previous to the day, on which I had seen her (spirit) racing round the room in her old home."[99]

If the appearance occurred at the time of death of the small animal, this vision could be attributed to telepathy; but if, on the contrary, the phenomenon took place some time after death, then it was indeed the phantom of the animal which was perceived by clairvoyance.

In the following example, if the phantom cat visions may be hallucinatory in nature, that is no longer the case with respect to the description of the dog that Mr. A. V. Peters had never known.

THE SURVIVAL OF ANIMALS AFTER DEATH

The medium A. V. Peters wrote to the British journal *Light* of Saturday, June 5, 1907:

"With reference to the 'survival of animals' I had a curious experience before I became a Spiritualist. I was ill and used to be visited by a cat which belonged to my landlady. Every evening, just before dark, it would come into the room and solemnly walk right round the room and then go out again. It was the only time it entered my apartments. One

---

[99] I left out four other cases, namely: *Proceedings of the SPR*, vol. x, p. 127; *The Phantasms of the Living*, vol. ii, p. 446; *Journal of the SPR*, vol. vi, p. 375, vol. xii, p. 21.

day I was told that the cat had been killed, but the thought passed from my mind, for every night the cat came as usual. However, one evening I suddenly remembered that the cat was dead. As I, at that time, knew nothing about psychic subjects and saw the cat quite plainly, I thought that I must be going mad through pain, but, after a while, I ceased to be visited by puss. On another occasion, after I had given a seance to a family, I sat talking to my host, when I suddenly saw a large brown dog come and place his head on his knees. The dog was so real to me that I described it, and my host recognized it as a much-loved family pet."

From a recent book by the Bordeaux medium, Madame Agullana, entitled *La vie vécue d'un Médium spirite* [*The lived life of a Spiritist medium*],[100] comes a case analogous to the previous one. Here it is:

"I was in Condom-en-Armagnac, at Mr. T——'s office, talking with him and his wife, when I had a singular vision of which I told them. I told them that I saw a spirit, a gentleman, whom I described to them. At the same moment, a dog appeared, of which I described the fur. It was walking through Mr. T——'s store, amid pottery and porcelain. It was constantly reminded by the gentleman: 'Come here, Medor!' As if he feared that the dog would do some damage to the fragile dishes. 'This gentleman died eight years ago already,' said Mr. T–. 'He was one of our best friends who had been like a brother for me. As for the dog which was called Medor, it died almost a year ago.'"

Now the case of Judge Austin is as interesting as the previous ones:

APPARITION OF A DOG

"*The North Somerset Gazette* reports the following story told recently by Mr. Robert Austin at a bulldog dinner in Bristol, and vouched for by him as true. His father, Judge Austin,

---

100 [Trans. note] R. AGULLANA, *La vie vécue d'un Médium spirite* (Bordeaux: Féret & Fils, 1923).

who, as most people know, is a great lover of dogs, possessed a spaniel who was devoted to its master. It was the judge's inseparable companion, and, said Mr. Roger Austin, 'we sometimes wondered whether the dog was thought more of than us children.' In the course of time the dog died. A week or so afterwards Judge Austin called upon a friend at Clifton, and sat talking for a while in the drawing-room. After he had gone, a young Scotch lady, who happened to be staying at the house, inquired who the gentleman with the dog was. The lady of the house replied that it was Judge Austin, but, she added, 'he had no dog with him.' The other replied that there was a dog in the room, and she proceeded to draw an absolutely faithful picture of the old spaniel, even describing its favorite attitude when resting beside its master. 'You may think what you like of this story,' Mr. Roger Austin added, 'but it is true.'"[101]

For inveterate supporters of the theory of thought transmission or cryptesthesia, the description of the animal could have been taken from an image of Judge Austin's subconsciousness – that hypothesis can hardly be sustained when the phantom apparition can also exert its action upon animals.

VISIONS OF ANIMAL PHANTOMS NOT RELATABLE TO ANY TELEPATHIC COINCIDENCE AND PERCEIVED COLLECTIVELY BY HUMANS AND ANIMALS

Well-known medium and author Madame d'Espérance relates a fact in *Light* (vol. xxiv, October 1904, pp. 511-512), involving the sight of a ghost animal that I will now reproduce, citing only the essential details.

While she was walking in a small wood near her home, she noticed that horses were often afraid at some point of the road they were crossing.

---

101 [Trans. note] *Light*, vol. xxxiv, February 21, 1914, p. 95.

"Once or twice, when accompanied by a couple of canine friends, they obstinately refused to enter the wood, but laid themselves down with their muzzles between their forepaws, deaf alike to threats or persuasion. They would joyfully follow me in any other direction, but, if I persisted in going through the wood, they would break loose from me and scamper off home with every symptom of fear.... I mentioned it to my friend, the lady of the manor, who said that such things had happened ever since she could remember ... She also told me that the part of the road running past the wood was looked upon by the peasantry as a rather eerie place....

One day in the autumn of 1896, my friend and I were out walking ...

We stood for a moment, perplexed and wondering, with our backs to the pathway. I was the first to turn, and there before me stood a red-brown calf. Startled by the unexpected and near proximity of such an animal, I uttered a surprised exclamation, and the creature ran into the wood on the opposite side of the pathway. As it darted into the brushwood a curious red brightness flashed in its large eyes, giving me the impression that they emitted fire.....

The sun was setting, and it instantly occurred to me that its level rays, shining full on the eyes of the animal, gave a sufficient explanation of this peculiarity ...

But (except when absent from home now and then) few days have passed that I have not walked or driven through the wood, and nearly always accompanied by two or three canine friends, without, however, encountering the mysterious calf, until, a few weeks ago, while out walking on an intensely hot day, I turned into the wood to find shelter from the sun and glaring whiteness of the roads. I was accompanied by two collies and a tiny terrier. The two collies laid themselves down at the entrance, refusing to proceed, but tried to induce me to go in another direction, exercising all their canine persuasions and arts for the purpose. Finding I persisted in going my own way, they accompanied me, but with visible reluctance. This, however, they seemed to forget after awhile, and gamboled on ahead of me while I strolled quietly along, picking blueberries as I went. Suddenly they came rushing back to me and crouched, whining, at my feet, while the little terrier sprang into my arms. I could not in the least understand what ailed them all. Almost at the same moment I heard a sound of many beating hoofs; they approached rapidly from behind, and before I could move out of the way there came a herd of roe deer in full stampede, galloping past, unheeding both me and the dogs, nearly throwing me down as they brushed past. I looked round, alarmed, for the cause of their terror, or what might be pursuing them, and saw a *red-brown calf* turn and lose itself in the brushwood. Then all was quiet. The deer had gone like the wind to another part of the wood. My dogs, who under ordinary circumstances would have given chase, yelping with excitement, crouched, still trembling and whining, at my feet, while the little terrier refused to leave my arms. For several days afterwards he refused to go through the wood, and the collies, though not refusing, only went under protest, showing plainly a considerable amount of suspicion and fear.

The result of all our inquiries only confirmed our first impressions, viz., that the red-brown calf, or, as the legend has it, 'the calf with the fiery eyes,' was no ordinary living, earthly creature."

The reality of a ghost calf is thus confirmed, not only by the vision of Madame d'Espérance, but especially by the terror felt by deers and dogs that no one had suggested.

The following is another case where the reality of the apparition of a bulldog after its death seems obvious.

A GHOST DOG

"*The Animals' Guardian* recently reprinted several stories of apparitions of animals contributed to The National Review by Captain E. T. Humphries, who had collected them in the course of his travels in many lands. Their general character may be judged from the following, which the captain

states was narrated to him by a friend and his wife, whose statements he has no reason to doubt:
'When resident in South Africa, their bungalow was situated Sclose to the railway, from which the garden was only fenced off by a dwarf wall. At this time they owned a fine mastiff dog which, owing to its perfect manners, was allowed to roam about. Unfortunately one evening, having strayed on to the line, and stepping out of the way of one engine it was run over and killed by another. Some months afterwards the engine-drivers of two evening trains always gave prolonged whistles with their engines. This was very annoying to the dog's late owner; the wife, too, was in delicate health and often lying down about that time. The husband waylaid one of the drivers after duty one evening and asked if the whistling was really necessary, as there were not any signals in view. The man at first resented being questioned upon the subject, but upon the plea of the wife's illness the request was further pressed. The man then suggested that the writer's friend had the remedy in his own hands, as the whistling was only done to prevent his dog being run over, for he was often trespassing on the line, and never moved unless so warned, when he usually passed off over the low wall already spoken of. The description given of the offending dog agreed in every detail with the one that was run over. This apparition continued for some months at frequent intervals.'"[102]

No telepathic action of the dog above can be invoked as an explanation. On the other hand, a visual hallucination of the engine drivers is improbable, since, on different occasions, they see the bulldog's ghost quite distinctly to whistle, in order to make it go away.

Note also that these apparitions took place a few months after the death of the animal, which indicates the survival of its form and the possibility for it to materialize. The following account still puts us in presence of a posthumous materialization of a dog and, remarkable thing, this

---
102 [Trans. note] *Light*, vol. xxxi, September 16, 1911, p. 442.

apparition occurred one hundred six miles away from the city where it had died.

THE LAUGHING DOG[103]

"The following apparition of the spirit of a dog, occurring 106 miles from the locus of his life experience and death, and at the very time of his 'passing out,' is vouched for by the writer, in every particular.

Jim, the dog whose ghost I refer to, was a beautiful collie, the pet of my family, residing at Cheyenne, Wyoming.

He had wide celebrity in the city as 'the laughing dog,' due to the fact that he manifested his recognition of and love for his acquaintances and friends by a joyful laugh, as distinctively such as that of any human being....

One evening in the fall of 1905, about 7:30 p.m., I was walking with a friend on Seventeenth Street in Denver. As we approached the entrance to the First National Bank, we observed a dog lying in the middle of the pavement, and coming up to him I was amazed at his perfect likeness to Jim in Cheyenne.

The identity was greatly fortified by his loving recognition of me, and the peculiar laugh of Jim's accompanying it. I said to my friend, then and there, that nothing but the 106 miles between Denver and Cheyenne would keep me from making oath to the dog being Jim, whose peculiarities I explained to him.

The dog astral, or ghost, was apparently badly hurt. He could not arise.

After petting him and giving him a kind adieu, we crossed over Stout Street, and stopped to look at him again. He had vanished.

The next morning's mail brought a letter from my wife saying that Jim had been accidentally killed the evening before at 7:30 p.m.

---

103 [Trans. note] *The Swastika*, Denver, CO, vol. II, no. 3, July 1907, p. 34.

I shall always believe it was Jim's ghost I saw." (Article signed by Gen. John Charles Thompson.)

What tends to rule out any idea of hallucination is that the ghost dog was seen by two people, including its master, to whom the dog showed its affection in its very special way; and also that its apparition coincided with the exact moment of its death.

The case of Mr. Charles L. Tweedale appeared in the journal *Light*:[104]

> "The Rev. Charles L. Tweedale tells a story of a ghost dog which belonged to his aunt, who died in 1905, the dog having died some time previously. In 1910 her apparition was seen by several members of her family in daylight and by full lamp light. It was sometimes accompanied by growlings and scratchings which puzzled them all greatly. At last the mystery was solved by the appearance of the aunt accompanied by the dog. The animal was twice seen with its mistress, on one occasion by four persons in broad daylight. One child present was so deceived by the apparition that she crawled under the bed after the dog, which she thought was real, only to find that it had vanished."

None of those who saw the ghost had known the animal during its lifetime. They had not seen any photograph of the dog either, since it did not exist. However, their descriptions of the ghost dog coincided absolutely and were consistent with what the animal was in its lifetime.

The collective vision of this dog and the hearing of his growling establish its survival several years after its death on Earth; here again, there was materialization of the phantom.

Here are two other cases reported by me in a memoir presented at the International Spiritualist Congress, held in London in 1898. I borrowed them from Mr. Dassier. The

---

104 [Trans. note] *Light*, vol. xxxv, March 6, 1915, p. 155. See also C. L. TWEEDALE, *Man's Survival after Death* (2nd ed. London: G. Richards Ltd., 1920), p. 146 *et seq*.

text does not allow one to know for certain whether we are in presence of posthumous or living animals, but it seems, if the descriptions are correct, that in both cases materialization was conclusive:

L. Dassier reports the testimony of a farmer who, on returning home at a late hour of the night, saw a donkey grazing in an oat field. He wanted to protect this field from such an inconvenient visitor. When the donkey was near, the farmer took him out of the field and brought him without resistance. He arrived thus to the stable door, but as he was about to open it, the animal disappeared from his hands like a shadow that vanished. Although he looked around him, he could see nothing. Seized with fright, he hurried home and woke his brother to tell him the adventure. The next day they went to the field to find out if such an extraordinary creature had caused great damage and found the harvest intact. The mysterious animal grazed an imaginary oatmeal. The night was clear enough for the farmer to see the trees and shrubs distinctly several meters from the road.

Here is another example told by the protagonist of another event. Mr. Dassier heard it from the narrator himself: "One evening, finding myself on duty (it is a customs officer who was talking) with one of my comrades, we saw, not far from the village where I lived, a mule which passed in front of us and which seemed charged. Supposing that the mule was carrying smuggled goods, and its master had fled when he saw us, we followed it, but the mule threw itself into a meadow, and after making various detours to escape, it returned to the village. While my comrade continued to follow it, I took a transversal road, in order to cut off its way, seeing that it was close up. The animal hurried its course and several inhabitants were awakened by the sound of the hooves resounding on the pavement. I arrived before it at the passage where it was leading to the street which it followed, when suddenly I saw it near me. I stretched out my hand to seize its halter, but the mule disappeared like a shadow, and I only saw my comrade, as astonished as I was." The place where this scene took place was a dead-end road, from which the animal could not have escaped without passing over the body of the customs officer.

The tangible objectivity of that form is demonstrated by the mule's noise as it fled, for the inhabitants of the village were inquiring the next morning about the noise they had heard in the middle of the night.

Apparitions of animals in experimental seances

In a seance held in November 1877 at the house of Commanding Officer Devoluette, the medium Amélie announced that something was developing on the table and precisely on a large sheet put there for mediumistic direct writing: "Here! an animal, I see paws! Ah! it is a small dog sitting on the paper, it is of such and such color, short nose, big round eyes, long ears, tail with long hairs, thin long paws." Soon all present could hear stamping of feet and shaking on the table, and the medium kept us informed of the movements of the animal. It jumps on the spot, it takes the paper between its paws, then scratches, twists and tears it. "Ah! I'm afraid, the dog jumped on my shoulder, it passed on the back of Ms. X (this lady felt the impact), now it has resumed its first position." All could hear some soft barking, and one of the sitters' wife could feel the animal's paws on her hands. It licked the hands of Amélie and of Mrs. X, then disappeared.

When lighting the room again we found the sheet of paper twisted, torn, and distinctly bearing the imprint of small claws.

The barking heard by all the sitters and the traces of the nails left on sheet the paper seem to establish the tangible reality of the ghost dog.

Visible materializations of animal forms

Materializations of animal forms are not a rare occurrence with Polish medium Franek Kluski. In the annotated minutes of the seances held by the Society of Psychical Studies of Warsaw, which will soon be published, I would like to point out especially a big bird of prey, which appeared at several seances and was photographed. Also a strange being, sort of intermediary between a monkey and a human being. This latter apparition is described as having the size of a man; a simian face, but a developed high forehead; its face and body covered with hair; very long arms, strong and long hands, etc. ... It seems to be always deeply moved, take the hands of the sitters and lick them like a dog.

Now, this being, which we called "Pithecanthropus," appeared several times during our seances. One of us, at the sitting of November 20, 1920, felt its big hairy head lean heavily on his right shoulder, against his cheek. This head was covered with thick, rough hair. A smell of wild beast, of wet dog, emanated from the being. One of the sitters having then offered his hand, the Pithecanthropus seized it, then licked it for a long time on three occasions. Its tongue was wide and soft.

Here are some details about this strange being, they were excerpted from the minutes of the sittings that took place in Warsaw in 1919:

> "He is a being the size of an adult man, heavily hairy, with a large mane and a bushy beard. He was clothed in something like a crackling skin; his appearance was that of a being reminiscent of a beast or a very primitive man. He did not speak, but he threw hoarse sounds with his lips, snapped his tongue and gritted his teeth, vainly trying to make himself understood. When he was called, he approached; he allowed his hairy skin to be touched, and touched the hands of the sitters, and scratched his hand very gently with claws rather

than nails. He obeyed the medium's voice and did not hurt the sitters by touching them very gently.

That was a progress, because at the previous seance, this being manifested great violence and brutality. He had a visible tendency and a tenacious will to lick the hands and the faces of the assistants, who defended themselves from these very unpleasant caresses. He obeyed every order given by the medium, not only when this order was expressed by speech, but even when expressed by thought."[105]

At other times we have felt, under our legs, contacts reminiscent of the rustling of a dog.[106] I know that, in the course of the year 1922, Dr. Geley, having gone to Warsaw, took note of materializations of dogs in seances with the medium Kluski. He most certainly published, at a later time, a report giving us the details of these peculiar sittings.

Nevi

The analogy between the spiritual principle of animals and that of humans can also be demonstrated by the influence of the imagination upon the body.

We know that during pregnancy, many women are taken by obsessive, sometimes bizarre, and even extravagant desires. It is a very old popular belief that, if such desires are not satisfied, the child will end up wearing on the skin, in the form of a stain or tumor, the indelible object coveted by the mother: strawberry, cherry, raspberry, wine, coffee, etc. These birthmarks are traditionally called nevi.[107]

---

105 [Trans. note] *Cf.* H. PRICE, *Fifty Years of Psychical Research* (London, New York and Toronto: Longmans, Green & Co., 1939), p. 89–90.

106 *Revue Métapsychique*, July–August 1921, p. 301; January–February 1923, p. 27 *et seq.* See also *Revue Métapsychique*, November–December 1923, p. 396 *et seq.*, "Materialization of animal forms with the medium Guzik."

107 [Trans. note] Plural of *nevus*, a birthmark or a mole on the skin, usually in the form of a raised red patch formed before birth.

In an article published by me in 1904,[108] I gathered a large number of examples, from which it follows that, as a result of violent emotions, pregnant women do imprint on the body of the unborn child the images which had hit them hard.

Weak impressions, when they last, produce the same result as violent and sudden impressions. French doctor Ambroise-Auguste Liébeault says that a winemaker looked amazingly like the statue of the patron saint of his village at the church. During her pregnancy, his mother had a fixed idea that her son would look like this saint.

On the other hand, Dr. W. de Sermyn wrote in the *Journal de Magnétisme* of March 1914:

> "I knew a lady who, having had three children whose hair was black and flat, one day saw a colored lithograph in a shop that represented a pretty little girl of about fourteen with blond, curly hair. She hastened to buy it, framed it, and placed it in her bedroom. 'How happy I would be if God granted me the grace of having a child just like this lithograph,' she often said to me.'
> To my surprise, her desire was fulfilled. She had not only one daughter, but two consecutively.
> At the age of fourteen, these two girls looked exactly like the one in the picture their mother had bought. They were taken for twins, so much were they both alike. The lithography seemed to be their portrait.
> Here the mother's constant attention to the image of the young girl ended up imposing a resemblance to her two children."

The fact below was published by the *Revue Métapsychique* of January–February 1922, under the title, "Un cas présumé d'idéoplastie" ["A presumed case of ideoplasty"].

---

108 *Revue Scientifique et Morale du Spiritisme*, November 1904, p. 321.

It is about a cat that had given birth to a kitten marked across the breast with the figure "1921," at Mrs. Davico, a baker in Nice. The fact was duly noted by Mr. Duquet, a veterinarian, and by a commission composed of Misters Bogdanof, Bizzet and Prozor. The hairs taken from the animal were not dyed and yet they are of a color different from the rest of the fur. Several photographs were taken which clearly show the "1921" figure surmounted by three small white spots.

How to explain this singular anomaly? When interviewed, Mrs. Davico said:

> "At one point, towards the middle of the gestation period, the cat was chasing a mouse that took refuge behind an unmarked bag full of flour. The good ratter would leap in that direction, when Mrs. Davico, fearing an accident that had already occurred before, threw on the full bag an empty bag she had on hand, to prevent the first one to be torn by the claws of the cat, which could cause the flour to spread. Disappointed in her hunt, the cat did not abandon it, and for hours on end remained on the lookout, lurking on a chair near the bag, eyes fixed on the empty one that covered the other and was marked with the figure '1921' surmounted by three stars. Mrs. Davico remembered it very well, the incident being engraved in her mind.
> Research conducted at Mrs. Davico's suppliers found bags of the same vintage with figures resembling those printed on the cat's fur. In addition, the figure of the year was surmounted by three stars.
> Therefore it seems that the figure '1921' on which the cat had the eyes fixed for long hours was reproduced on the small kitten which was still in formation, or more exactly, it is the perispirit of the embryo which received this impression, since it only became visible when the hairs had grown."

This is a genuine case of nevi found in the animal race, which seems so similar to those found in humans.

Bozzano published in the *Annales des Sciences Psychiques*[109] a classification of the phenomena of animal metapsychics, which I briefly reproduce below.

Knowing the author's critical acumen, and his high criteria and caution when evaluating the stories he relates, I can assure total confidence in the authenticity of the facts he has gathered.

Mr. Bozzano has thus enumerated the phenomena:

1st category: Telepathic Hallucinations in which an Animal acts as an Agent (12 cases, 8 cited).

2nd category: Telepathic Hallucinations in which an Animal acts as Percipient (1 case).

3rd category: Telepathic Hallucinations perceived collectively by Animals and by Humans (17 cases, 4 cited).

4th category: Visions of Human Phantoms occurring outside of any Telepathic Coincidence, and perceived collectively by Animals and Humans (18 cases, 8 cited).

5th category: Visions of Animal Phantoms occurring outside of any Telepathic Coincidence, and perceived collectively by Animals and Humans (5 cases, all cited).

6th category: Animals and Phantasmogenic Localities (22 cases, 9 cited).

Only 69 cases are narrated among those Mr. Bozzano collected, and he points out that the number of reports already known to him in 1905 could easily reach the double that number. This observation suffices to show that the few examples I have reported are, so to speak, only types of each of these psychical manifestations.

Therefore, from now on, the following seem to be extremely probable:

1) That telepathic communication between humans and domestic are a fact;

---

109 *Annales des Sciences Psychiques*, August 1906. [Trans. note: In English, refer to *Annals of Psychical Science*, vol. II, July–December 1905, pp. 80–120.]

2) that animals sometimes exhibit phenomena of spirit sight, that is, they can perceive invisible beings;
3) that they are capable of having presentiments;
4) that they have a fluidic form that allows them to duplicate themselves and have out-of-body experiences;
5) that this animal perispirit survives death in an invisible form that can be described by seeing mediums;
6) that the materialization of this principle which individualizes the animal soul has sometimes been observed in Spiritist seances.

If we recall the stories about the Elberfeld horses, the dogs Rolf, Lola and Zou, it is impossible to deny that there is an intellectual kinship between these animals and humans. Evidently the degree of development of the animal psyche in these still relatively lower forms is scarcely comparable to ours, except their extraordinary faculty of calculation when compared to that of our children. Yet the identity of the thinking principle in them as in us seems undeniable, and the hypothesis that we had to pass before, successively through lower stages before arriving at humanity appears to be very probable today, which must be taken seriously by all those who pursue the solution of the problem of our origins.

I therefore fully agree with the conclusions made by Mr. Bozzano in the remarkable work from which I have borrowed so many examples.

These are the final words of his study:

> "What perplexing psychic problems to solve! However, the time has not yet come for attempting this task. I will therefore confine myself to remarking that in the day when we shall come to obtain the scientific proof that the phenomena of supernormal psychic perception which occur in human experience are realized in an identical manner in the experience of animals, and complete this proof by the further fact that the higher forms of instinct proper to animals are found to exist in the subconsciousness of man, on that day we shall also have arrived at the demonstration that there is

no qualitative difference between the human and the animal psyche. So also at that day we shall have arrived at a better understanding how, to the biological evolution of species elucidated by science, there corresponds a parallel psychical evolution which dominates the former, and which (if we are to judge by the guidance of the marvelous faculties latent in the subconsciousness, and manifestly independent of the law of natural selection), far from having to be considered as a mere product of functional synthesis of cortical centers, far from being made to consist in a simple epiphenomenon, we shall be logically compelled to recognize as deriving its origin from a sovereignly active immaterial principle which exhibits organizing force, a principle in virtue of which alone the law of natural selection is enabled to act efficiently in view of the biological-morphological evolution of species. To psychical science belongs the glorious task of demonstrating this in a not far distant future."[110]

---

110 E. Bozzano, "Animals and Psychic Perceptions," in *Annals of Psychical Science*, vol. II, July–December 1905, p. 120.

6

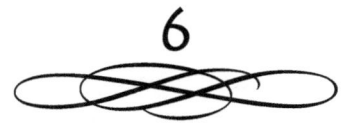

THE INTEGRAL MEMORY

EXPERIMENTAL TEST DEMONSTRATING SUCCESSIVE LIVES · SOME NOTES ON MEMORY · CONDITIONS OF A GOOD MEMORY ACCORDING TO RIBOT · INTENSITY AND DURATION · MEMORY DOES NOT RESIDE IN THE BRAIN, IT IS CONTAINED IN THE PERISPIRIT · EXPERIENCES OF MISTERS DESSOIR AND DUFAY · ECMNESIA ACCORDING TO MR. PITRES · REGRESSION OF MEMORY · ASSOCIATION OF PHYSIOLOGICAL AND PSYCHOLOGICAL STATES, THEY ARE INSEPARABLE · HISTORY OF JEANNE R. · EXAMPLES CITED BY PIERRE JANET · HISTORY OF LOUIS V. · INDISSOLUBLE LINK BETWEEN PHYSICAL AND MENTAL STATES · LATENT MEMORY AWAKENED BY DIFFERENT PROCESSES · AWAKENING OF OLD MEMORIES DURING ANESTHESIA · VISION BY MEANS OF CRYSTAL BALL · OBSERVATION BY MR. PIERRE JANET · CRYPTOMNESIA

INTEGRAL MEMORY

SINCE I SHALL HAVE TO STUDY, in the remainder of this book, phenomena which tend to establish the reality of previous existences in humanity; and since this demonstration rests partly on the resurrection of past memories; it seems to me indispensable to establish that memory is not merely an organic faculty indissolubly linked to the substance of the brain, but that instead it resides in that indestructible part of ourselves which Spiritists call the perispirit. If this is true, the reincarnating soul brings in itself in a latent state all the memories of its previous lives. Hence, it is possible, sometimes and exceptionally, to have reminiscences about one's ancient past. Just as in certain subjects we can revive the memory of events of their present life that have entirely disappeared from normal consciousness, so we can sometimes penetrate the depths of these ancestral archives, allowing us to properly qualify it as *integral memory*.

There cannot be a question here of accomplishing a complete study on memory, because that would require many more pages than I am allowed to use in the current book. So, it will suffice for me to highlight some important phenomena which, I hope, will demonstrate with evidence, that everything that has once acted upon a human being is engraved in oneself in an indelible way; and that such preservation does not take place, as we are taught by mainstream psychology, in the nervous system, but in this imperishable part of one's being that imparts individuality to it, and from which it is inseparable.

In order to avoid sounding too extraordinary, I must again recall that materialized apparitions, which temporarily reconstitute the ancient physical body that such beings had on Earth, with all its anatomical features and details, prove that they have always had the organizing power which gives the fleshly envelope its form and properties; while all the intellectual faculties are also reconstituted, when the spirit has become the complete master of the process of materialization. That is so because often phantoms speak, write; and their style, handwriting and draftsmanship are identical to those they once had in their lifetime. Thus, memory and the ideomotor mechanism of writing are preserved after death, ready to manifest themselves physically when circumstances allow.

Definitely, it was not only in the nervous system that all these acquisitions were recorded, since the being, which always survives, takes away its dynamic associations and memories, even after the former is destroyed by death.

The case of the spirit Mrs. Estelle Livermore,[111] writing under the watchful eyes of her husband more than two hundred messages after her death, shows with evidence, not only the preservation of her personality, but also that her memories had lost none of their completeness, for al-

---

111 [Trans. note] See Robert Dale Owen, *The Debatable Land* (New York: G. W. Carleton & Co., 1872), p. 482 *et seq.*

though she was American, she retained, after her death, the knowledge of the French language which she commanded perfectly in her lifetime. Furthermore, these messages are autographs in every respect identical to her writing during her earthly life.

This fact is confirmed by a quantity of others obtained, either by mechanical mediums or through direct writing between slates, so that we can, as Spiritists, affirm categorically that all the intellectual acquisitions made during one's lifetime are not located in the encephalon, but actually reside in the fluidic double which is the true body of the soul.

If so, what role does the nervous system play during life? It is undeniable that the integrity of one's memory is related to the proper functioning of the brain, because many diseases that reach this organ have the effect of weakening and even completely suppressing the memory of recent or old events, either entirely or partially.

So it seems obvious that during life the brain is an indispensable condition of memory. But here comes a second consideration that seems to me of utmost importance as well: The forgetfulness observed during the course of one's life, or after some organic disorders, is not fundamental and insurmountable, but rather only apparent. By means of various processes, it is sometimes possible to revive those memories that seemed to be destroyed and lost forever.

This is what I will try to show by giving various examples.

But first, it will not come amiss to recall some basic notions regarding this mysterious phenomenon which can resuscitate the past and make it, so to speak, current.

According to French Psychologist Théodule-Armand Ribot, in the ordinary meaning of the word, memory comprises three things in people's general view: the preservation of certain states, their replication, their location in the past. This, however, is only a certain type of memory, the one which may be called perfect. These three components are of unequal value; the first two are necessary, indispensable;

the third, which in jargon is called recognition, completes memory, but does not constitute it.

This seems to be all the more true in that memory, during one's lifetime, is linked to the proper functioning of the nervous system. However, if one's memory appears deficient, this in no way proves that one's recollections are annihilated, but rather only that the power to awaken them has been momentarily paralyzed, and that it can reappear when the causes which had suppressed them cease to exist.

I would also like to point out that memory, as a general term, includes many varieties, and that across different individuals, the power of renovation of old sensations is markedly dissimilar. Some have a highly developed visual memory, as is the case of painters such as Horace Vernet or Gustave Doré, who could make a portrait entirely from memory. In others, it is the musical sense which reaches a very high degree of perfection, as when Mozart noted down the *Miserere* of the Sistine Chapel after having heard it only twice. But without mentioning such exceptional faculties, it is a well-known fact that everyone has an aptitude for representing the past in a satisfactory way, for it is to this faculty that we owe the feeling of the continuity of our being, of our self. However, for a sensation to register in us, at least two conditions are required: intensity and duration.

Let us see, according to Ribot,[112] the importance of these two factors.

> "Intensity is a condition of extremely variable character. States of consciousness are continually striving to supplant it, but the victory may result either from the strength of the victor or the weakness of the other combatants. We know – and this point has been made very clear by Herbart and others – that the most exalted state may continue to decrease until the threshold of consciousness is passed – that is to

---

112 T. Ribot, *Diseases of Memory* (Trans. W. H. Smith. New York: D. Appleton & Co., 1882), p. 33–34.

say, until one of the conditions of existence fails. We are justified in saying that there may be every possible degree of consciousness, as small as desired, to the lowest modality – conditions named by Maudsley subconscious – but there is no authority for believing that this decrease has no limit, even although it escapes us."

1. But nothing authorizes one to say that this decay has no limit, although it escapes us.

2. We have scarcely dealt with duration as a necessary condition of consciousness. It is nevertheless capital. Here we can reason about it using precise data.

Research carried out over the past thirty years has determined the time required for the various perceptions: sound = 0" 16 to 0" 14; tact = 0" 21 to 0" 18; light = 0" 20 to 0" 22; for the simplest act of discernment, the nearest reflex is 0" 02 to 0" 04. Although the results vary according to experimenters, according to persons, according to circumstances and the nature of the psychic acts studied, it is at least established that each psychic act requires an appreciable duration and that the so-called infinite speed of thought is only a metaphor.

That being said, it is clear that any nervous action whose duration is shorter than that required by psychic action can not awaken consciousness.[113]

Allow me to add that, in my view, a sensation must draw one's attention in order to become conscious. It is well known, indeed, that if we are absorbed by an interesting work, we will no longer hear, for example, the sound of a clock pendulum which, however, always strikes our ear with the same force. But our mind occupied elsewhere does not transform this sensation into perception, that is, we are not conscious of it. It is very curious to observe that these sensations, unnoticed by the normal self, can reappear if we plunge a subject into magnetic sleep. Here is an example borrowed from German psychologist Max Dessoir:

---

113 It should be noted that this refers exclusively to the functioning of memory, during one's lifetime, when it uses the brain.

"Mr. X., absorbed in reading in the midst of chatting friends, suddenly had his attention awakened when he heard his name spoken. He asked his friends what had been said about him. He was not answered; Max Dessoir hypnotized him instead. In his magnetic sleep he could repeat the whole conversation that had eluded his waking self. Even more remarkable is the fact reported by Edmund Gurney and other observers that a hypnotic subject can grasp the whisper of his/her magnetizer, even when he/she is in the midst of people who are talking aloud."[114]

In these examples, the duration and the intensity were sufficient to engrave the words uttered in the person's nervous system and in his/her perispirit; but, because attention was lacking, the conscious memory at the waking state has not occurred, and the individual does not know what has been said of him/her. However, when magnetically put to sleep, as that general vibrational state that physiologists call *cenesthesis*[115] was increased, the auditory vibrations became more intense and the subject was then able to take cognizance of them.

It is not only memories of the waking state that somnambulism can reconstitute, but also those of earlier entranced states, so that it seems to exist in the same individual two series of perfectly coordinated memories, completely ignoring each other. The following observation is a striking example:[116]

---

114 I apologize to readers for repeating these facts already mentioned in my previous books, but since they are still very little known and quite demonstrative for the study at hand, I will not hesitate to use them again. [Trans. note: For the unsourced Max Dessoir's episode, *cf.* Albert MOLL (Trans. A. F. Hopkirk. London and New York: Water Scott Publishing Co., etc., 1913), p. 250.]

115 [Trans. note] *Cenesthesis* (or *cenesthesia*), in psychology, is the general consciousness or awareness of one's body.

116 PITRES, *Leçons sur l'Hystérie et l'Hypnotisme*, p. 200 [Trans. note: See also F. W. H. MYERS, *Human Personality*, vol. I, "Appendices to ch. V," p. 512.]

"Dr. Dufay, a senator from Loir-et-Cher, published his observation of a young girl who, in a bout of somnambulism[117], had squeezed jewels belonging to her mistress into a drawer. The latter no longer found her jewels in the place where she had left them, accused her servant of having stolen them. The poor girl protested her innocence, but could not give any information on the causes of the disappearance of the lost items.

She was put in prison in Blois. Dr. Dufay was then a doctor of this prison. He knew the defendant for having made some experiences of hypnotism on her. He put her to sleep and questioned her about the crime she was accused of. She told him then, with all the necessary details, that she had never intended to steal her mistress, but that one night it had occurred to her that certain jewels belonging to that lady were not safe in the piece of furniture where they were placed and that, since then, she had tucked them in another piece of furniture. The investigating judge was informed of this revelation. He went to the lady who had been stolen and found the jewels in the drawer indicated by the somnambulist. The innocence of the defendant was thus clearly demonstrated, and the patient was immediately set at liberty."

What is remarkable is that the second state, when it is deep, designating by this expression what is produced by somnambulism, embraces all kinds of memories, including those of sleep and awaken ordinary life. It is truly the old life that resurrects with all the complexity it entails.

Professor Pitres, in his already quoted book, gives a very curious example. He names it *ecmnesia*. Here is what it consists of:

Suppose for a moment that a 30-year-old person suddenly loses the memory of everything he/she has known and learned during the last fifteen years of his/her life. By the

---

117 [Trans. note] *Somnambulism* was the preferred word in the 19th century until the first quarter of the 20th century to designate both sleepwalking and trance mediumship, which are quite different things.

very fact of this partial amnesia, a radical transformation will take place in the subject's mental state.

This person will speak, act, and reason, as he/she would have done at the age of fifteen. He/she will have the knowledge, tastes, feelings, manners that he had at age of 15, since all the memories of the last fifteen years will have vanished. From a mental point of view, it will no longer be an adult, but a teenager.

> "A 28-year-old patient, Albertine M., during an ecmnesiac delirium episode reverted back to the age of seven, when she was busy keeping her wet nurse's cow.
>
> After having observed the whole series of auras which usually precede the explosion of her delirium fit, the patient began to walk slowly, stooping from time to time, as if she had picked up flowers on the side of a road. Then she sat down on the floor humming a ditty. A few moments later she made the gesture of rummaging in her pocket and began to play knucklebones,[118] not without often interrupting her part to speak to her cow. We questioned her at that moment, and she, thinking that she was dealing with the village kids, immediately offered to share her game. *It was impossible to make her understand her mistake.* To all the questions we asked her about her cow, her grandmother, and the inhabitants of the village, she answered with the naivety of a child, albeit with imperturbable precision. If, on the contrary, we spoke to her about the events that she witnessed or acted in the course of her life, after the age of seven, she seemed very astonished and did not understand anything about it.
>
> I must point out two peculiarities of no minor importance. Until the age of 12, Albertine remained in a small hamlet in the Charente, in the midst of poor peasants who barely spoke French. She herself spoke at that moment only the patois of Saintonge; it was not until much later that she learned French.

---

118 [Trans. note] The game of jacks.

Also, throughout the duration of the fit, *she spoke in patois*, and if we asked her to speak French, she answered invariably, and *always in patois*, that she did not know the language of the gentlemen of the city.

The second particularity is no less curious. At the age of seven, Albertine had not yet had any hysterical accidents and, in all likelihood, she did not have any hemianesthesia or hysterogenic zones yet. However, during the bout of ecmnesiac delirium, which we are dealing with herein, her cutaneous sensibility was normal on both the left and right sides, and all the spasmogenic[119] zones had lost their action, except the left ovarian zone, that if vigorously pressed had immediate effect of stopping delirium. Upon returning to the normal state, the patient had no recollection of what she had said and done during the delirium episode."

Let us note here the close connection that exists between the psychic state and the physiological state of the subject. They are so closely associated that the mere fact of reverting Albertine to a period of her past life, during which she did not present any nervous disorders, suppressed those in which she was afflicted by them at the time when the experiment was made.

OTHER CASES OF ECMNESIA

The phenomenon of resurrection of forgotten memories of part of a life, which Mr. Pitres named ecmnesia, has been pointed out by many authors who have dealt with somnambulism.

This is how Dr. Charles Richet, in his book *l'Homme et l'Intelligence*[120] [*Man and Intelligence*], draws our attention to the vividness of the ancient sensations which the magnetic (hypnotic) state can revive.

---

119 [Trans. note] *Spasmogenic*: having the potential of causing a hysterical bout.

120 C. RICHET, *l'Homme et l'Intelligence* (Paris: F. Alcan, 1884), p. 194.

"If active memory is deeply troubled, passive memory becomes rather exalted. Somnambulists can describe with an incredible luxury of details the places they once saw, and the facts they witnessed, always with great accuracy. During their magnetic sleep, they have exactly described such and such a city, such and such a house, as they once visited or had a passing view of them. But once they wake up, they can hardly say that they were there once at all, and X., who was singing the air of the second act of Meyerbeer's opera *l'Africaine* during her sleep, could not recall one single note when she was awake."

The following is a woman who, fifteen years ago, spent an hour or two at Versailles, and who had almost completely forgotten this short walk. She is even absolutely unable to say whether she did it. However, if one hypnotizes her into sleep and speaks to her of Versailles, she will be able to describe very faithfully the avenues, the statues, the trees therein. She will promptly see the park, the alleys, the big square, and, to the utter astonishment of those present, give extremely precise details.

It is not only the visual or auditory memories that are preserved, but also all the intellectual acquisitions, as testified by the story of Jeanne R., thanks to doctors Bourru and Burot (abridged citation):[121]

"Jeanne R., aged 24, is a very nervous and deeply anemic young woman. She is prone to fits of crying and sobs; no seizures, but frequent fainting; she is easily hypnotized, she falls in a deep sleep and on waking she has lost the memory. She is told to wake up at the age of 6. She is at her parents' home: we are at a moment of vigil, we peel some chestnuts. She wants to sleep and asks to go to bed! She calls her brother André to help her finish her job, but André enjoys making small houses with chestnuts instead of working. 'He is very lazy, he enjoys peeling only ten, and I have to peel the rest.

---

121 Doctors H. BOURRU and P. BUROT, *Variations de la Personnalité* (Paris: J. B. Baillière, 1888), p. 152–158.

In this state, she speaks Limousin patois, cannot read, hardly knows her A–B–C. She cannot speak a word of French. Her little sister Louise does not want to sleep. 'Always have to lull my sister who is nine months old', she said. She has a childish attitude.

After putting his hand on her forehead, she was told that in two minutes she would be at the age of 10. Now her physiognomy is entirely different; her attitude is no longer the same. She is at Les Frais, in the castle of the Moustier family, near which she lived. She sees paintings on the walls and admires them. She asks where are her sisters who have accompanied her, she will see if they are coming on the road. She speaks like a child who is learning how to speak; she has been attending the Catholic nuns' school for two years, but she spent a long time without going there; her mother was often ill, so she was forced to look after her sisters and brothers. She learned how to write since six months ago, she remembers a dictation she took on Wednesday, and she writes down an entire page very fluently and by heart; it's the dictation she took when she was 10 years old. She says she is not very advanced: 'Marie Coutureau will make fewer mistakes than me, I'm still behind Marie Puybaudet and Marie Coutureau, but Louise Roland is behind me. I think Jeanne Beaulieu is the one who makes the most mistakes.'

In the same way, she is told to retrieve the age of 15. Now, she is a servant to Mortemart at Mrs. Brunerie's. 'Tomorrow we go to a party, to a wedding, to the marriage of Baptiste Colombeau, the marshal. It's Leon who will be my escort. Oh! I won't go to the ball, Miss Brunerie does not want me to; I'm going there for a quarter of an hour, but she doesn't know it.' Her conversation is more coherent than earlier. She writes the *Petit Savoyard*. The difference of the two writings is very great. When she wakes up, she is very surprised to have written down stanzas of *Le Petit Savoyard*,[122] which she does not know anymore. When she is shown the dictation she made at age 10, she says she did not write it."

122 [Trans. note] A. GUIRAUD, *Le Petit Savoyard* (Paris: A. Lemerre, 1897), the rhymed story of a poor little boy taught to children at French schools.

I would like to point out that the phenomenon of re-awakening a period of past life occurred spontaneously in Albertine, the subject of Mr. Pitres's experiment, as a consequence of a crisis of hysteria, whereas in the case of Jeanne R . this regression of memory is due to a hypnotic suggestion.

These accounts show that, whatever the process used, when one reaches the deepest layers of consciousness, one always finds faithfully recorded all the events of the past, because they have left an indelible impression that subsequent sensations may cover up to the point of making them completely forgotten; but they are never destroyed. It is a superposition of impressions which do not mix with one another, which always have a perfect autonomy, and which embrace all the states of the personality. Thus, Jeanne R., when sent back to the age of 6, has the feelings of a small child, does not yet know French and expresses herself only in Limousin patois; that is, at that moment, all her subsequent life has completely vanished for her. However, as I said above, we notice that each layer of memories awakes with a freshness and liveliness that is equivalent to the impressions of real life.

As a result of a second suggestion, a larger part of the memory domain is retrieved, still with the same luxury of details regarding the most minute circumstances of everyday life.

Jeanne R. reproduced from memory the dictation she took Wednesday at the nuns' school. The handwriting is childish and the spelling defective. It is therefore the precise state of the age of 10 which was retrieved. It did not get mixed with the 6-year-old writing, nor did it amalgamate with the memories of the following periods, when the subject was reverted to her fifteenth year of age. This time the handwriting had changed, and it is quite interesting to point out that, if the ideomotor mechanism of writing occupies the same parts of the subject's nervous system, it has however undergone successive modifications, each of which has obviously left footprints which have never faded.

We can therefore imagine that successive memories build up by layers, that all those which are contemporaries are closely connected to one another, so that not only psychological memories survive, but all their respective physiological states as well. If one of them is resuscitated, the other inevitably reappears. I will insist on this point by quoting the testimony of Mr. Pierre Janet,[123] Professor of Psychology at the Collège de France, which clearly shows this indissoluble connection of the psychic and physical states of the body at any time in the life of one same person:

(One can make all the scenes of his/her own life unfold to one subject and to see, as if they were happening right now, details which the subject thought to be completely forgotten and could not normally recollect. P. Janet's subject, Léonie, stayed two hours transformed into the 10-year-old girl she once was, and was living her own existence again, with a liveliness and a very strange joy, shouting, running, calling her doll, talking to people she did not remember anymore, as if the poor woman had really returned to the age of 10. Although she was still anesthetized on the left side, *she recovered her full sensibility, that is., her full physical functionality, to play this role.*)

> "These modifications of sensibility and nervous phenomena by a suggestion of this kind sometimes give rise to singular phenomena. Here is an observation which may seem facetious, but which is truthful and exact, and in fact quite easy to explain. I suggested to Rose that we are no longer in 1888, but in 1886, in the month of April, to simply observe what changes of sensibility might occur. But then there was a very strange occurrence; she moaned, complained of being tired and unable to walk: 'Well, what have you got?' 'Oh, nothing, but in my situation.' 'What situation?' She replied

---

123 P. JANET, *l'Automatisme Psychologique* (6th ed., Paris: F. Alcan, 1916), p. 160.

with a gesture, her belly was suddenly swollen and stretched by a sudden manifestation of hysterical tympanitis: I had, without knowing it, brought her back to a period in her life when she was pregnant. It was necessary to suppress the suggestion to put an end to this embarrassing faux pas. More interesting studies were made by this means on Marie; I have been able, by successively reducing it to different periods of her existence, to record all the different states of sensibility by which she had passed, and the causes of all modifications. So she is now completely blind of the left eye, and claims to be so since birth. If she is brought back to the age of seven, she is still anesthetized in the left eye; but if it is suggested to her that she is only six years old, one realizes that she can see with both eyes, and one can determine the period and the very curious circumstances in which she lost the sensibility of her left eye. The memory automatically realized a state of health of which the subject had kept no recollection."

The three subjects of Pierre Janet, especially the last two, demonstrate well this indissoluble bond of the successive states, namely, the bodily and spiritual one, of which I spoke above. It is quite remarkable that one can retrieve an intellectual period of the past life by reproducing, through suggestion, or by a physical process, a pathological state which the subject once had. For example, if at the age of 12 an individual was insensitive on the right side, and that disability has since disappeared, but one artificially induces anesthesia on his/her right side, immediately this subject takes up the character, manners, and memories he/she used to have at the age of 12.

History of Louis V.

The story of Louis V.,[124] again borrowed from Bourru and Burot, confirms this statement in an absolute way. Since

---

124 [Trans. note] Louis Vivet (also Vivé or Vive)

the story narrated by these scholars is a bit long, I thought it would be worth to summarize it below:[125]

"Louis V. was a hysteric who, after a robbery, was shut up in the colony of Saint-Urbain (France). At the moment he is docile and intelligent. He occupies himself with agricultural work. After the emotion produced by the sight of a viper, he became paralyzed in his lower limbs.

Transported to Bonneval, his facial expression was open and sympathetic; the character, sweet and docile; he deeply regrets his past and says that in future he will be more honest and correct. He is being taught tailoring. One day, he was seized with a crisis that lasted fifty hours, after which he was no longer paralyzed. He has completely lost the memory of his transportation to a new place; he thinks he is still at Saint-Urbain and wants to go to work in the fields. Morally, he is no longer the same subject, he has become quarrelsome, greedy and thievish; he responds impolitely. In 1881, he seems to be cured and leaves the asylum.

After a stay with his mother, in Chartres, he is placed in Mâcon, at a farm owner's house. Having fallen sick, he was transferred to the asylum of Saint-Georges, near Bourg (Ain). We noticed that he was sometimes exalted, sometimes almost stupid and imbecile.

In 1883, believed to have been cured and in possession of a nest egg, he leaves Saint-Georges to return to his country. He arrives in Paris, we do not know how. He is admitted first to Sainte-Anne and lastly to Bicêtre. On January 17, 1884, he had a another very violent attack, which recurred on the following days with thoracalgia (thoracic-mid back pain), paralysis and contractures on the left and right sides of his body. On April 17, following a mild seizure, contracture on the right side disappeared. He wakes up the next day and believes to be still on January 26th. During the last six months of 1884, Louis V. did not present any new phenomenon. His character has changed. He was gentle

---

125 Doctors H. BOURRU and P. BUROT, *Variations de la Personnalité* (Paris: J. B. Baillière, 1888), p. 127–138.

during the period of contracture; *outside these periods, he was undisciplined, teasing and thieving.*
On January 2, 1885, after a scene of induced somnambulism, followed by an attack, he escaped from Bicêtre, stealing clothes and money.
After a few weeks spent in Paris, he joins the naval infantry and arrives in Rochefort. At the barracks, he commits robberies and is submitted to a council of war. Charges against him were dismissed and on March 27 he enters the hospital. On the 30th, he presents a contracture of his whole right side, which is dissipated after two days, yet he remains paralyzed and numb in all the half of his body. When this subject was placed in Rochefort hospital, he had a paralysis with insensibility on the right side, and he could recall of his life only the second part of his stay in Bicêtre; and finally his stay in Rochefort, where he is now. The action of metals and the magnet was tried on him; it was possible by these means to reduce all the previous pathological states, and at the same time to awaken the memory of all the concomitant psychic states. It is also in this way that the previous history of Louis V. was reconstituted in its entirety by these gentlemen who did not know its particularities; and the investigation they conducted revealed the perfect authenticity of all details provided by the subject in each of these states, while he lost memory as soon as he returned to his current state."

These changes were obtained – and this is a very important detail – by physical agents which determine physiological changes revealed by transformations in the distribution of sensitivity and motility. At the same time as these physical alternations occur, there are regular transformations of the state of consciousness, which are so constant that, in order to make a particular psychological state disappear at will, it suffices for the experimenter to induce by the proper application of the magnet, of a metal, of electricity, such or such a modification of the sensibility and the motility.

THE INTEGRAL MEMORY

Figure 3. LOUIS VIVET AGED TWENTY-TWO

And this state of consciousness is complete for the memory state it embraces; memory of time, places, people, acquired knowledge (reading, writing), learned automatic movements (tailor's craftsmanship), own feelings and their expression through language, gesture, physiognomy; the concordance is perfect.

> "Considering only the sudden changes in the physical state, these are already very surprising. To transport and, better still, to make one's sensibility, motility, anesthesia disappear in the whole body or in a determined part of the body, seems to border on the marvelous. This astonishing change does not begin to approach the amazing transformation that takes place simultaneously and by the same agent in the realm of consciousness. Earlier, the subject knew only a limited part of his existence; after an application of the magnet, he is transported to another period of his life with the tastes, habits, and attractions he had then. Should the transference be well conducted and rid of all infirmity of movement or sensibility; at the same time, *the brain becomes almost entirely free*, the book of life is thus completely open and one can read easily through all its pages.
>
> It is this book that we had to leaf through to get to know the life of our patient which *we absolutely ignored*. There were many pages torn off, so to speak; they had to be reconstituted. It was enough to apply a magnet on the thighs to reveal *a particular physical state causing its own memory*, but under no condition was it possible to display the full memory, because in no case the absence of physical disorders was complete. There was still one complementary test to be done: to act directly on the state of consciousness and to see if the physical state would be transformed in parallel.
>
> To act on the psychic state, there was no other way than suggestion, in the following form: 'Louis V., you will wake up at the Bicêtre Hospital, in Cabarnis's room, on January 2, 1884.' Louis V. obeys; at the end of the induced somnambulism, his intelligence and affective faculties are exactly the same as in the second state. *At the same time, he is paralyzed*

> *and insensitive in the whole left side of his body.* In another suggestion, he was ordered to be in Bonneval while he was a tailor. The mental state obtained is similar to that described *in the fourth state,* and *simultaneously a paralysis appeared with contracture and insensibility of the lower parts of his body."*

The verification has been complete; it is certain that contemporary psychic and physical states register together in the organism, where they are linked to each other in an indissoluble manner.

Let us not think that this integral resuscitation of memories is only the privilege of somnambulists. In fact, each and every one of us keeps them. I will show that ordinary people can, under certain circumstances, retrieve life events down to the smallest details.

Latent memory

Suggestion during hypnotic sleep are not the only way of awakening the memory of the past. Normally, in certain cases of illness, it has been possible to observe the retrieval of previous periods of one's life completely forgotten in the waking state. This is how memory resurrection occurs in cases of acute fever, manic excitement, ecstasy, and the incubation period of certain diseases of the brain.

As I cannot dwell on these particular examples, it seems to me interesting to point out memory awakening that normally occurs as a result of certain circumstances.

> "A lady, in the last stage of a chronic disease, was carried from London to a lodging in the country; – there, her infant daughter was taken to visit her, and, after a short interview, carried back to town. The lady died a few days after, and the daughter grew up without any recollection of her mother, till she was of mature age. At this time, she happened to be taken into the room in which her mother died, without knowing it to have been so; – she started on entering it, and,

when a friend who was along with her, asked the cause of her agitation, replied, 'I have a distinct impression of having been in this room before, and that a lady, who lay in that corner, and seemed very ill, leaned over me and wept.'"[126]

Another example:

"A man with a strong artistic temperament (this detail is worth noting) went with friends to party near a castle in Sussex County that he had no memory of having visited. As he approached the front door, he had an extremely keen impression of having seen it before, and he saw not only this door, but people on the top, and donkeys down under the porch. This singular conviction imposing itself on him, he addressed his mother for some clarification on this point. He learned from her that, when he was sixteen months old, he had been brought to this place, that he had been carried in a basket on the back of a donkey; that he had been left down with the donkeys and the servants, while the older ones of the group had settled down to eat over the castle gate."[127]

It is interesting to note that impressions that probably were not conscious were stereotyped in the brain of this 16-month-old child and with enough intensity to reawaken many years later with the fullest fidelity.

Anesthetic sleep, due to chloroform or ether, can produce the same effects as febrile excitement:

"An old forester had lived during his youth on the Polish border and spoke only Polish. After that, he lived only in German districts. His children assured that for thirty or forty years he had not heard or spoken a word of Polish. During an anesthetic that lasted nearly two hours, this man could speak, pray, and sing, in Polish only."[128]

---

126 J. ABERCROMBIE, *Intellectual Powers* (Edinburgh: Waugh & Innes, 1830), p. 117.

127 [Trans. note] T. RIBOT, *Maladies de la Mémoire* (Paris: F. Alcan, 1888), p. 144.

128 DUVAL, entry "Hypnotisme" in the *Nouveau Dictionnaire de Médecine* ..., p. 144.

Even during ordinary life, certain violent emotions result in suddenly triggering the mechanism of memory with truly extraordinary intensity. The following two examples can give us an idea of what often happens at the moment of death, or shortly after disincarnation.

> "There are several stories of drowning, rescue from an imminent death, that agree on this point that at the moment of asphyxiation one seems to see, in a fleeting moment, one's whole lifetime with its smallest incidents. One of them claims that he seemed to see all his previous life unfolding in retrograde succession, not as a simple sketch; but with very precise details forming a panorama of his entire existence, of which each action was accompanied by a feeling of good or evil.
> In a similar circumstance, a man of a remarkably clear mind was crossing a railroad track as a train came at full speed. He only had time to stretch between the two lines of rails. As the train passed over him, the feeling of his endangerment made him recall all the incidents of his life, as if the book of judgment had been opened before his very eyes."[129]

Therefore it seems obvious from the examples cited above that all the sensations we have felt have registered in us, leaving indelible marks. Without doubt, this immense mass of knowledge of all kinds has not remained present to the consciousness, for, as has been rightly observed, the oblivion of an enormous quantity of insignificant events is one of the conditions of memory. However, what is quite remarkable is that oblivion does not imply the annihilation of recollections. Experiments show that everything that has acted upon us is fixed forever in the depths of our being, somehow in the lower part of consciousness; and that all these memories, even though we seem to be unable to retrieve

---

[129] About this retrospective view of one's current lifetime, see in *La Revue Spirite*, year 65, September 1922 (p. 333) onwards, the remarkable articles signed by Mr. Ernest BOZZANO, and published under the title, "De la Vision panoramique ou Mémoire synthétique dans l'imminence de la mort" ["Panoramic Vision or Synthetic Memory in the imminence of death"].

them, continue to live in a latent state and constitute the foundations of our personality. Each physical or intellectual memory contributes to the building of our mental life.

In his book *Névroses et Idées fixes* [*Neuroses and Fixed Ideas*] (Paris, 1898), Pierre Janet demonstrated this thesis with a number of most illustrative clinical observations. His method consisted in discovering the fixed idea, often unknown to the patient, which is the cause of all his/her mental and physical disorders. Here is what he says about it:

> "Often the existence of a fixed idea can only be revealed during bouts, dreams, somnambulisms, or by subconscious actions and automatic writings. In a word, these ideas remain beneath, or rather outside, normal consciousness, and yet exert a preponderant influence, since they are the origin of the subject's malady."

To the immense stack of auditory, olfactory, tactile, kinesthetic, visual sensations, etc., which we have consciously felt, are added other impressions which have entered us, so to speak, in a furtive manner. They are fixed without our knowledge; so that, the day they reappear, they seem supernormal phenomena to us, coming from higher faculties.

Vision through crystal ball

One of the means used to exteriorize mental images is that of the crystal ball. We know that some people, in fact, after having stared at it for a few moments, first see a cloud, then, within it, stars, bars, numeral figures, letters, color pictures, personalities, animals, trees, flowers. Sometimes these images are mobile; the protagonists come and go and can even talk to each other.

Where do these visions come from?

According to British authors who have studied them better than anyone else, those are visual hallucinations that exteriorize the images contained in the brain of the experimenter.

What causes the surprise of the seeing subject is that, often, he/she does not recognize these landscapes or objects, but a meticulous research sometimes allows one to find proof that these are things which he/she saw unconsciously, which are thus resurrected and projected into the glass ball. Here are three examples borrowed from the British *Proceedings of the SPR*:

> "One young woman relates that on looking at a mirror, she was always haunted by the same picture, a house with large, dark, dismal walls, on which grew an extraordinary clump of white jasmine. She had never, she thought, seen a similar house in the town where she had lived for a long time. But, after a searching inquiry by the London Society for Psychical Research, it was proved that there was a house in London which had this appearance and which this person had seen. When passing it she had been thinking of something else, but she had seen it. Another person, when placed in front of the crystal ball saw a number suddenly appear.' I have never seen this number,'she said.' Why is it that I see this number 3244 more than any other ?' But it was proved that during the day she had changed a bank-note which bore this number. A third person, something of a mystic, saw an article from a newspaper appear in the glass. She thought it odd but sought to read it: it was the announcement of the death of one of her friends. She related the fact : those present were astonished. There was found in the house a copy of the newspaper placed before the fireplace as a screen, and on the visible side, spread out plainly enough, was the article in question with the same characters and form as seen in the crystal."[130]

It was therefore the exteriorization of a visual cliché that had been recorded unconsciously.

---

130 [Trans. note] E. BOIRAC, *Psychic Science* (Trans. D. Wright. London: William Rider & Son, Ltd., 1918), p. 139.

This last example shows us how cautiously we should be when appreciating apparently supernormal facts. What often makes the study of Spiritism very difficult is that, nearly always, the true Spiritist phenomenon is coupled with another one which is only a counterfeit. Thus automatic writing simulates the mechanical writing of true spirit mediums; a true hallucination may resemble a true apparition; the objectification of the types may resemble the facts of an incarnation; and ideoplasty is sometimes as difficult to distinguish from true spirit materialization, just as paramnesia – as we shall see later – can be taken for a memory of a previous life. Without exaggerating the importance of these phenomena of mere animism,[131] we must, however, know them well, if we do not wish to expose ourselves to some serious miscalculations. The following are facts which resemble those of clairvoyance and spirit sight, and which belong only to cryptomnesia, that is to say, latent memory.

Cryptomnesia

A Mr. Brodelbank loses a pocket knife. Six months later, without being worried in the least about this loss, he dreams that this knife is in the pocket of a pair of trousers he had put in the discarded clothes basket. Waking up the idea came to him to check whether his dream was correct: he went to fetch his pants and found the knife in a pocket

This was obviously a case of forgotten memory that reawakened during sleep. The same can be said of the following story:

In his book, *Le Sommeil et les Rêves* [*Sleep and Dreams*] (Paris, 1885), Professor Delboeuf says that in a dream, the name **Asplenium ruta muraria** seemed familiar to him. On waking, he searched his head in vain to discover where he could have learned this botanical designation. Long after,

---

131 [Trans. note] See footnote 31 above.

he discovered the name 'Asplenium ruta muraria' written by himself in a collection of flowers and ferns, beside which he had inscribed the names as a friend dictated them.

In the following example, there is more than just a memory reminder. It seems that a certain number of visual impressions have been recorded unconsciously, as we will soon see that this is perfectly possible; then, under the influence of attention, they were found by the soul during sleep. Here is what happened:

> "On reaching Morley's Hotel at 5 o'clock on Tuesday, 29th January, 1889, I missed a gold brooch, which I supposed I had left in a fitting room at Swan and Edgar's. I sent there at once, but was very disappointed to hear that after a diligent search they could not find the brooch. I was very vexed, and worried about the brooch, and that night dreamed that I should find it shut up in a number of the Queen newspaper that had been on the table, and in my dream I saw the very page where it would be. I had noticed one of the plates on that page. Directly after breakfast I went to Swan and Edgar's and asked to see the papers, at the same time telling the young ladies about the dream, and where I had seen the brooch. The papers had been moved from that room, but were found, and to the astonishment of the young ladies, I said, 'This is the one that contains my brooch'; and there at the very page I expected I found it."[132]

I will try to draw conclusions from all these observations, and we shall see how they confirm the teachings of Spiritism, both by the spirits and the experimental results obtained by scientists for half a century all over the world.

---

132 [Trans. note] *Journal of the SPR*, vol. 4, no. 63, Oct. 1889, p. 142.

7

EXPERIMENTS IN MEMORY RETRIEVAL

THE PERISPIRIT IS THE PRESERVER OF ALL PHYSIOLOGICAL AND INTELLECTUAL ACHIEVEMENTS – AFTER DEATH, THE PERISPIRIT PRESERVES ALL ITS EARTHLY SENSATIONS · THE DISTURBANCE PERIOD CLOUDS ONE'S INTELLECTUAL FACULTIES · AS ON EARTH, ON THE SPIRITUAL PLANE MEMORY IS FRAGMENTARY IN LESS EVOLVED BEINGS · IT CAN BE AWAKENED LIKE THE ONE FROM HERE BELOW THROUGH MAGNETIC ACTION · DR. CAILLEU · STUDIES OF SEANCES WHERE ALLEGED REVELATIONS OCCUR REGARDING PREVIOUS LIVES OF THE SUBJECT OR SITTERS–DIFFICULTIES OF MAGNETIC EXPERIMENTATION TO OBTAIN THE REGRESSION OF MEMORY TO PAST LIVES–1ST. SIMULATION, 2ND. FICTITIOUS PERSONALITY, 3RD. CLAIRVOYANCE · THE CASES OF MISTERS ESTEVAN MARATA, GASTIN, CORNILLIER, HENRI SAUSSE, AND BOUVIER · REINCARNATION IN ENGLAND · THE SUCCESSIVE LIVES OF MR. ROCHAS D'AIGLUN. FROM INDIA TO MARS, PROFESSOR FLOURNOY · THE CASE OF PRINCESS SIMANDINI · AWAKENING OF MEMORIES DURING TRANCE, STILL IN ENGLAND · THE REPORT OF PRINCE WITTGENSTEIN · AWAKENING IN A SUBJECT OF THE MEMORY OF A FOREIGN LANGUAGE, IN GERMANY · THE CASE OF THE MADMAN SUCIAC · SUMMARY

THE FEW EXAMPLES CONCERNING MEMORY that I have just mentioned are only particular cases taken from a very large number of others, authorizing us to believe that any action exerted on a human being leaves an indelible trace of itself. Also that, while ordinary memory usually reminds us only of the most important facts of our existence, it is none the less true that the most insignificant events are etched in us as well, and that they may reappear under the influence of various causes, both spontaneous and induced.

Where are these sensations recorded? In what part of our being does it take place? This is a problem that has not yet been solved, and it is very curious that science, which has revealed the world with its laws to us, has remained powerless to penetrate into the depths of the human being. Neither physiologists nor psychologists have been able to explain a fact so simple and commonplace as sleep, for, according to Swiss psychologist Edouard Claparede, there are twenty-one theories about sleep, which clearly proves that none of them is accurate, each considering only one aspect of the issue. The same can be said of memory.

Materialistic scientists claim that it is contained in the nervous system, but it is impossible for them to indicate in a precise way what are the modifications of this system which take place at the moment when an impression enters the nervous mass, and how it can be reborn to produce memory.

Actually, Maudsley states that there are residua from motor reactions in the nerve centers. The movements determined or effected by a particular nerve center leave, similar to ideas, their respective residues which, repeated several times, become organized or embed so well in its structure, that the corresponding movements can take place automatically.

Below is a sample of the vagueness and imprecision of terms that obscure the thought; besides, the British author seems to feel it himself, for he adds:

> "When we speak of a trace, vestige or residuum all we mean to imply is that an effect is left behind in the organic element, a something retained by it which disposes it to a similar functional act ..."[133]

Ribot agrees that it is impossible to say what such a modification consists of. Neither the microscope, nor the reagents, nor histology, nor histochemistry can teach us.[134]

In short, these authors admit that the molecules of living matter which have received the action of an external force no longer vibrate in the same manner as before, being in a new state of balance, and if an impulse of the same nature

---

133 H. MAUDSLEY, *The Physiology of Mind* (3rd rev. ed. London: Macmillan & Co., 1876), ch. v, p. 270.
134 T. RIBOT, *Maladies de la Mémoire* (Paris: F. Alcan, 1888), p. 14.

is once again exerted upon them, the movement this time will be more easily performed than the first time, and will be embedded, so to speak, in the substance to which it has communicated a new property.

T. Ribot sees in the association of these movements of all parts of the nervous system an essential condition of memory, and mentions a certain number of facts which seem to strongly support his manner of interpreting these phenomena. Thus, the movements of walking require the participation of a very large number of motor and nervous elements which need to be coordinated and associated in order to produce the desired displacement. Cells differing in volume, form (fusiform, giant, pyramidal, etc.), by their position in the various parts of the cerebrospinal axis, all come into play, since they are widespread from the lower extremity of the marrow to the cortical layers.

All these elements play their part in this concert. Ribot summarizes his observations as follows:[135]

> "Therefore, we believe that it is of the utmost importance to draw attention to this point: that organic memory does not only involve a modification of the nervous elements, but *the formation among them of associations determined for each particular event*, the establishment of certain *dynamic* associations which, by repetition, become as stable as primitive anatomical connections. In our eyes, what matters as the basis of memory is not only the modification printed on each element, but the way in which several elements group together to form a complexus."

According to this view, psychological memory, properly speaking, suggests the same reflections, for our ideas are associated with each other according to laws determined by contiguity, resemblance, difference, etc.

Moreover, it should be noted that one of these secondary associations can enter, in turn, into other groups, in order to

---

[135] [Trans. note] T. RIBOT, *Maladies de la Mémoire* (Paris: F. Alcan, 1888), p. 16.

play a different role, because dynamic relationships which were created, for example, for walking, can be used with other modifications for skating, swimming or dancing.

But is it really in the nervous mass that these associations are organized, and can we conceive rationally that this is the place of their conservation? I do not think so, and here is why: if we admit, with Claude Bernard, that all these movements produced in the organism require the destruction of the living substance, the brain which functions with an uninterrupted activity must renew itself a considerable number of times during one's lifetime, so that the movement imparted to a nervous cell would become weaker and weaker as the number of renovations of this cell increased. Therefore, it is difficult to imagine how stable dynamic relations could be maintained in the midst of a perpetual change of molecules constituting the billions of small organisms that form the fabric of the nervous substance. This means that, at the end of one's life, when these reconstitutions would have occurred hundreds of times, the memory of the first years should have disappeared completely.

But it turns out that observation has shown that in old age it is the memories of young age that last over more recent ones. This anomaly would be inexplicable, if it really were the nervous system that recorded all sensations as those researchers claim.

This is where Spiritist teaching comes in: it brings a new explanation, as I have already said several times. We know that the human soul is associated with an infinitely subtle substance to which Allan Kardec gave the name of *perispirit*. This spiritual body exists throughout one's lifetime and survives death. It is the mold into which physical matter is incorporated, or, more exactly, the ideal blueprint or matrix which contains the organogenic rules of the human being. The perispirit is attached to the body through the nervous system; every sensation which shakes the nervous mass releases this kind of energy to which we have given the most varied names: nervous fluid, magnetic fluid, ectenic force, psychical force, biological force, etc. This energy acts on the perispirit to communicate to it the particular vibrational movement according to the nervous zone which has been excited (visual, auditory, tactile, muscular vibrations, etc.), so that the attention of the soul is awakened, thus producing the phenomenon of perception. From that moment on, this vibration is forever part of the perispiritual organism, since, by virtue of the law of conservation of energy, it is indestructible. Without a doubt, it will be able to disappear from the field of consciousness, but, as we have seen, it will persist unaltered in the depths of latent memory, which nowadays is called the unconscious. Spiritist experiments have established with absolute certainty the existence of this spiritual body, which makes itself visible during the doubling (OBE) of the human being, and which testifies to its persistence after death, through apparitions, and especially by means of materializations. These last phenomena, which momentarily reconstitute the human being as it existed on Earth physically and intellectually, prove with a luminous evidence that it is the perispirit that organizes and maintains the human body and which, borrowing the clear expression of Claude Bernard, contains the guiding idea, the structure and functions. It is in the perispirit that lies the ultimate reason for the biological and psychological functions of all living beings.

It is because the perispirit is indestructible that we carry away after death the entirety of all our earthly acquisitions, and that memory awakens whole and integral in sufficiently evolved beings, so as to make us embrace the panorama of our past existence.

We shall see a little further, the resulting consequences in spiritual life, and why the memory of past lives is not equally retrieved by all spirits which inhabit the spiritual plane.

At this time it is still difficult to accurately describe the conditions of life beyond the grave; however, numerous mediumistic communications obtained for half a century all over the world allow us to get a general idea of the psychological state of the soul after one's death. We know that the separation between spirit and matter produces a period of disturbance during which the soul does not have an exact awareness of its new situation; it is as if in a dreamy state, and sometimes it does not know much about the material world which it has just left. Sometimes it has vague perceptions which, blending with its memories, give it some sort of abnormal existence similar to the delirium that accompanies certain earthly diseases. It is in this category that we must include those spirits which believe to be still physically alive and whose manifestations sometimes give rise to phenomena of obsession which have been so often noted. If we address the beings which are in this situation, we usually only get incoherent answers, but little by little this kind of perispiritual disease comes to an end, either spontaneously or under the influence of protector spirits; and then the soul awakens in its new environment, and the memories of earthly life can be resuscitated in their entirety.

We have found that memory is part of the perispirit, in successive layers so to speak, since in phenomena of regression of memory, as signaled by Pitres, Bourru, Burot, Pierre Janet, and others, each age resuscitates all its respective contemporary events, and those retrieved from the age of 19, for example, are associated with one another in an indissoluble manner, and do not blend with those of previous ages or with those which followed them.

Better still, in certain subjects, such as Louis V., the physiological state is inseparable from the psychological state which is associated with it. This allows us to understand how, during a materialization, the spirit recreating momentarily a physical body which is the representation of the one it once had at a period of its earthly life, can do it by a simple act of its will, that is, by autosuggestion.

It is possible to compare the action of the spiritual body with that of a field of magnetic or electric force, because we know that these can act upon matter by means of lines of force which form in a more or less complicated way – in a magnet, for example, following the shape of the poles. It is therefore possible to imagine that all earthly organs are represented in the perispirit; that at the moment of materialization, it is the energy provided by the spirit medium that puts this mechanism into action. This exteriorized material to which today we give the name of *ectoplasm*, which also emanates from the same medium, is mechanically incorporated in the same fluidic matrix to which it passively obeys, should this exteriorized material not be thwarted by any disruptive influences.

It is easy to imagine that such an abnormal phenomenon is accompanied by more or less pronounced disturbances as regards the psychological state, and that during tangible apparitions, the being which manifests itself in this way has, in the beginning, great difficulty in using its perispiritual brain that has just been so deeply, and so suddenly, modified. These remarks should help us understand why the apparitions of living beings or those which occur shortly after death are, in general, little talkative and very sparing of information, if one decides to question them. But that is no longer the case when we are dealing with spirits that have gradually become accustomed to this new state, because then, we see that their intellectual faculties gradually resume their normal functioning, as it was on Earth. This is what was observed with Katie King, who, in the last days of her apparitions told the children of Mr. Crookes about the events of her life in India; or, for that matter, with Mrs. Estelle Livermore who ended up, after two-hundred seances, being able to write her messages in French, a language she commanded perfectly in her lifetime, but which was totally unknown to the medium Kate Fox. I cannot stress it enough that, for me, these experimental observations have a first rank value, since they show that it is the spirit that has the power to organize matter, that it is in it that the intellectual faculties reside and not in the physical body which has disappeared and whose elements are now scattered in nature. If the memory of the last earthly life is restored after death, this does not happen in many cases with that of previous existences – and enemies of Spiritism have tried to use this argument to fight the theory of *reincarnation*. Yet, here again, observing the facts allows us to understand this apparent anomaly.

We have seen that there are series of superimposed memories and that the superficial layers are accessible to ordinary consciousness. If one wants to penetrate deeper into the stacks of memory, it is necessary to plunge the subject into a somnambulic (trance) state, the latter having the result of partially disengaging the soul from the body by restoring to the perispirit its proper vibrational action. Then, just as in a ray of white light there exist different wavelengths that extend far beyond its visible part, so in the spiritual body there are different zones of tremendous vibrational intensity. The perispiritual layers of past lives have a minimum vibrational action which renders them unconscious for undeveloped spirits, so that they do not know if they have lived before, thus they can affirm in good faith that there is only one earthly lifetime. But it is possible to awaken older memories in such spirits by magnetizing them, and then unfold before them the panorama of their remote past. for those who do not believe this explanation, and claim it was invented for the needs of the Spiritist cause, I once again stand firmly on experimental grounds – and it is quite remarkable, that it is our spirit instructors themselves that put us on the path of this discovery. At a time when nobody knew of experiments on the regression of memory yet, Allan Kardec taught us that, on the spiritual plane, any spirit can be magnetized just as on Earth, and by this means regain the fullness of memory, its integral memory. Here is what we read the *Revue Spirite* of

1866, volume IX, page 175 *et seq.* (I quote this passage because it seems to confirm the opinion above):

(It is the spirit of a highly respected doctor, Dr. Cailleu, who recounts through the medium Morin that, although he had been free from disturbance for a long time, he found himself one day in a state similar to a sort of lucid sleep.)

> "When my spirit suffered a kind of numbness, I was somewhat magnetized by the fluid of my spirit friends; it must have been result in moral satisfaction which, they say, is my reward and, moreover, an encouragement to walk on the path that my spirit has been following since many lives. I was therefore asleep in a mystic-spiritual sleep; I saw the past rendered in a fictitious present; I recognized individuals that had disappeared in the course of time, or rather that had only been the one and same individual. I saw one starting a medical book, another, later on, continuing the book left blank first, and so on. I have come to see, in less time than I can tell you, an idea form, grow and become a science, that in the beginning was just the first attempt, the first steps of a busy brain studying how to bring relief to a suffering humanity. I saw all this, and when I arrived at the last of these beings who had successively brought a complement to the previous work, only then, I recognized myself. At that point, everything vanished and I became again yours truly, the spirit still behind your poor doctor."

Here the teaching of our spirit guides has preceded science, and this story proves to us that the laws of magnetism are the same in the spiritual world as on Earth. So, mutatis mutandis, if we magnetize an earthly subject enough to exteriorize his/her fluidic body; and if we continue on the disengaged spirit until we reach the deeper layers of the perispirit; we may eventually resuscitate the memory of past lives of this subject.

This is what Spanish Spiritists have done, as it is easy to check by referring to the account of the Congrès Spirite et Spiritualiste International of 1889. Later, following indications of Léon Denis, Colonel Rochas d'Aiglun was committed in the same way and got some interesting results, which are recorded in his book *Les Vies Successives* [*Successive Lives*] (Paris, 1911). Unfortunately, these experiments are not exempt from criticism, especially as regards the suggestion that the magnetizer even involuntarily exerts upon his subjects. I am convinced, however, that we will be able to protect ourselves from these causes of error, and that we will be able to eventually acquire new proofs of the great law of evolution which governs the whole universe. So, taking into consideration the power of the perispiritual body to retain forever all the influences that have acted upon it during all its transitions on Earth, we will have a clear and simple explanation of the problems of heredity that contemporary science is powerless to solve. It will be another immense service that Spiritism will have rendered to humankind, and our successors will finally pay tribute to it as it so rightfully deserves. In the meantime, we will briefly review the results obtained in Spiritist seances with magnetically asleep subjects, or by mediums serving as intermediaries for discarnate spirits.

Study of seances where alleged revelations about the subject's or participants' past lives have occurred

If it is perfectly exact, as we will see later, that one can actually push the regression of memory back to previous lives in certain somnambulic subjects. It is equally certain, unfortunately, that the study of this issue is bristling with difficulties of all sorts.

In these researches, we should be very cautious in the first place against simulations, which are always possible when dealing with professional subjects. Secondly, even with perfectly honest somnambulists, one must always be suspicious of their imagination, which often gives itself free rein by forging more or less truthful stories, which Professor Flournoy has so aptly called "subliminal novels." These kinds of personifications of imaginary individuals have been frequently produced in experiments, among others by Professor Charles Richet, who has designated them by the term "objectification of types"; and we know that by autosuggestion it is perfectly possible for a subject immersed in this state to imagine that he/she is such and such personage, and to compose the type with such a great luxury of attitudes and characteristic traits, that It would seem that one is really in presence of a true individuality.

Other causes of error, depending on the case, may still occur if the subject possesses a faculty of clairvoyance or cryptesthesia that allows him/her to become acquainted with the thoughts of the seance participants, or, if he/she is a psychometer, to resurrect with a perfect likelihood scenes that took place far away from him/her, and in past eras.

Here is first a category in which the good faith of the subject and experimenters seems certain to me. These facts have been, for the most part, spontaneously observed by Spiritists, and as they differ from the systematic inquiries of Misters Flournoy and Rochas d'Aiglun, I will relate them first, because they do have priority.

At the Congrès Spirite et Spiritualiste International of 1900, Mr. Jacinto Esteva Marata gave the following interesting account, which shows how one might sometimes succeed in resuscitating, during the somnambulic state, memories borrowed from past lives:[136]

> "It was in 1887; there was in Spain a Spiritist group called Peace, whose founder and president was Fernandez Colavida, nicknamed, on the other side of the Pyrenees, the Spanish Kardec. In all its seances, this group was studying and

---

136 [Trans. note] See *Compte rendu du Congrès Spirite et Spiritualiste International*, 1900 (Paris: Librairie de Sciences Psychiques, 1902), pp. 349–350.

controlling [verifying rigorously] Spiritist issues. My wife and I were members of this group at the time.

Now, one day, Mr. Fernandez Colavida wanted to check to see if he could induce on a somnambulist the memory of his past lives. This is how he acted. The medium being magnetized to a high degree, he commanded him to say what he had done the day before, the day before that, a week, a month, a year before, and thus pushing him back in time, so in the end, the medium reached his childhood which he explained in all its details. Pushing him further back in time, the medium then told about his life on the spiritual plane, the death of his last incarnation and, pushed continuously to the past, he totaled four incarnations, the oldest of which had been a totally wild existence. It must be remarked that at each different existence the features of the medium were completely modified. To bring him back to his normal state, Mr. Colavida made him come back to his current existence, then woke him up.

Not wishing to be accused of having made a mistake, he had the same medium magnetized by a different magnetizer who was to suggest to him that past lives did not exist. Despite this suggestion, the medium again exhibited the four aforementioned existences, as he had done a few days earlier. I got the same result of the same nature, with another medium:[137] I magnetized my wife until she fell into somnambulism, to control a poetry that Mrs. Amalia Domingo Soler had offered her, in which a spirit told her a fact that had happened to her in a previous existence; and indeed the case was confirmed by my wife in this state of trance.

I believe that if anyone wants to undertake these studies, they can achieve the same results, but the medium must be surrounded by all possible precautions, because extremely dangerous accidents may happen.

Do not push your research too far and try these studies only with perfect somnambulists who are used to parting with their body and remaining linked only by their perispirit."

---

[137] The first studies were controlled by the members of the Spiritist group "Peace."

It is clear that here we have no effective demonstration of the reality of these retrocognitions, because the second experiment involving suggestions that these visions do not exist could not have any hold on the subject's somnambulistic consciousness. Moreover, since no verifiable revelation is given in relation to these past lives, there is nothing to allow us to see a true resurrection of the past. Let us now turn our attention to experiments in other settings.

Unforeseen revelation

I owe to the kindness of Mr. Louis Gastin, a well-known Occultist, the following account:

"Dear Mr. Delanne,

I am pleased to confirm below the very curious experiment that I obtained a number of years ago in a quite impromptu way.

It was in 1906. I was still living in Avignon and I was already busy with the systematic study of psychical phenomena, apart from any doctrine or theory.

I had not yet managed to form an opinion on the value of the Spiritualist hypothesis, and my positivistic tendencies inclined me to rather find in suggestion and autosuggestion a sufficient explanation for all psychical and parapsychical phenomenism.

I went frequently to Romans-sur-Isère, in the Drôme (France), where my uncle lived with a family of Spiritists composed, apart from the father and the mother, of two young girls, of whom I had no difficulty in making two subjects of experiments.

In hopes of gaining a more serious control over the phenomenon, I was simultaneously sleeping near the two girls and trying to obtain somnambulic clairvoyance in them, while my uncle, a writing medium, received spirit communications a few steps from there.

Aimée, the youngest of the two subjects, presented frequent and very interesting manifestations of lucid somnambulism. I will not tell you about it here, although some of these events were really interesting.

On the other hand, the eldest, Juliet, did not present any interesting phenomenon: she remained in a kind of unconscious lethargy from which I in vain tried to pull her out by opening her eyes and looking at her. A cataleptoid state was coming, and she closed her eyes as soon as my eyes, for one reason or another, left hers. Apart from this trivial fact, nothing, absolutely nothing, had make me hope for any realization of experimental interest with this mediocre subject. However, the loss of consciousness was obvious.

One day, renewing an attempt I had unsuccessfully made so many other times, and besides, without any specific goal or objective, while the two sisters were asleep and my uncle at the table, in front of his writing paper, I approached Juliette, the mediocre subject, and opening her eyes I looked at her as usual, when suddenly she said to me, looking surprised: 'How curious, I do not see you anymore ... or rather I see you old, bald and stern in appearance, but no it's not you ... it's your expression, but it's not you, it's an old man who looks like you, and behind that cold and stern face that frightens me I see you, as I know you, alive and smiling.'

As I asked for more details, Juliette added, 'Ah, the old man's face has disappeared ... but another is replacing him.' And successively, in an order that I did not have time to notice, so much the fact had been unexpected and fast, the subject described a long series of faces of all ages, men and women, who came, like masks, alive but cold, to stand in front of my own living physiognomy, and always it was the same expression on the look. This door of the soul, according to the physiognomists, that the subject recognized to be my own expression, is like the characteristic of my individuality.

Then suddenly all visions disappeared and Juliette could see only my present and current self.

I then asked the subject what, in her opinion, could represent the curious kaleidoscopic visions. Juliette replied clearly that she knew nothing about it. I approached her sister, who was still sleeping a few steps away, and asked her if she had seen them too.

'Yes,' she answered me, 'there were even more figures than my sister reported, but they passed so fast that sometimes my sister could not grasp them.' What do you think these visions could mean? 'Your previous lives.'

At this precise moment my uncle wrote mediumistically: These are your previous incarnations. Evidently there was in this succession of facts, for me who found myself at this moment outside any spiritualistic doctrine and willing enough to see everywhere the role of suggestion or autosuggestion, nothing demonstrative about the possibility of a vision of past incarnations. I was at the home of Spiritists and I thought it was only natural to receive, from Aimée and my uncle in a subconscious relationship with Juliette, an explanation of Spiritist character.

To better observe the phenomenon, I decided to induce it again, and, approaching Juliette, I asked her to open her eyes again, suggesting that she would see the same visions unfold again.

In spite of all my efforts of suggestion (I was then in good form as a hypnotist), it was impossible for me to reproduce, even embryonically, the same vision, and I must add, because the fact is of paramount importance, that Juliette later became again the mediocre subject that she had been until then, and that no more event ever came to assert itself. Thus the explanatory argument of suggestion and autosuggestion disappeared. It is not with you, dear Mr. Delanne, that I have to develop this point of logic; you will do it with more precision and authority than me, if you think you should use the story in your books. I just related to you an experiment which was the starting point for a series of studies on my part regarding the duality of the inner being and the fundamental difference which we should establish in their nature as well as in their relations between the living personality and the spiritual individuality that this personality reflects without knowing it, and of which it is only an extension.

Thanking you, I remain your fraternal friend,

Louis Gastin"

It seems obvious that any suggestion on the part of Mr. Gastin must be eliminated, but as the scene occurred in a Spiritist environment, in which ideas of reincarnation were familiar, we can suppose that there has been a temporary irruption of subconscious ideas that have exteriorized themselves in visual forms related to such theory. However, the second subject confirming the descriptions of the first would have been of great value if this second subject had not heard her sister make those descriptions. The same applies to the mediumistic writing of Gastin's uncle.

Finally, as no clarification is provided on these retrocognitions, which would allow for later verification, I am logically obliged, without denying the possibility of a genuine revelation, to classify this phenomenon among those which do not offer sufficient proof of their reality. The same can be said of the following case:

Subliminal novel or reminiscence

In his interesting book, *La Survivance Humaine*[138] (Paris, 1920, pages 535–536), Mr. P. E. Cornillier recounts one of his seances with his medium, Reine, a young artistic model who had no knowledge whatsoever of Spiritist theories.

> "'Here they are,' said she, now in contemplation before the lake and talking – and it is with a reality so prodigious that we seem to be a third party in their conversation. The lucidity of the medium is increasingly more clarified. The

---

138 [Trans. note] In English, see P. E. Cornillier, *The Survival of the Soul* (London: Kegan Paul, Trench, Trubner & Co. Ltd., 1921).

sight of this blue lake brings back memories of her past lives in Italy and the Orient. She relates some incidents to her two companions, makes descriptions, comparisons. She tells about her life in Naples and Capri.

She speaks of Sicily, describes aspects of Vesuvius with extreme precision. At Capri, she knew a house that Vetellini[139] would later inhabit; she gives her exact location; she makes observations on the landscapes of Nature; she saw the boiling sea when the lavas of Vesuvius were engulfed there; the absolute lack of birds in this beautiful sky, etc. Then she appreciates the Orient, surprised that Old Friend never had the curiosity to go there since he is a spirit.

'It would be so easy! Why do you not go there? Ah! you like the banks and the stock market better; well, we should go there together sometime. I'll take you there. Oh! I know Egypt well ...' Then she came back to the time when she was a healer. In Egypt, doctor of the body and soul. In that life she was with Vetellini; they were friends; he, already more advanced, above her (above him rather) and protecting her. She notices that in the Orient, because of atmospheric conditions, life of the astral is perceptible. The incarnate, when a little advanced, can feel so to speak the constant grazing of the discarnate.

All this talk is prodigious; despite our being used to it, we are still amazed. But many times already Reine has noticed that she will never be able to get Mr. Cornillier informed of all this. Vetellini reassures her, tells her that he makes her speak aloud. She only half believes it; it seems to her impossible that she could have spoken aloud to Paris what she saw and felt here in America. We must come back, so that she can check if it is true.

The spirit guide Vetellini had already said in another seance that Reine ("Queen") had lived in Egypt. After a stone from a necklace of this country was put in her hand, she said: 'That. Comes from Egypt Is it psychometry?"'

---

139 Vetellini was Reine's spirit guide, as well as guide of the group directed by Mr. Cornillier.

Here again, no precise indication of these so-called past lives is given, and the descriptions made by Reine could at the very least be the result of previous readings or conversations, or even a clairvoyant action [or remote viewing] by the subject. This calls for the greatest caution when assessing this curious phenomenon.

It seems that with the following cases we take a small step towards something more demonstrative.

I borrowed the following narrative from a short brochure published by Mr. Henri Sausse. Having known the author personally for a very long time, I can attest to his absolute good faith and the veracity of his accounts.[140]

> "While coming to our meetings, Mrs. Conte Calix was accompanied by Miss Sophie, her lady's company. The latter, after having seen the ease with which the mediums were put into somnambulism and the state of well-being in which they awoke, asked me to try to put her to sleep to see if she had, at a latent state, faculties that could be useful to us. At the end of a seance, I said to Miss Louise before waking her up: 'Help her disengage from her body, I'm going to make Miss Sophie fall asleep.' She replied nervously and in a low voice, 'No, I don't want to. I don't want to, so do as you please.' I was surprised at the tone of her reply, but I did not insist. The next day I saw Miss Louise, and without telling her the purpose of my visit, I put her in somnambulic trance, and asked her the cause of her behavior the day before. She persisted for a long time in wanting to keep for herself a secret which did not concern me; however, at my insistence, she finally declared to me: 'I opposed it because this person was the cause of my misfortune in another existence; we swore eternal hatred, I despise her, I hate her and I will never forgive her – never, do you hear? Oh, all the harm she has done to me!'

---

140 H. Sausse, *Des preuves? En voilà!* [*Need proofs? Here they are!*] (Orig. 1911, FLV reprint 2012), p. 32 in the original edition..

'But I believe,' I said to her, 'that it is not chance alone that has put you on the same path again, but our spirit friends which thus are giving you the means of reconciling with each other.' She rebelled against this idea, but with patience and good arguments, I finally made her promise that she would help me to put Miss Sophie to sleep and forgive her. In the next seance I did not tell anyone about this last interview. After having at the same time put Miss Louise, Mrs. Maria, and Mr. Molaret into magnetic sleep, I put the latter in my place, with Miss Louise on the right and Mrs. Maria on her left, and placing myself in presence of Miss Sophie, I began to induce her into somnambulic trance. At this moment Mrs. Maria and Mr. Molaret took Miss Louise by the waist, saying:

'Now come, Louise, have courage, we must help her freed herself from her body; we must also forgive her, we must forget. Yes, forgive and forget; it is our spirit friends who ask you to do it; this hatred must end and a sincere pardon reconcile you.'

Miss Sophie had fallen asleep in her turn; then Miss Louise took her by the hand and said to her, 'See and remember.' Miss Sophie stood for a moment stupefied, dumbfounded, and then burst into tears, saying, 'No, you can't forgive me, I have done you so much wrong that you can't forget it. Where to hide? I'm ashamed of myself.' And she cried so much she flooded her blouse. Louise and the others were crying too. Finally, Miss Louise said: 'Since our spirit friends have asked for it, let everything be erased from this sinister past, let everything be forgotten.' And having stood up spontaneously, the four mediums were holding each other in a strong embrace, now weeping with joy and rapture. I had a hard time bringing all four back to the feeling of reality and awakening them back. The other members of the group had followed this deeply moving scene without understanding it. I had to give them the key to the riddle. It was the end of a posthumous hate.

Elsewhere I observed two other similar cases.

In September 1887, in a seance, one of the spirits which helped us in our work, the spirit friend Joseph, said to us: 'I come to bid you farewell, I will not return to your meetings where you have so fraternally welcomed me, I will now reincarnate.' 'If you wish to tell us in what conditions we could look for you to still take care of you.' – 'No, it's useless; it would be against the law of God. If the mystery of our past is hidden from us, it is because there are serious reasons for it and we can't break it by seeking to lift the veil that hides our destiny.' That was his last visit.

If we did not know of any instances of psychical contagion occurring among somnambulic subjects, we might class this fact of reciprocal recognition among the good proofs of reincarnation.

Unfortunately, here again, no precise information is given on the past lives of the two subjects, which leaves us indecisive and does not allow us to express an absolute opinion on the value of this mutual recognition.

Now here is another ambiguous case where the earthly action producing an obsession would have been determined by a hatred contracted in a previous existence. I borrowed it from a study on reincarnation conducted by Mr. Bouvier.[141]

Tenacious hatred

"Towards the end of 1886, a lady from Saint-Marcel Street, now Sergent-Blandan Street, had been locked up as insane for fifteen years in various health centers. After a while, her condition seemed to improve, she went out to return to her family, but new crises of great intensity forced them to lock her up again. Seeing that this state would not subside, the interested parties resorted to magnetic action, believing with good reason that it would be possible to obtain a result which mainstream science had failed to give. And, indeed, this is what took place under the following conditions:

---

[141] Talk given by Mr. Bouvier at the Allan Kardec Auditorium, p. 10.

At the second seance, wanting to show through my subject Isidore what was the cause of the cerebral disturbance which afflicted this lady, she told me that the lady was suffering from obsession and that, if I wanted to call and counsel the spirit that was the culprit of his disorder, it would soon make me assured of that. That is what I did and little by little the obsessor made known the reason that made him act that way.

In a previous existence, he [the spirit] told me, 'I was part of a Russian princely family. We were three children, two girls and a boy. My sisters, in order to enjoy my patrimony, made me be locked up in a house from which I could only escape through death. There I swore to myself that, if I could, sooner or later, I would avenge myself. God in his goodness allowed us to be reincarnated in the same environment, so that by the bonds of marriage we came to be brother-in-law and sister-in-law. Despite this, during my life, we could not sympathize with each other for any apparent reason. I died in the world of matter thirteen years ago; I could recognize myself quickly enough to see that my sister from the past was my sister-in-law of the present. Hence our aversion to each other; and from there also my vengeance: I was dead locked up; I wanted her in turn to suffer the same fate. Now I understand my wrongs, since, despite my vengeance, suffering is always my lot; so I want to ask her forgiveness and promise to let her live in peace.' Forgiveness took place, it was a touching scene to see the medium and Mrs B. crying in each other's arms regretting the past. You must have seen it to feel that there could be no acting out. From this moment on the cure was radical; this lady lived for another twelve years in perfect lucidity and died very slowly at the age of 72 from influenza. As to whether it is true that these beings were or were not part of a Russian princely family, which would constitute more evidence in favor of reincarnation, the thing is difficult to control [i.e., to verify], but what is absolutely certain is that, 16 years earlier, a brother-in-law of the patient bearing the name given by the entranced medium and with whom she had never sympathized had died. Moreover, it was verified that one year after his death, Mrs. B. was locked up once; better still, the realization of the promise made after reciprocal forgiveness shows us well that there was a cause conscious of itself. But just as all these controllable facts are true, there are also probabilities that may be not true as well."

Reincarnation in England

Opponents of Spiritism have often asserted that there was frequently an absolute contradiction between the teachings of discarnate spirits that manifest in France and those in England regarding reincarnation.

Undoubtedly, the majority of the Anglo-Saxon discarnate spirits do not admit that the evolution of the soul takes place on our globe by a succession of earthly lives. They teach that this evolution occurs on different planes of the spiritual world and on other planets. However there are many centers in which the teachings of the Hereafter are in line with those of so-called Latin countries (France, Italy, Spain, etc), and this is an interesting point to report, since, increasingly, the theory of palingenesis is gaining ground among the British and even in North America. Here is an example among many others that I could highlight.

Can reincarnation be proved?

The author begins by saying that in England the majority of the spirits refuse to believe in reincarnation, because all the mediums speaking in the state of trance declare, not that reincarnation is certainly a myth, but that they have no notion about it. In addition, humans find the sojourn on Earth so sad, that they cannot conceive of the idea of returning to it. Finally, most Spiritualists themselves keep caution by asking for more evidence, as they do not think that we still have enough.[142]

"But is this so? I used to adopt this attitude and was as strongly opposed to the theory as anyone could be, and, as a trance medium, my controls [spirits] have delivered addresses through me against reincarnation. B u t some three years ago a band of spirits came to our circle (a private one), and through me claimed that reincarnation is a fact and not merely a theory. I strongly objected when informed afterwards of what had been said. I argued that as I was opposed to the theory, it was unfair that I should be used for upholding it. But the same spirits came again and again, and we became interested. We said, 'If, as you say, reincarnation is a fact, and not merely a theory, can you prove it?' They replied that they not only could but would. But they said, 'Let us first prove ourselves and our powers in matters which you can easily test, and then when we have gained your confidence, we will proceed further.'

This seemed reasonable and we agreed. Time after time they gave us most convincing proofs of their identity and of their knowledge of things past and present, and in many cases also of the future.

Speaking generally, we found that they were thoroughly to be trusted. They guided us in earthly matters as well as in spiritual, and we all, to this day, feel deeply grateful to them. But now to the proofs promised us. They said they would bring us into touch with people we had known in former incarnations, and would show us scenes in our past lives that we could recognize. One evening a lady was described, and I was told that I should shortly meet her. Ten days afterwards I went by appointment to a south coast watering place. It was my first visit there, and I knew nobody, all my arrangements having been made by letter. On my arrival I was informed by my hostess, whom I had never met

---

142 *Revue Scientifique et Morale du Spiritisme*, November 1903, p. 314 [Trans. note: French article based on an English letter published by *Light*, no. 1186, vol. xxiii, October 3, 1903, p. 479, faithfully reproduced above].

before, that there was a lady staying in the house who was rather 'anxious to meet me. She had come there two days previously, a complete stranger, and had taken apartments. In the course of conversation she remarked that she was a vivid dreamer, and that she frequently saw people in her dreams whom she afterwards met in the flesh. 'For instance,' she said, 'I am waiting now for the fulfillment of a dream. I am going to meet a Mr. W. this week. I don't know where but I know I shall.' ... On my arrival I was duly introduced and instantly recognized the lady I had been told I was to meet.

A still stronger proof was given to another member of our circle. She was introduced to a gentleman, and her memory instantly flew back to a former life when she had known him under other conditions. The recognition was mutual, for he smiled and said, 'Do you remember me?' She replied that she did. 'Then, as a test, let us write down the names by which we knew each other,' he said. This was agreed to. The names were written on slips of paper, and the papers were exchanged. The names on each were identical. If this is not proof, it is something which at least is difficult of explanation. But I prefer to accept the explanation given by our spirit friends, that this was a meeting of two people who had been friends in a former incarnation, and that they had brought about the meeting as a proof for us...."

In these two examples, unfortunately too little detailed, the certainty of previous lives results from the affirmation of spirit guides; but the simultaneous evocation of memories relating to a previous existence, if they do not result from a spiritual suggestion, would prove that it is really a resurrection of the past that has occurred for each experimenter, and this in their ordinary normal state, which increases the value of the case.

Successive lives

This is the title of a book published in 1911 by Colonel Rochas d'Aiglun,[143] a former director of the French École Polytechnique. The author is well known for his extensive research on the exteriorization of sensibility, the superficial and deep states of hypnosis, and lastly for his experiments with prenatal memory. In the book in question, he relates his experiments from the years 1892 to 1910 with nineteen subjects, to try to awaken in each of them, by plunging them deeper and deeper into magnetic states, the memory of their past lives.

His process consisted in giving longitudinal passes, in order to lull the subjects more and more to sleep; and to make suggestions to them, so as to awaken in them all the memories of current life until birth, and, by pushing the experience even further back, to obtain from them revelations about existences that would have preceded the current one.

All these subjects gave him more or less probable accounts of past lives. Unfortunately, in the majority of cases, it was impossible to ascertain the reality of these retrospective visions. The author did not focus enough on the names, dates, and locations of these regressive visions. I believe that if Rochas d'Aiglun had better known and practiced Spiritist experiments, he could have benefited greatly from his very real fluidic power, by asking the discarnate spirits to help him in this search by acting on their side upon the soul of the subject when it was exteriorized, since it is during this period that resuscitation of the integral memory takes place.

Mr. Rochas d'Aiglun was very fortunate in another attempt in the opposite direction: that of making the sensitives foresee what was going to happen to them in future.

---

143 ROCHAS D'AIGLUN, *Les Vies Successives* (Paris: Chacornac, 1911).

To bring back the somnambulist to his/her normal state, Rochas d'Aiglun used transverse passes and continued them after the subject's waking, which put the latter in another state where he/she would supposedly be able to foresee the future.

I believe that in this case the magnetizer's suggestion was really the efficient cause, for the relation between him and his subjects was always very close, and it is to be supposed that his mental action was transmitted to those upon whom he operated with the greatest facility.

Whatever the case may be, here is how the author thus sums up the long work he has done:[144]

> "I have related a certain number of experiments in which, under the influence of magnetic passes, the sensitives, whose souls were more or less freed from the bonds of the body, seemed to revive lives already lived or to live future lives. This phenomenon takes various forms depending on the individual. In some, the various transformations have the appearance of absolute reality and are always consistently identical and in the same order. Several months apart, the subject lives them in a striking manner with physical and intellectual states that characterize him/her. In others, they vary somewhat and are more like memories in which one can easily recognize the intervention of previous magnetic readings; they are none the less interesting, because they prevent us from having a blind confidence in the former and put on the path of a purely physical explanation. A constant, however, is reproduced in all these manifestations: the atonement, in the following lives, of faults committed in previous lives.
> What are the conclusions that can be drawn from the facts I have reported?
> There are of two kinds, some certain, others simply problematic. It is certain that, by means of magnetic processes, we may, in certain subjects endowed with sufficient sensitivity,

---

[144] *Op. cit.*, p. 495 *et seq.*

provoke a series of phases of lethargy and of somnambulic states which succeed one another regularly, as nights succeed days, and during which the soul seems to free itself more and more from the bonds of the body and to leap into regions of space and time generally inaccessible to it in the normal state of sleep.

It is certain that by means of certain magnetic operations we can gradually revert the majority of sensitives to earlier periods of their current life with intellectual and physiological peculiarities characteristic of these periods in time and up to the moment of their birth. It is not the memories that are awakened, but the successive states of the personality that are evoked. These evocations always occur in the same order and through a succession of lethargic and somnambulic states. This phenomenon occurs spontaneously in some patients, but only in relation to certain periods of their existence.

It can be explained by supposing that memories are registered in the successive layers of the brain, the oldest being located in the deepest layers, and that, owing to various circumstances, the vital activity which, ordinarily goes to the outer layers, returns to this or that part of the cerebral mass which has become inert by the passing of time. Yet, a more probable explanation, because it is based on the testimony of seeing subjects, is that the phenomenon is due to the concentration of the fluidic body which resumes the forms that it had successively during the development of the subject's life.

It is *certain* that by continuing these magnetic operations beyond birth, and without the necessity of resorting to suggestions, the subject passes through analogous states corresponding to previous incarnations and the intervals which separate these incarnations. The process is the same through successions of lethargy and somnambulic states. These revelations, when we have been able to control them, do not generally respond to reality, but it is difficult to understand how the same physical practices that first determine the regressions of real personalities up to the time of birth can suddenly give rise to quite false hallucinations."

Rochas d'Aiglun quite rightly remarks that, ideas of hell and purgatory being very widespread in all the places where he took his subjects, it is astonishing that none of them mentioned them, when he was between two alleged incarnations.

We shall now see another experimenter who was more fortunate than Mr. d'Aiglun, since at least once he obtained exact details relating to a subject's previous life.

The medium Hélène Smith

In his book *From India to the Planet Mars*,[145] Mr. T. Flournoy, professor of psychology at the Faculty of Sciences of the University of Geneva, made a very scholarly and very thorough study of the faculties of a medium he calls Miss Hélène Smith.

It is quite remarkable that this young girl of good education, full of sincerity and absolute good faith, would give herself freely for years to the investigation of scholars, and present imaginary personifications beside other clearly spiritualistic phenomena.

To be frank, Flournoy endeavored to explain all the phenomena as mere autosuggestion by the medium, whose inward and refined nature would have subconsciously led her into reveries to imagine that she was not in the social position she should have occupied, so that by frequenting Spiritist circles, where the ideas of reincarnation are common, she would have successively forged subliminally, that is to say, during her periods of unconsciousness, at least two novels relating to her past lives.

One of her 'novels' represents her as the reincarnation of Queen Marie Antoinette, and the other as the wife of a Hindu prince who lived in the 14th century and ruled over Kanara.

---

145 T. Flournoy, *From India to the Planet Mars* (Trans. D. B. Vermilye. London and New York: Harper & Bros., 1900).

A third hypnoid creation is relative to the planet Mars, of which Miss Smith gives descriptions that are fanciful. Even better, she would have made known the language of the inhabitants of our nearest neighbor planet.

Mr. Flournoy has very cleverly shown the probable genesis of this so-called Martian language and proved by the analysis of texts that it was, in reality, only a counterfeit of the subject's French language and that only the representative signs of the letters had a true originality. But that does not go beyond what schoolchildren can produce when they imagine secret alphabets in the classroom to match each other. I also acknowledge that Mr. Flournoy's skepticism toward Miss Smith's claim of being a reincarnation of the unfortunate Queen of France is very justified, because the memories of this royal cycle are full of anachronisms and the writing of the alleged personality of Marie Antoinette has nothing in common with the texts the actual Queen has left. Moreover, for historical events, as it is easy to find them everywhere, they cannot be mentioned, since the subliminal memory has certainly recorded a great many of them through reading, theater plays, and conversations.

This commentary applies to all cases of the same kind, and when we bear in mind the great fidelity with which the somnambulic memory retains all the visual or auditory clichés, we must, in good methodology, ascribe this knowledge to the normal acquisitions of everyday life and not to memories of an earlier existence.

An exception must be made, however, in the case of historical events not found in ordinary history textbooks or in historical or biographical dictionaries, but only in a few documents which are unknown to the public. The latter had to be discovered through laborious research, the contents of which could not have been previously available.

If this particular information relating to a non-European civilization is accompanied by descriptions relating to the country and reminiscences of the language which has been used there, then the probability of this knowledge being due to genuine memories of a past life becomes very high. That is why I will now cite briefly what Mr. Flournoy calls Miss Hélène Smith's Hindu cycle.

A preliminary remark must be made: this resurrection of the past has occurred during many sittings, without any previous suggestion from the sitters, and the somnambulic sleep occurred spontaneously in the subject, whether during seances, during normal life, and mainly in the morning when waking up. Then the visions reproducing scenes of the previous life took place by visual and sometimes auditory hallucinations, and are known only from the letters which Miss Smith regularly addressed to the learned professor at Geneva.

I will content myself with making here, for lack of space, an extremely short summary of the Hindu cycle, referring the reader for details to the book as quoted.[146]

Mr. Flournoy tells in this enigmatic chapter how his medium Helen Smith, pretending to be the reincarnation of the Hindu princess Simandini, mime her character in the most realistic, most accomplished way.

> "Mlle. Smith is really very wonderful in her Hindu somnambulisms. The way in which Simandini seats herself on the ground, her legs crossed, or half stretched out, nonchalantly leaning her arms or her head against Sivrouka [her husband], who is sometimes real (when in her incomplete trance she takes me for her prince), sometimes imaginary; the religious and solemn gravity of her prostrations when, after having for a long time balanced the fictitious brazier, she crosses her extended hands on her breast, kneeling and bowing herself three times ... the agile suppleness of her swaying and serpentine movements, when she amuses herself with her imaginary monkey, caresses it, embraces it, excites it, scolds it laughingly, and makes it repeat all its tricks – all

---

[146] *Op. cit.*, pp. 294, 296.

this so varied mimicry and Oriental speech have such a stamp of originality, of ease, of naturalness, that one asks in amazement whence it comes to this little daughter of Lake Leman, without artistic education or special knowledge of the Orient – a perfection of play to which the best actress, without doubt, could only attain at the price of prolonged studies or a sojourn on the banks of the Ganges."

However, adds the wise psychologist T. Flournoy:

"Two points remain, which complicate the case of the Hindu romance and seem to defy – thus far, at least – all normal explanation, because they surpass the limits of a simple play of the imagination....

These are the precise historical information given by Leopold [the medium's spirit guide], some of which can be, in a certain sense, verified; and the Hindu language spoken by Simandini, which contains words more or less recognizable, the real meaning of which is adapted to the situation in which they have been spoken. But, even if Hélène's imagination could have reconstructed the manners and customs and scenes of the Orient from the general information floating in some way in cosmopolitan atmosphere, still *one cannot conceive whence she has derived her knowledge of the language and of certain obscure episodes in the history of India.*" (My emphasis.)

So here is a fact of the first importance which can be explained very well by a resuscitation of memory, and which simply cannot be explained otherwise.

But Mr. Flournoy did not want to agree.

He sought specialist advice on the historical points, by consulting with qualified experts on Asian history. There was no knowledge of the characters or localities mentioned. Yet they were scholars of historical science. However, in his own words, "while professional science was administering to me these cold douches," he continued, on his own account, to search the libraries at his disposal, until he came across an old book: *Histoire de l'Inde* by Marlès. Therein he found a passage which has irrefutably proved that the story told by Hélène was not a myth. Of course, the scholars, the experts who were previously consulted, treated Marlès, the author of the venerable book, with aloof arrogance, and refused to consider him as a serious colleague. This is certainly very fortunate for the repute of Marlès.[147]

As for Flournoy, notwithstanding the implausibility of such a supposition, he does not hesitate to consider that the subliminal memory of Hélène Smith has drawn the information from the obscure and unknown book by Marlès; he scarcely detains himself at the orthographic differences between the text of the latter and that of the medium. The only thing that bothers him, and he admits it, is that *he cannot say where, when, and how Miss Smith could have read that book.*

> "I admit frankly that I know nothing about it, and I give full credit to Hélène for the indomitable and persevering energy with which she has never ceased to protest against my hypothesis, which has the faculty of exasperating her in the highest degree – and one readily understands that it would naturally do so. For it is in vain that she digs down to the very bottom of her memories ; she does not discover the slightest trace of this work ... I only know in Geneva of two copies of the work of De Marlès, both covered with dust ... It could only have happened, therefore, by a combination of absolutely exceptional and almost unimaginable circumstances that the work of De Marlès could have found its way into Hélène's hands; and how could it have done so and she not have the slightest recollection of it?"[148]

In short, and by Flournoy's own admission, this Hindu 'novel' (or 'romance') remains a psychological enigma not yet satisfactorily solved, because it reveals and implies in Hélène, with regard to customs and languages of the Orient,

---

147 [Trans. note] Jules Lacroix de MARLÈS, *Histoire de l'Inde Ancienne et Moderne* (Tours: A. Mame & Cie., 1845).

148 T. FLOURNOY, *From India to the Planet Mars* (Trans. D. B. Vermilye. London and New York: Harper & Bros., 1900), pp. 305–306..

Figure 4. Swiss medium Hélène Smith

the East, a knowledge whose source has been impossible to be determined for certain until now.

In spite of this formal restriction which removes all authority from the anti-spiritualist or extra-spiritualist hypotheses, our opponents have not hesitated to annex all this portion of Flournoy's work and still use it today as a deadly projectile, without realizing that he is actually turning against them. It is impossible to see telepathy, hallucination, or autosuggestion in those phenomena. All that remains is to admit what the medium herself constantly repeated: that she was resuscitating the distant memory of the Hindu princess Simandini. In the sittings in which it manifested itself, it was not an incarnation of this princess that the medium made, it was a resurrection of ancient memories. Hélène Smith really feels Princess Simandini returned in the form of a modern girl. Both seem to be the same individuality. This individuality was manifested successively over time in the form of Simandini, in India, and later in Switzerland with the mentality of Hélène. This kind of event was worth noting; it has nothing in common with habitual incorporations (i.e., mediumistic psychophonies) or incarnations in the medium of a personality that is entirely and completely extraneous to her. It is a distinct phenomenon. What authorizes me to make this assertion is that, since her youth, Miss Smith had artistic tastes quite different from what she could have drawn from her Geneva environment. Here is what Mr. Flournoy noted:

> "[According to her mother and herself] ... Mlle. Smith, since from her school-girl days ... has shown herself to be of a sedentary and domestic temperament, preferring the quiet companionship of her mother to the games of her comrades, and her needle-work to out-door recreations.... It is to be noticed also that the designs, embroideries, varied artistic works, which were always the favorite occupations of her moments of leisure and in which she excels, were almost always, from her infancy, not copies of exterior

models, but the products of her own invention, marked with the bizarre and original stamp of her internal images. Moreover, these pieces of work grew under her fingers with an ease and rapidity that astonished herself. They made themselves, as it were."[149]

With judicious common sense, Mr. Flournoy rightly points out that mediumship is by no means incompatible with a normal and regular life, that a medium is not necessarily a neurotic, as some short-sighted doctors have attempted to portray it. The subject being really important, I again allow myself to quote the authorized opinion of the famous Swiss psychologist:

"If one is astonished at the prominent place that this fear of passing for a sick or abnormal person has held in Miss Smith's worries, it must be said in her defense and that of mediums and scholars unduly incriminated, that the blame lies with gossips and loose talk of all sorts, with which the ignorant public poisons the existence of mediums and those who study them. It is clear that one can often find among the ranks of the learned academic or in official scientific organizations, as in any other numerous groups, a few narrow minds, very strong perhaps in their fields of specialty, but all too ready to throw anathema on whatever does not fit in their ready-made ideas, and quick to class as illness, pathology, or madness, anything that deviates from the normal type of human nature, as they conceive it based on the model of their narrow personality. This is, of course, the unfavorable, but self-conscious, verdict of these blinkered doctors and so-called learned individuals, who preferentially peddle and eventually reshape interested ears. As for the reserved and cautious judgment of those who do not like to pronounce themselves lightly and do not rush to conclusions on issues whose solution is still impossible

---

149 [Trans. note] T. FLOURNOY, *Des Indes à la Planète Mars* (3rd ed. Paris: F. Alcan, 1900), pp. 41–42. The extensive excerpt above is absent from the English version of the book

at the current time, it goes without saying that it has no bearing on the matter, because the mass of evidence is decidedly clear.

You do not dare to affirm that mediumship is a good, healthy, normal, enviable thing, that one has to develop and cultivate wherever one can, and that mediums put you in touch with a higher invisible world. Instead, you hold this nasty disposition against it, for being disastrous, unhealthy, morbid, detestable, worthy of being extirpated or annihilated, wherever mediumship attempts to manifest itself; and you regard all psychics as mad people. Such is the imperturbable logic of the vulgar, the ax-chopping dilemma in which the Spiritist and non-Spiritist milieus sometimes amuse themselves in shutting me up, and keep buzzing in Miss Smith's ears. It should be admitted that this explains and amply justifies that she is sometimes worried about what is said and thought of her health, and that Leopold [her spirit guide] himself thinks he ought to interfere."

Mr. Flournoy is very adroit in his well-expressed remarks.

Awakening of the Past During Trance

Now let us examine a case borrowed from the UK:[150]

"Here is an incident which I think may interest your readers. Some twenty years ago I returned, one sunny spring day, from the City, and on my way home by chance purchased a copy of the *Saturday Review* just published. Arriving at home I found my wife suffering from a severe headache, I advised her to go to bed and said I would send her off to sleep with a few mesmeric passes. In five minutes she was comfortably asleep, and I, ensconcing myself in a snug armchair by the window, took out the *Saturday Review* and commenced to

---

150 [Trans. note] *Light*, no.1247, vol. xxiv, Saturday, December 3, 1904, p. 598.

digest its contents. Turning over the leaves I soon became absorbed in an article dealing with some phase of current French politics, I was somewhat puzzled over an abstruse sentence when, to my surprise, my wife commenced to speak on the subject in question, and gave me a most interesting and instructive little lecture on the political state of affairs in France, relative to this aforesaid article, showing a most intimate knowledge of and acquaintance with French history. At first I thought some spirit was controlling her to speak, and asked who it might be. She replied, 'This is no strange spirit, but myself. When you mesmerized me my body went to sleep, but my spirit is, for the time, free, I perceived your puzzled interest in the article you were reading and proceeded to elucidate it for your benefit.' I said, 'But how comes it that you are so well up in French history and politics when in your normal state you know nothing about them, and take no interest in them?' 'When I return to my body these things, and many other matters which I am cognizant of in my spirit state, are shut out from me and I have no remembrance of them.' 'But how came your spirit to be acquainted with the facts you have just told me? You appear to have a most astounding knowledge of French diplomacy!' 'Well, yes! I do know France and Frenchmen well, having one time been a French woman, and one who played a considerable part in French history.' After a little more conversation she said, 'I must go back to my body now. It is tune. Goodbye.' My wife in a minute or so awoke much refreshed and free from headache. I may mention that her spirit's discourse with me was marked by the most refined and cultured style of delivery. In her normal state she is decidedly fluent in speech but a trifle brusque and outspoken. Outside the body her spirit spoke, if I may use the term, ethereally, with the utmost refinement and delicacy of style and phraseology. I always found in this trance state her spirit could answer any question I put to her. The knowledge evinced was marvelous, and appears to me to be most valuable testimony as to the capacity of our spirits, when free from the body. Although this experience occurred so many years ago it made such a great impression upon me that it seems but yesterday

Robert H. RUSSELL-DAVIES,
27, Buckingham-place, Brighton."

This example confirms the awakening of knowledge acquired in a previous life, during a period of trance induced by the somnambulic state. Having been observed spontaneously it is even of bigger value, since the author could not know of the work of Rochas d'Aiglun or Flournoy, his observation being from a much earlier date.

A COMPLEX CASE OF REMINISCING

The Prince Emile of Sayn Wittgenstein is well known to Spiritists. The researcher Aksakov (French spelling Aksakof), in his book *Animisme et Spiritisme* [*Animism and Spiritism*], quotes his testimony about Baron Korf's will, whose spirit told the Prince, in Paris, where this document had been hidden in Russia. He was a sincere and honest individual whose testimony we can accept with confidence. This is what he reported:[151]

"Prince Wittgenstein in one of his articles in *The Spiritualist*, published September 18th, 1874:

A very distinguished French writing-medium, Madame C——, had come (in the summer of 1869) to spend some weeks at my house, at Nieder Walluf, and we had asked our leading spirits whether it was possible or not to evoke during the sleep of the body, the spirit of a person now alive? Soon after there fell from the ceiling, on the table where Madame C—— was writing under spiritual control, a small oval bronze medal, quite tarnished, with some dry yellow earth sticking to it, bearing on one side the likeness of Christ,

---

[151] William H. Harrison, *Spirits before our Eyes* (London: W. H. Harrison, 1879), vol. I, p. 175 *et seq*.

on the other one that of the Virgin Mary, and seeming, by its style, to belong to the sixteenth century. We were then told that this medal had been buried a long time ago, with a person who had constantly worn it, and who had died a violent death – that this person was now reincarnated in Germany – that an object which bad belonged to her formerly was necessary to establish between her and us a fluidic connection, which might enable her to come and appeal to us for assistance against a sort of painful obsession under which she was laboring that her name began with an A and that we were to call her *'In memory of the town of Dreux.'*

Accordingly, on the following and some other evenings we set to work, Madame C—— (whom I had mesmerized to sleep for better control) holding the pencil: and presently the spirit wrote, in small hasty writing : 'I am here.'

Quest.—How is it that you are already asleep? (It was only ten o'clock.)

Ans.—I am in bed, ill of fever.

Quest.—Can you tell us your present name?

Ans.—Not yet. When I wore the medal I was in France; in the reign of Louis XIV. I was killed by a man who was carrying off a lady from the monastery where I was a nun.

Quest.—Why did he kill you?

Ans.—He did so unintentionally. I had just returned from Dreux, where I had been sent on an errand by our Abbess. I overtook them unawares and threatened to scream; he then struck me on the head with the pommel of his sword, in order to stun me into silence, and killed me.

Quest.–How did he manage to enter the convent?

Ans.—By bribing the man who kept our doors, and who feigned to be asleep while they were stealing his keys. When he saw that I was dead he was frightened. He and his servant bore me off and buried me in the first place they found fit. There are now houses built all over it, but my grave exists, still unknown, in a garden.

Quest.—What place was it?

Ans.—The Près-aux-Clercs, Paris.

Quest.—Was the man who killed you a nobleman?

Ans.—Yes. He belonged to the Lesdiguières.

Quest.—Who was the nun he carried off?

Ans.—A novice of a noble family. He had led her already to a coach, which was to carry her off in another direction than the one he intended to take; they were to meet again later. So she knew nothing about my death. They fled to foreign countries. She died soon after.

Quest.—What did your spirit do when it left your body?

Ans.—I hastened straight to our Abbess, but she was terribly frightened when she saw me, thinking it was a nightmare. I then roamed about the chapel, always thinking myself alive still. I only understood that I was dead when those who were burying me said a prayer before covering my body with earth. A great trouble overcame me then, and I felt it a hard task to pardon them. I had great difficulty in obeying your call, because as soon as I am asleep, I am usually forced to return to Dreux and to haunt the church under my former aspect, as I used to do before my present incarnation. It is a terrible subjection, a constant hindrance to my progress, as it paralyzes all my efforts to come into contact with the good spirits who guide and comfort those who are in the flesh and asleep. Emile! You must help me to free myself.

After some words of advice and encouragement, and my promise to help her, we continued:

Quest.—In which street at Paris was your monastery situated?

Ans.—Rue de l'Abbayie.

Quest.—Under the patronage of which Saint?

Ans.—Of St. Bruno; the congregation of the Ladies of the Passion.

Quest.—Does the monastery still exist?

Ans.—Destroyed; plundered during the Revolution.

Quest.—Is there anything now remaining of it?

Ans.—A wall.

(Having, after this, written to Paris for information, the friend to whom we wrote informed us that, after many long searches, he had indeed found out, encrusted between houses, an old wall, which once, as was said, belonged to a ladies' monastery.)

Quest.—Have you, in your present incarnation, any recollection of the one gone by?

Ans.—I have a sort of apprehension, as if I were to die of a violent death – an injury to the head. It makes me very nervous at times! I see now that it is only a reflex of the past. I also dream of phantoms in monastic gowns, and of murderers rushing at them; also of a specter in an ancient dress, who grins at me.

Quest.—Do you live far off?

Ans.—In Germany.

Quest.—Is your name a German one?

Ans.—Yes. Those questions hurt me!

Quest.—Do I know you?

Ans.—To be sure you do!

Quest.—Where do you live?

The medium then begins to trace with great difficulty:- F... Fu... I exclaim, under sudden inspiration, *Fulda!* and at the same moment Madame C—— gives a shriek and a violent start, nearly upsetting her chair. She says she felt a commotion, as of a strong electric discharge. I understand at once that the controlling spirit is that of my cousin, the Countess Amelie of Y—— who lives in Fulda (a small town about five hours' journey away by the railway), where she occupies a high charge in a Protestant Chapter of noble ladies.

Quest.(after a long pause).—Why did you give the medium such a shock?

Ans.—I did not want you to know yet.

Quest.—Did your body awake?

Ans.—No; but I was startled.

While we were still (Madame C—— and I) debating whether it were really my cousin or not, the medium's hand unconsciously wrote down a name which cut short all my doubts, as it referred to a secret known only to the Countess of Y—— and myself.

Quest.—How am I to ascertain your identity, and make sure that you are not a frivolous spirit, mocking us?

Ans.—When you meet me, before long, ask whether I have any dreams, in which it seems to me as if I were killed! I shall say, No, and add, that I dream sometimes of a priest murdered by ruffians. You may also show me the medal: I shall feel then as if I had known it before.

With this communication we closed our evocations of Amelie, which had taken us several evenings.

A few months later I met my cousin at my sister's country seat. Amelie, as was her wont, began joking with me about my faith in Spiritualism, declaring that it was all delusion and deception. I bore her merry attacks merrily, defending, however, my theories about dreams, reminiscences, spirit messages, and so on, till I came to ask, as in a joke, whether she, for example, never dreamt that she was being murdered. She answered 'No,' adding, after a slight pause, that, in fact, she had sometimes a disagreeable dream, always the same-a sort of nightmare-which made her nervous and uncomfortable for the whole day after. On my insisting upon receiving the particulars, she said at last, that she dreamt of a. Catholic priest in sacerdotal dress, flying from a burning church, with armed men at his heels, who wanted to kill him. After changing the conversation, I took the medal out of my pocket and showed it to her, feigning to have bought it at an antiquary's. She handled it about for some moments, and then began to examine it so long and so closely that I, at last, asked her, 'What is the matter?' whereupon she answered that she could not understand how that object seemed as familiar as if she had possessed or seen it formerly, although she could not, for the world, recollect under what circumstances.

I now told her all about our evocations ; and she, being very much struck by my narrative, requested to be shown the medial writing. This writing, I had thought, was not like her own. I had known hers only by her letters, in German, written with pen and ink, while the former, traced by a French medium, was written in French. When she saw it she exclaimed that it was positively her writing, when she used a pencil instead of a pen; and forthwith she wrote some words which I dictated, and which proved to be exactly like the original.

She got into a great fright at the thought of her soul haunting an old church, and I advised her, in order to paralyze the attraction, to pray every evening for help to her guardian angel, and to say three times aloud, before going to bed, 'I will not go!'

Since she has done this, I was informed by my leading spirits that she has entirely succeeded in ridding herself of the aforesaid subjection.

This, my dear sir, is my personal experience of a fact, interesting enough I think, to find a space in your columns; and I would be thankful for every explanation of it, given in the non-reincarnationist sense, in favor of the French proverb which says, *Du choc des opinions jaillit la vérité* [The clash of opinions shakes forth the truth]."

In this case, it seems certain that it was indeed the spirit of the cousin of Prince of Wittgenstein which manifested itself, since the mediumistic writing is identical to that of the living person. No previous rapport having been established between the medium and this lady, there is no need to involve clairvoyance or remote viewing.

If this assassination story is false, one would have to imagine not only that this pious and well-bred lady took pleasure in lying, and that without gaining anything from it; but also that, during her spiritual release, she would use it to endorse the theory of successive lives in which she refused to believe in the waking state.

Personally, I am inclined to accept her story as truthful, because nothing allows me to suspect its veracity.

A RESUSCITATION OF THE PAST

I will now borrow the following case from a book by my friend Léon Denis, *The Problem of Life and Destiny*.[152]

(I have personally known Prince Wiszniewski, who has always seemed to me worthy of the greatest trust. Mrs. Noeggerath, the author of the book *La Survie, Échos de l'Aude-là* [*The Survival, Echoes of the Hereafter*], heard the prince tell the same story and reported it to Mr. Rochas d'Aiglun. Here it is:)

"Prince Adam Wiszniewski, of 7 Débarcadère street, Paris, communicates the following narrative. He cites the witnesses themselves, some of whom still live and have agreed to be named only by initials:
'Prince Gallitzin, the Marquis de B——, and the Count of R——, were all together at the German spa of Bad Homburg during the summer of 1862.'
'One evening, after a very late dinner, they were walking in the park of the Casino, when they noticed a poor woman lying on a bench. Having approached and questioned her, they invited her to come and dine at the hotel. After she had supped with great appetite, prince Gallitzin, who was a magnetizer, had the idea of lulling her to sleep. After performing many passes, he succeeded. To the utter astonishment of the people present, the woman who, in the night before, spoke only a bad German dialect, once asleep began to speak very correctly in French, saying that she had reincarnated in poverty as a punishment for committing a crime in her previous life, in the 18th century. She was then living in a castle by the sea in Brittany. Having taken a lover, she wanted to get rid of her husband and hurled him to the sea from the top of a rock. She described the crime scene with great precision.'
'Thanks to her indications, prince Gallitzin and the marquis de B—— were able, later on, to go separately to Brittany,

---

152 Léon Denis, *The Problem of Life and Destiny* (Trans. H. M. Monteiro. New York: USSF, 2018), p. 247.

in the Côtes-du-Nord, and make two inquiries, the results of which were identical. Having questioned many people, at first they could not gather any information. Finally they found old peasants who remembered hearing their parents tell the story of a young and beautiful chatelaine who had killed her husband by throwing him into the sea. Thus all that the poor woman of Homburg had said in a somnambulistic state proved to be exact?

'On his return from France, prince Gallitzin went back to Homburg, where he asked the chief of police about this woman. This officer told him that she had no education, spoke only a vulgar German dialect, and lived on very meager means as a prostitute."

This time, amnesia with regard to the past has disappeared so well during somnambulism that the unfortunate woman has not only resuscitated her tragic past, but did so by using the French language, of which she did not know a single word in her normal state. If we had so many such characteristic examples, the certainty that everyone will come back to Earth a very large number of times would be beyond anyone's doubt. It is to be hoped that impartial scientists will engage in the study of these phenomena, and I am convinced that it will not be long until they collect facts as conclusive as this one.

The following is an excerpt from a Conference on Reincarnation given at the Congrès Spirite de Liège, on August 28, 1923, by Dr. Torres:

"Twenty-three years ago, a brother and a nephew of my father living in a small village in my province were murdered as a result of local quarrels.

Some time after this violent death, my uncle communicated through a medium in my family. He was very happy with everything that had happened to him. He explained to us how, in an earlier life, in a very distant city in Daroca, province of Aragon, in a house which he described very carefully, and on the date he specified, in agreement with the murdered nephew who happened to be my current father's wife, they got along to kill my father in order to satisfy carnal passions.

My uncle was satisfied with his state on the spiritual plane and having undergone the test chosen in his last existence. He thanked God for allowing him to settle this painful debt. The inquiries made at Daroca, a city completely ignored by all of us, confirmed in every respect the precise details given by my uncle's spirit. The names of the street and the house, the date of the unpunished crime, the names of the characters involved, everything was exactly checked and verified."

There is reason to suppose that clairvoyance on the part of the medium cannot be invoked as an explanation in this case, since it was spontaneously that these revelations were made by the spirit of the doctor's uncle.

After reading this story, I wrote Dr. Torres to ask him for some details concerning the medium, the seance group, and whether a report had been drawn up. Here is the information he provided:

"The seance took place at home, in my family circle where seances are very frequent. We do not take down minutes; as we are all very convinced of the spiritual truth, we consider the spiritual phenomenon as a natural fact in our life. The seance was attended by six people.

The medium belonged to my family and only knew of the murder of my uncle and my father's nephew. However, he knew nothing about the city, the hidden drama and the circumstances indicated by my uncle's spirit, as well as the names of the actors of the human tragedy unfolded at Daroca. Mediumship took place by trance or complete "incorporation," with the medium totally unaware of these facts upon awakening."

An Atonement

Let us end this too brief review of experimental cases by citing a report borrowed from the archives of the group of the city of Huesca (Spain) directed by Mr. Domingo Montreal. It is quite instructive as can be clearly judged by the following:[153]

> "From 1881 to 1884 there was an individual in the streets of Huesca known only as Suciac, the village idiot. He was dressed in a burlesque manner, spoke by himself, sometimes ran aimlessly, sometimes walked solemnly, and did not answer any of the questions addressed to him. In the end, as he became dangerous, he had to be closely watched. In the same town a group was formed among people of average culture for conducting Spiritist studies, having Domingo Montreal as president and Sanchez Antonio as medium. The latter had this characteristic that, being quite illiterate, he would often write without punctuation, but at other times with perfect correctness, long communications.
> The group's president decided to evoke the madman's spirit when he seemed to be asleep, and thus received several messages. At last the madman Suciac died, and, spontaneously, shortly after, gave through the illiterate medium Antonio a message stating that he had been lord of Sangarren; that he had had a guilty behavior and that the life in which we had known him had been imposed on him as atonement. He said that we would find the confirmation of his words in the archives still existing in what used to be his castle.
> I went with Mr. Severo Lain and Mr. Marvano Ballestar to the old stately home, where we were told that there was no trace of any archives. Deeply disappointed, we met in a seance to report on the result of our mission. Antonio wrote that if we returned to the castle, we would find near the kitchen hearth, in a hiding place, all the documents we wanted.

---

153 *Revue Scientifique et Morale du Spiritisme* (Spanish edition), year 1912, p. 442.

That was done, and, having returned to Sangarren, we obtained permission to probe the wall, and to our astonishment we found in a small recess a whole series of parchments. They were reported to Huesca, where they were translated by Professor Oscariz, and confirmed in every respect the affirmations of made by the spirit."

In this case again the moral law was applied in an indisputable manner, and the documents discovered as a result of the indications given by the madman's spirit establish the very great probability of this spirit's affirmations regarding its previous lifetime.

Summary

As we have seen, both in the course of the preceding chapter and of this one, memory is not a faculty as unstable as it might seem at first sight. It is perfectly true that we do not preserve the integral memory of all the events that have occurred to us during the course of our life, oblivion being an essential condition so that the spirit is not overwhelmed by an innumerable multitude of insignificant recollections. But contrary to what is generally believed, the loss of memories is not absolute. All the visual, auditory, tactile, kinesthetic sensations, etc., which have acted upon us, remain indelibly engraved in the permanent part of ourselves, which scholars call the subconscious, and Spiritists, the perispirit.

These sensations, as seen above, can be reborn either spontaneously or during natural or induced somnambulism (trance). Each previous state of one's current existence is reborn with a freshness and intensity that is equivalent to reality. Therefore it seems that each period of life leaves in the fluidic framework of the spiritual body successive, indelible imprints, similar to clichés, or better, sound and image recordings formed by stable dynamic associations which are superimposed without being confused, but whose vibrational motion diminishes as time goes by, till the moment when these feelings or memories fall below the threshold of ordinary consciousness. Since things are so and the perispirit is indestructible, as it is in it that the archives of all mental and physical life are embedded, it is natural to suppose that if we revert the fluidic body to vibrational patterns similar to those which it has recorded at some point in its life, all concomitant memories of this period of the past will be at the same time resuscitated.

This is what happens, as we have seen, in Charles Richet's, Bourru and Burot's, and Pitres's experiments, among others. Therefore, it is logical to continue the regression of memory beyond the limits of a subject's current life by means of the magnetic action. This is what the Spiritists and scientists that I have mentioned in this chapter have done. Undoubtedly, results are not always satisfactory; not all subjects are able to retrieve the past. This is certainly due to several different causes, the main one seems to me to result from what might be called the density of one's perispirit, that is to say, the relative coarseness of one's fluidic body whose vibrations would then not be able to regain the necessary intensity to resurrect the past in a sufficient way – even with the artificial stimulation of magnetism. However, it sometimes happens that during the state of ordinary sleep, the exteriorized soul, temporarily disengaged of the body, momentarily regains favorable conditions for the retrieval of the past to occur. It may be that this resuscitation of the past happens accidentally, as by sudden insights, in the normal state. We then witness a retrieval of old sensations which give the one who feels them the impression of déjà vu, that he/she has already seen certain cities or landscapes, albeit having never been there before. Such cases will be studied in the following chapters; and it will be seen that they too, despite their great variety, can be understood and easily fall within the framework of integral memory, once we admit that it resides in the spiritual body which accompanies each and every soul throughout the course of its continuous evolution.

8

HEREDITY AND CHILD PRODIGIES

A FEW REMARKS CONCERNING HEREDITY · SPECIFIC HEREDITY IS CERTAIN · PSYCHOLOGICAL HEREDITY DOES NOT EXIST · SCIENTIFIC HYPOTHESES TO EXPLAIN HEREDITY · EXAMPLES OF SCIENTISTS WHO COME FROM COMPLETELY UNEDUCATED FAMILIES; CONVERSELY, INDIVIDUALS OF GENIUS WHO GIVE BIRTH TO DEGENERATE CHILDREN · DIFFERENT CATEGORIES AMONG CHILD PRODIGIES · MUSICIANS · PAINTERS · SCHOLARS · WRITERS · POETS · MENTAL CALCULATORS

CHILD PRODIGIES

SOME WORDS ABOUT HEREDITY.

In my book, *Évolution Animique* [*Animistic Evolution*],[154] I have briefly dealt with the issue of heredity in its relation to the theory of reincarnation. I can only send the reader back to its pages. Suffice it to say briefly that the status of the problem has not changed in recent years. As we have seen previously, the spirit after its disincarnation can, during seances of materialization, reconstitute by means of the matter and energy furnished by the medium, the physical body which it possessed in its previous life. It has the power to organize matter according to the particular type that used to be its own. It is very likely that it will do the same when reincarnating on Earth; but then, if no extraneous influence acts upon it, it should be reborn with a physical type similar to the one it had before. However, this is not so because it is often observed that children are more or less like their parents and that the progenitors can even transmit to their descendants special traits of their organism. Thus the strong

---

154 G. DELANNE, *Évolution Animique* (Paris: Chamuel, 1897).

muscles of the blacksmith, the callous hands of the peasant or the blue-collar worker, the smaller hands in the families where one never did a physical work, the development of the most different abilities by the use, the stamp impressed on the outside of an individual by the profession he/she practices, are all familiar occurrences; and, although not based on any precise observation, the idea of their being transmitted has always been raised.

According to T. Ribot, the different forms of heredity should be classed as follows:[155]

"1. *Direct heredity*, which consists in the transmission of paternal and maternal qualities to the children. This form of heredity offers two aspects :

(1.) The child takes after father and mother equally as regards both physical and moral characters, a case, strictly speaking, of very rare occurrence, for the very ideal of the law would then be realized.

Or (2), the child, while taking after both parents, more specially resembles one of them; and here again we must distinguish between two cases.

a. The first of these is when the heredity takes place in the same sex—from father to son, from mother to daughter.

b. The other, which occurs more frequently, is where heredity occurs between different sexes—from father to daughter, from mother to son.

2. *Reversional Heredity*, or atavism, consists in the reproduction in the descendants of the moral or physical qualities of their ancestors. It occurs frequently between grandfather and grandson, grandmother and granddaughter.

3. *Collateral*, or *indirect heredity*, which is of rarer occurrence than the foregoing, subsists, as indicated by its name, between individuals and their ancestors in the indirect line—uncle, or grand-uncle and nephew, aunt and niece.

4. Finally, to complete the classification, we must mention the *heredity of influence*, very rare from the physiological

---

[155] T. RIBOT, *Heredity* (London: H. S. King & Co., 1875), p. 147.

point of view, and of which probably no single instance is proved in the moral order. It consists in the reproduction in the children by a second marriage of some peculiarity belonging to a former spouse."

Such are the various formulas in which all the facts of heredity are classed. For us Spiritists, there are, in short, two things to be distinguished in the phenomenon of heredity. Firstly, the specific character of the being which is born, and, secondly, its intellectual faculties. Next, I shall briefly examine these two points below.

It is quite certain that progenitors belonging to a specific species give birth to a child of the same species. This is a general and absolute law, but, in each species, from the morphological point of view, there are different races, and in these there are great differences among the offspring of a same couple, according to the preponderance of one sex over the other. In short, it must be admitted that the structural type is functional in animals and in humans. It is due to the action of the perispirit upon matter; but the secondary traits, such as the color of the eyes and hair, the shape and size of certain parts of the face or body, and even the internal organs, are the result of physical heredity.

It has sometimes been observed that the father can sometimes transmit the brain to the child, and the mother the stomach; one the heart, the other, the liver, and so on.

By through what mechanism this transmission takes place remains a profound mystery; and all theories devised for half a century to explain it have remained totally powerless to solve this problem.

It is known today that the being that will be born does not exist in the sexual organs like a microscopic reduction which would only have to grow by developing all its parts. The starting point is a simple cell which, when it is fertilized, goes through a series of successive and different forms before reaching the end of its evolution which aims to represent a complete being of the specific species.

What are the causes that require this evolution and through what agents can they occur? The following is a list of the most notable scientists who have devoted themselves to this study. The vast majority of theories conceived as an explanation for the phenomena of life and, consequently, of heredity, are based on this assumption that between the chemical molecules and the components of a cell visible under the microscope, there would still exist a category of units, initial protoplasmic particles which, by their character and their mode of grouping themselves, would determine the various properties of living matter.

It is by defining the properties and arrangements of these infinitesimal particles that each author has endeavored to explain complex cases of heredity. British philosopher, biologist, anthropologist, and sociologist Herbert Spencer, in 1864, first laid the foundations of the theory of *physiological units*. It was developed in 1868 by Darwin under the name of *pangenesis*. In its system, the particles are called *gemmules*. In 1884, Naegeli imagines that these small units were ultra-microscopic molecular aggregates which he called *micellae*. According to him, these formed networks composing what he termed *idioplasm*, and those undirected would form the *nutritious plasma*.[156]

In 1902, August Weismann further complicated this system by imagining not only two kinds of plasma, but also determining what he calls *ids* and *biophores*.

All these theories, albeit ingenious, do not yet provide a really scientific explanation of the phenomena of heredity. This is what the authors of the book *The Theories of Evolution*[157] do not hesitate to declare. Indeed, they ask, what in the composition of protoplasm determines its type of life? There we are entirely reduced to hypotheses. These

---

156 [Trans. note] All the terms in *italics* in the paragraphs above have since become obsolete and are now only of historical value.

157 [Trans. note] Yves DELAGE, M. GOLDSMITH, *The Theories of Evolution* (Trans. A. Tridon. New York: B. W. Huebsch, 1912).

are not directly verifiable and can be judged by us only from this point of view alone: can such a conception give a likely explanation of different vital phenomena, namely, ontogenesis, heredity, variation, etc?

These assumptions are necessary because we should not resign ourselves to having no idea about these issues that fascinate us more than all the others.[158]

In short, morphological inheritance is the law, although it presents so many exceptions for secondary characters that there is almost never an identity between the progenitors and their descendants.

From an intellectual standpoint, it is quite the same, because there is a considerable number of examples of great scientists, who were born from most ignorant circles. Thus, for example, Roger Bacon, Berkeley, Jacob Berzelius, Blumenbach, David Brewster, Auguste Comte, Copernicus, Claude Bernard, Descartes, Galen of Pergamon, Galvani, Hegel, Hume, Kant, Kepler, Locke, Malebranche, Priestley, Réaumur, Rumford, Spinoza, Pope Sixtus V, Young, and so many others, came from uneducated backgrounds; and nothing could have predicted the remarkable faculties which distinguished them to such lofty degrees. Conversely, there is a considerable number of great geniuses whose descendants were mediocre, even below average. Pericles of Ancient Greece fame begot two fools, Paralus and Xanthippus. The wise Aristippus gave birth to a madman such as Clinias; from the great historian Thucydides, was born the inept Milesias.

Socrates and Themistocles only had unworthy offspring. Among the Romans, the same applies to Cicero and his son; Germanicus and Caligula; Vespasian and Domitian; and the great Marcus Aurelius had a madman in his son Commodus. In more recent history, the children of Henry

---

158 *Op. cit.*, p. 110. Mirroring DELANNE's text almost word by word is the French original, DELAGE, GOLDSMITH, *Le Théories de l'Évolution* (Paris: Flammarion, 1920), p. 100.

IV, Louis XIV, Cromwell, Peter the Great, like those of La Fontaine, Crébillon, Goethe and Napoleon, represent so many other examples that one could cite. Even better, cases of child prodigies prove to us, with irresistible evidence, that intelligence is independent of the organism that serves to its manifestation. For the highest forms of intellectual activity show themselves at an age when the brain has not yet fully developed. This is one of the best arguments there is against materialistic theories.

The highest forms of art and science are found in children from the earliest age. Many examples will be given below, in order to leave no doubt in this regard.[159]

Musicians

There are examples of prodigious precocity in all eras and in all countries. In the 17th century, Handel, at the age of ten, composed motets for charity at the church of Halle, Germany. The case of Mozart is famous. It is well known that at the age of four he performed a sonata, and his musical faculty developed so rapidly that at eleven he composed two small operas, *La Finta Semplice*, and *Bastien and Bastienne*. We know with what great success he continued his brilliant career as for the one known as the God of Music, Beethoven, he was already distinguished at ten years age by his remarkable talent as a music performer.

Of another genre, the precocity of the great violinist Paganini was such that at the age of nine he was applauded in a concert in Genoa, Italy.

At the age of six, Meyerbeer already had enough talent to give much appreciated concerts. Liszt, a wonderful piano virtuoso from a tender age, composes, at just fourteen years old, an opera in one act called *Don Sanche or the Castle of Love*.

---

159 See Léon Denis, *The Problem of Life and Destiny* (New York: USSF, 2018); Théophile Pascal, *Reincarnation: A Study in Human Evolution* (London: T. P. Society,1910); and C. Lancelin, *La Vie Posthume*.

The great Arthur Rubinstein, brought from Russia to Paris at the age of eleven, aroused universal admiration for the virtuosity of his piano playing.

The Spanish composer and violinist Sarasate, at age eleven, showed his qualities of purity of tone and style that made him one of the greatest violinists of our time.

French composer Saint-Saëns, a precocious virtuoso, also at eleven years of age, gave his first piano concert, and was not older than sixteen when his first symphony was performed.

Even in current times, certain children have revealed remarkable musical talents.

I had the pleasure of hearing at International Psychical Congress in 1900 the little Spaniard Pepito Arriola play and improvise on the piano various tunes at the tender age of three and a half years.

Professor Charles Richet published about Pepito's case a study in which he said that, "He played before the king and the queen mother of Spain six compositions of his invention, which were noted down, because he himself does not know the notes and cannot yet read or write."

> "He has devised a special fingering: he replaces the octave by *arpeggios* deftly and very skilfully executed. It is often very difficult, when hearing an adult improviser, to tell what is invention from what is reproduction from memory of tunes and pieces already heard. However, it is certain that when Pepito begins to improvise, he is almost never brief, and he often finds extremely interesting melodies that sound more or less new to the audience. There is an introduction, a middle, and an end; and at the same time a variety, a richness of sound which, perhaps, would astonish listeners even if it were a professional musician, but which, *in a child of merely three and a half years of age, become absolutely astonishing.*"(Abridged.)[160]

---

160 [Trans. note] *Cf.* full article by C. RICHET in *Les Annales de Sciences Psychiques*, vol. x, year 1910, p. 324 *et seq.*

Even more recently, the American-born Italian Willy Ferreros, at the age of four years and a half, conducted the Folies-Bergères Orchestra with remarkable certainty and mastery. All the Parisian press, usually so skeptical, praised it.

Le Journal wrote:

"Michelangelo had not finished wearing his boy's trousers when his master Ghirlandaio sent him away from the studio, seeing that he had nothing more to teach him. At age two, Christian Friedrich Heinecken spoke three languages. At age four, Jean-Baptiste Raisin displayed a rare virtuosity on the violin. At the age of six, Mozart composed his first concert. Today, it is Willy Ferreros who amazes Paris by the assurance, the attention to detail, the artfulness and the fantasy with which he directs the orchestra in the Revue des Folies-Bergères. There are no more children therein."

La Comœdia magazine stated

"He is a very little fellow who is already wearing the black coat, the satin pants, the white waistcoat and the patent leather shoes. The baton in his hand, he directs with a clarity, an assurance, and incomparable precision, an orchestra of eighty musicians, attentive to the smallest detail, conscious of the nuances, a scrupulous observer of rhythm ...
Not long ago, on the occasion of a trip to the South, Mr. Clement Bannel discovered this little prodigy, became enthusiastic for such a musical instinct, and brought the child back to Paris, which he conquered last night, during the Revue des Folies-Bergères. Willy Ferreros conducted the cadets of Souza, *Sylvia* of Léo Delibes, then our National Caroline, etc., etc., etc ... It was a dazzling success."

The *Intransigeant* of June, 22, 1911:

"Aged five years at most. Long brown curly hair, chubby face like a little cupid of painter François Boucher. Our friends saw him at the Trocadero conducting his orchestra with imperturbable phlegm and staggering authority.
I saw him at his parents' in a bright little room with the flowery wallpaper, which he animates with his well-behaved

Figure 5. MUSIC VIRTUOSO PEPITO ARRIOLA
aged three

kid's turbulence. Then nothing in him remains of the child prodigy. He is not in the least infatuated with his merits and he does not even think about it for a moment.

I placed on my knees the youngest orchestra conductor in the world: 'Hey! tell me a story, would you?' – 'I'm leaving Monday, I'm happy to go to Turin where I will see grandma, and then I'll lead classical music concerts, I like it better than waltzes and ditty songs.'

'Now tell me: what are your favorite among all these that you know?' – 'I like Haydn's Symphony and Wagner's *Tannhäuser March*, and most of all Grieg's *Anitra's Dance*. I heard it in a classical concert at Cannes with dad and I said: I have to learn that, daddy; I want to conduct it. Then daddy taught it to me, I'm going to direct it at the Turin exhibition. I'm happy.'

'Look, Mr. Bannel gave me all these toys at the Folies-Bergères and then those ... He's nice ... But all the same, four and a half months in the same music hall, oh, that's so boring.'

And after his confession, the young musician slipped off my knees and went to play with a wooden toy, while his parents told me that for a year now he was performing longer pieces and rushing on the stage to greet the public after the number where his father and mother had played."

I could extend indefinitely the list of these prodigious children, who show from an early age a remarkable talent they could not have acquired in this life through education or training, and which they must necessarily have brought with them as a legacy from one or more previous lives devoted to the development of their art.

I will show, always through examples, that the other faculties of the spirit assert themselves in certain individuals with a power as evident as in the musicians. I am referring to painting, and we will notice that manifestations of this art, which is so ancient and so painstakingly difficult to acquire through practice, appear in certain truly predisposed individuals.

Painters

The great Giotto (1267–1337) is yet another example of the innate dispositions that one may bring from birth. While still a child, a humble shepherd, he was already instinctively drawing sketches so natural that the painter Cimabue, having met him, took him away with him.

Another great genius of Italy, Michelangelo, at the age of eight, already knew enough the technique of his trade; so much so that his master, famous painter Ghirlandaio, told him that he had nothing left to teach him.

From his childhood, the renowned Dutch painter Rembrandt showed so much passion for drawing that Lombroso states that he must have known how to draw as a master before even learning to read.

In France, more recently, the painter Marcel Lavallard had his first painting accepted at an official art exhibition, when he was only twelve years old.

On August 12, 1873, aged only ten years and eleven months, died the young Frédéric Van de Kerckhove, of Bruges, who left 350 paintings, some of which, says Adolphe Siret, member of the Royal Academy of Sciences, Letters and Fine Arts of Belgium, could have been signed by illustrious name such as Diaz, Salvator Rosa, Corot, and others.

Another critic, the powerful French colorist Richter, having accidentally had the opportunity to see twenty panels of the young prodigy, congratulated the owner to have sketches of Theodore Rousseau in such a large quantity. Some went to great lengths in order to fool him, a complete expert, and when he knew the truth, he could not restrain a tear for that much talent cut off from life so early.

Scholars, writers and poets

Hermogenes of Tarsus, at age fifteen, taught rhetoric to the wise Marcus Aurelius.

Blaise Pascal was undoubtedly the most beautiful genius of the 17th century. At the same time a geometer, a physicist and a philosopher, he was also a major literary talent. From an early age, he had a taste for study and especially for geometry. At the age of thirteen, he had found Euclid's first thirty-two propositions and published a treatise on conic sections. His genius was later confirmed by his researches on the gravity of the air, the invention of a two-wheeled litter and a barrel-carrying cart.[161] But it is especially as a philosopher that his mind has risen to the highest peaks of thought.

French nobleman Pierre de Lamoignon, also from his early teens, composed verses in ancient Greek and Latin, which were very remarkable; and he was no less advanced in the culture of law than in cultivating literature.

German astronomer and mathematician Carl Friedrich Gauss, from Brunswick, could solve arithmetic problems when he was only three years old; and we know with what success he continued his career in mathematics.

Nils Ericson, who died in 1870, showed such a genius for mechanical sciences that at the age of twelve he was appointed Inspector of Sweden's Göta Canal by that country's administration. He was in charge of six-hundred workers.

The great French poet, Victor Hugo, at the age of thirteen already gave signs of his magnificent talent for versification by winning first prize at the renowned Floral Games in Toulouse. At the time, he had been called 'the sublime child'.

William James Sidis, from the state of Massachusetts, USA, could read and write at two years of age. At four years old, he spoke four languages, and at the age of twelve, he could solve

---

161 [Trans. note] These ingenious vehicles were very specific: the *brouette* or *vinaigrette* was a two-wheeled litter usually dragged by one man on foot, whereas the *haquet* was a very simple two-wheeled open cart dragged by horses to carry barrels.

geometry problems, and was admitted to the Massachusetts Institute of Technology (MIT), where the age of admission is normally twenty-one. He also gave, at Harvard University, to the astonishment of high mathematics professors who listened to him, a lecture on the 4th dimension of space.

British polymath and physician Thomas Young, who imagined the theory of the ripples of light, possessed a great intellectual development from the tenderest age, as proven by his ability to read fluently at the age of two years, and at eight years old he knew six languages thoroughly.

Another child, William Rowan Hamilton, an Irish mathematician, learned Hebrew at age three; at age seven, he had more extensive knowledge than most candidates for the high-level competitive examination for teachers.

"I can still see him," said one of his parents, "answer a difficult question of mathematics, then go trotting away, dragging behind him his wheelbarrow." At thirteen, he knew twelve languages. At the age of eight, he surprised everyone around him to the point that an eminent Irish astronomer said of him:

> "This young man, I do not say *will be*, but *is*, the First mathematician of his age."[162]

Scaliger[163] called Jacques Christon, a fifteen-year-old Scotsman, a monstrous genius, for expounding in Latin, Greek, Hebrew, or Arabic, any subject posed to him.

The Italian Giovanni Pico della Mirandola was extremely precocious in his extensive knowledge of Latin and Greek, and later Hebrew and Arabic. At the age of twenty, he was considered to be the most cultured mind of his time.

German scholar Jean-Philippe Baratier, born in 1721 in Schwabach near Nuremberg, Germany, died in 1740. At age five, he knew German, French, Latin and Hebrew. Two

---

162 [Trans. note] A. MACFARLANE, *Ten British Mathematicians* (New York: J. Wiley & Sons, 1916), p. 36.

163 [Trans. note] That could have been Julius Caesar Scaliger (1484–1558) or his equally scholarly son Joseph Justus Scaliger (1540–1609).

years later he collected materials for a dictionary of the most difficult Hebrew words. At the age of thirteen, he translated from Hebrew to French, the itinerary of Rabbi Benjamin of Tudela, and the following year he was admitted master of arts at the University of Halle. At the same time he published several scholarly dissertations at the Germanic Library. He died from work exhaustion at the age of nineteen.

Christian Henry Heineken, born in Lübeck, Germany, in 1721, spoke almost at birth; at two, he knew three languages. He learned to write in a few days and soon practiced short speeches. At two and a half years old, he took an exam on geography and modern history. He lived only on his wet nurse's milk. They wished to wean him; he wasted away and died in Lübeck, on June 17, 1725, in the course of his fifth year of age, affirming his hopes in the afterlife. The blade had worn out the scabbard, so to speak.

Among the linguists who distinguished themselves early on, our contemporary, the Italian Mr. Trombetti, should be mentioned. He far surpasses all his predecessors. As a young man he learned French and German at school; then read Voltaire and Goethe. He learned Arabic just by reading a biography of Emir Abdelkader. A Persian passing through Bologna taught him his language in a few weeks. At twelve, he learned Latin, Greek and Hebrew simultaneously. Since then he has studied almost all living or dead languages. His friends say that he now knows 300 Eastern dialects.

Mental calculators

Ability to perform mathematical calculations with extreme speed has already been found with a surprising singularity in the Elberfeld horses, as well as in the dogs Rolf and Lola. Now, we will see that the same happens to humans.

The Frenchman Henri Mondeux, born in 1826 near Tours, a peasant devoid of all instruction, revealed himself very early to be a prodigious 'calculating machine'. At the age of fourteen, he was introduced to the Paris Academy of Sciences. He had no other special talents.

In 1837, a very young shepherd, Vito Mangiamele, still almost a child, attracted scientists from all over the world for his incomparable faculty of calculation. To a mathematician who asked him the following question: what is the number which, raised to the cube and added to the sum of five times its square, is equal to 42 times itself plus forty? He answered in less than one minute, "It's the number five."

Another humble shepherd, Giacomo Inaudi, performed the most complicated calculations with disconcerting ease and speed. He was examined at the Academy of Sciences in 1892 and gave with amazing speed the solution for exceedingly difficult problems.

It is also possible to point out the faculties of calculation of the young Franckall and the incredible Diamandi.

North and South America also offer us various examples of precocity of all genres. Thus in mechanical sciences Georges Steuler conquered at the age of thirteen a degree in Engineering. H. Dugan traveled the United States when he was not yet ten years old, getting for the house he represented the best deals.[164]

According to the often-dubious American press, a five-year-old Willie Gwin was reportedly granted a doctor's degree by the University of New Orleans, and an eleven-year-old child recently founded a newspaper, with a circulation of 20,000 copies.

The immortal author of *Jerusalem Delivered*, Torquato Tasso, composed verses remarkably well around the age of seven. Elsewhere, the little Joan Maude (five years old), daughter of British actor Charles Maude, publishes her first book, *Behind the Nightlight* (London, 1912).

---

164 [Trans. note] Some of these child-prodigy names are very obscure, reproduced above in DELANNE's approximative French spellings.

These numerous and varied examples of intellectual precocity are irreconcilable with the theory that intelligence is a product of the organism. Even if heredity played a part in the genesis of these prodigious faculties, it would be incomprehensible that a barely formed brain would be capable of generating the highest and most powerful forms of intelligence, for these are not found at all in such degree other than in some adult individuals, when they reach full development of their brains.

The Spiritist hypothesis of the preexistence of the human being is the only one that gives a logical explanation of child prodigies.

One wonders how the soul of a Baratier has been able to manifest, almost from breastfeeding, knowledge that requires not only a wonderful memory, but also the necessary gifts of assimilation and reasoning for the comprehension and use of languages as difficult to assimilate as ancient Greek and Hebrew. It is very likely that the spirit of these young prodigies was not yet fully embodied, or that it was during periods of exteriorization that it embraced the memory of the past, and instead of learning was only reminiscing.

Some Spiritists may wish to explain these astonishing cases by assuming that these children were mere mediums. This interpretation seems flawed to me, because in good logic it is useless to needlessly multiply the causes. Since we know, as Spiritists, that the soul existed before the current life, there is no need to involve the presence of extraneous entities. Moreover, mediumship is not a constant faculty; it does not obey the will of the medium, while the children of whom I have spoken could at any time and in any circumstance immediately give proof of their surprising aptitudes.

Undoubtedly, child prodigies are exceptions; nevertheless, although to a lesser degree, some of our schoolchildren have the most varied predispositions for the arts and sciences. Even when they come out of less cultured circles, they develop with such speed that they surpass all their classmates. It is not an intuition proper that gives them the power to assimilate new notions, but a kind of reminiscence that allows them to take possession of the most recent subject matters that, in reality, only awaken in their subconsciousness.

I will now examine some phenomena in which these reminiscences seem to actually be memories of past lives.

REMINISCENCE STUDY

General remarks on the interpretation of phenomena · Difficulties in identifying the true causes of a phenomenon · Reminiscences should not be confused with feelings of déjà vu · Examples of clairvoyance during sleep · This one when it wakes up during life is a reminiscence of things perceived during one's current existence · The cases Berthelay and of the English Lady · Reminiscences seemed to be caused by the vision of certain places · The stories of Major Wellesley and a clergyman · Curious coincidence · Reminiscence or clairvoyance of Mrs. Krapkoff · Persistent memories during youth of a previous life

Feelings of déjà vu

Spiritist phenomena vary greatly in their manifestations. For half a century, they have been subjected to the most severe and repeated controls (i.e., verification), not only on the part of Spiritists, but also by scholars who have taken the trouble to examine mediums' faculties.

It was then perceived that, besides certain indubitable facts, induced by spirits, there existed other ones which have, with the former, only an outward resemblance, but which are not really spirit communications.

Already Allan Kardec, Hudson Tuttle, Aksakov, Dr. Metzger, and others, had taken care to warn us against such causes of error, while critics among the incredulous have focused on these pseudo-phenomena to try to remove from Spiritism its true strength, that is, the demonstration of our contacts with the souls of those who have departed Earth.[165]

Thus they attributed all communications through writing to automatism, and the information contained therein to

---

[165] See G. Delanne, *Recherches sur la Médiumnité* (Paris: Librairie des Sciences Psychiques, 1902).

cryptesthesia on the part of the subjects or to transmissions of thought which would be made to them telepathically. In the same way, phenomena of communications by discarnate spirits did not actually take place; according to P. Janet, Flournoy or Morselli; but rather self-suggestioned mediums would imagine themselves to represent extraneous personalities. This is the thesis that Charles Richet has just taken up again in his resounding book on *metapsychics*.

For scholars who admit the reality of materializations, one would be in any case in presence of a phenomenon of duplication of the medium or ectoplasm modeled by the subject's ideoplasty. In the same way spirit photography would be due to an identical cause.

What makes the experimental study of such phenomena so delicate is that, in fact, automatism, autosuggestion, duplication, and ideoplasty sometimes blend in an almost inextricable manner with the real phenomena, so that it already requires great experience not to be deceived by these disappointing occurrences. Once we are able to tell the difference between real mediumistic phenomena and those coming from animism[166] (i.e., from the subjects themselves), we can advance more boldly in the experimental field.

In this way a real service to Spiritist science is made by pointing out to researchers the pitfalls they may encounter, thus preventing them from taking for revelations from the beyond mere ruminations of pseudo-mediums, or from attributing to certain phenomena a demonstrative value that actually they do not possess.

In this vein, I find it useful to draw readers' attention to a category of facts presenting analogies with certain proofs which serve to establish the validity of the theory of successive lives, but which are not usually considered as such: I am referring to memories related to previous existences.

Quite often we are told that reincarnation is only a philosophical speculation not based on any material proof. To

---

166 [Trans. note] See footnote 31 above.

these I reply that if the memory of past lives is not generally found, it nevertheless occurs with some frequency, so that these reminiscences can only be explained if the soul has lived before.

"Not at all," some doctors will answer, "what you take for memory of past lives is only attributable to a memory disease," as pointed out long ago by Mr. Ribot, who calls it *false memory*, or, according to Dr. Chauvet, *the feeling of déjà vu*, that is, of something already experienced before; or still, *false recognition*. It was also given the name of *paramnesia*.

According to Dr. Napoléon-Magloire Chauvet, the phenomenon consists exactly in the following:

> "Sometimes it is a man who, in the presence of a woman unknown to him, suddenly recognizes her silhouette, her attitudes, her gait, the expression of her face, her voice. In other cases – the most numerous and frequent – it is an indoor scene, or a landscape, or the aspect of a town that gives the impression of déjà vu.
>
> Upon entering an environment hitherto unknown, and surrounded by people we have just met, we suddenly feel that we have already witnessed, a long time ago, the same scene, in the same setting, with objects confusedly familiar, with the same persons having the same attitudes, and the same play of physiognomy, expressing the same ideas with the same words and the same intonations, underlining them with the same gestures. Or if we were in the same places talking, suddenly discovering that in the same context, being in the same emotional state as the first time, we end up doing and saying what we already did: this is a fairly common way of feeling the illusion of déjà vu."[167]

According to Dr. Chauvet, this feeling of déjà vu has special characteristics, it would be obvious from the outset, and cover all perceptions. Then the subject is intimately convinced that what he/she sees is the reproduction of a scene previously perceived. These impressions arouse the

---

167 [Trans. note] Original source not mentioned by DELANNE.

same emotional states that one would have felt before: joy, boredom, indifference, and so on. Finally, such sensations are usually extremely short, but in some subjects they are accompanied by a feeling of anguish, of annoyance.

Jules Lemaître[168] experienced the impression in question several times. About the Verlaine verses he quoted, he wrote in 1888:

> "The poet wants to render here a very bizarre and painful mental phenomenon, which consists in recognizing what has never been seen before. Has this happened to you sometimes? We think we remember, we want to continue and specify a very confused reminiscence, but which we are sure it is a reminiscence, it melts and dissolves progressively, and it becomes atrocious. It's at these times that you feel like going crazy. How to explain that? Oh! That we certainly do not know ourselves enough. It is because our intellectual life is largely unconscious, objects continually make impressions on our brains without our noticing them, and which are stored there without our being warned. At certain moments, when exposed to an external shock, these ignored impressions half awake in us; we suddenly become aware of them with more or less clarity, but always without being informed of where they came from, without being able to clarify them, or to bring them back to their cause, and it is this impotence that make us uneasy."[169]

Dr. Arthur Wigan, in his well-known book *The Duality of the Mind*,[170] reports that while attending the funeral service of Princess Charlotte in the Windsor Chapel, he suddenly felt that he had once been a witness of the same scene. The illusion was only fleeting. George Henry Lewes rightly compares this phenomenon with some other more frequent ones. It happened in a foreign country, that the abrupt detour

---

168 This case was related by E. LEROY, paraphrased above.
169 J. LEMAÎTRE, *Les Contemporains* (Paris: Société Française d'Imprimerie, 1890), p. 105.
170 [Trans. note] A. L. WIGAN, *The Duality of the Mind* (London: Longman, Brown, Green & Longmans, 1844), ch. IX, p. 85.

from a path or a river puts us in front of some landscape which it seems to us to have once been contemplated.

Introduced for the first time to a person, we feel that we have already met him/her. Reading in a book of new thoughts, one feels that they have been present to in one's mind previously.

What is the explanation that psychologists give for these phenomena?

According to T. Ribot, this would only be a reminder of sensations previously recorded within us, which would be enough to make us believe that this new state would be its repetition.

If this hypothesis can be accepted for simple cases where the feeling of déjà vu is vague, it is hardly acceptable in the following case, reported by Ribot himself:[171] [172]

> "An educated man, who seems to have understood his disease, and who himself gave a written description of it, was seized at the age of thirty-two with a singular mental affection. If he was present at a social gathering, if he visited any place whatever, if he met a stranger, the incident, with all the attendant circumstances, appeared so familiar that he was convinced of having received the same impressions before, of having been surrounded by the same persons or the same objects, under the same sky and the same state of the weather. If he undertook any new occupation, he seemed to have gone through with it at some previous time and under the same conditions. The feeling sometimes appeared the same day, at the end of a few moments or hours, sometimes not till the following day, but always with perfect distinctness.
>
> In this phenomenon of pseudo-memory there is an anomalous condition of the mental mechanism which eludes

---

[171] [Trans. note] T. RIBOT, *Maladies de la Mémoire* (Paris: F. Alcan, 1888), pp. 188–189.

[172] On this subject, see ANGEL, ARMAND, DUGAS, FOUILLÉE, JENSEN, MAUDSLEY, WIGAN, LEROY, among other authors.

investigation and which is difficult to understand in a state of health."

What is relevant to us is to remark that when the sense of déjà vu is imposed on the observer for contemporary events, conversations or readings, this results from a memory disease, and that there is no point in taking it into account when gathering evidence to establish the reality of past lives based on memories.

In fact, this feeling of déjà vu, which projects, so to speak, the same visual or auditory sensations at two different levels, cannot in any way inform the person who experiences it on circumstances that are not contemporary. That is to say, they do not allow him/her who is attending a scene – even though he/she seems to have already seen it – to foresee, for example, an accident that would occur a little later; or, in presence of a landscape that already looks familiar, to indicate aspects of such a landscape that are beyond its visual range.

Paramnesia, while giving the feeling of something already perceived, does not reveal anything really new to the one who experiences it.

It is quite different when it comes to reminiscences. At the sight of a landscape which he/she has never laid eyes on before during their current lifetime, not only is the subject sure that he/she has known it before, but this feeling is accompanied and completed by the knowledge of things and details regarding this landscape, which he/she cannot currently see; and which, nonetheless, the person describes with perfect accuracy. Likewise, we must beware of another, more elusive cause of error, which would be produced by our ability of disengaging from the body while asleep.

Camille Flammarion, in his book *L'inconnu – The Unknown*,[173] cites several cases in which sleepers have dreamed of cities they had never visited, but which they recognized

---

[173] C. FLAMMARION, *L'inconnu – The Unknown* (New York and London: Harper & Bros., 1900), p. 435 *et seq.*

immediately when they were actually there. Here are some examples.

Visions of unknown places by subjects during sleep

"I will introduce myself as Pierre Jules Barthelay, born at Yssoire, Puy-de-Dôme, on October 25, 1825, a former pupil in the Lycée at Clermont, priest in the diocese of Clermont in 1850, vicar for eight years at Saint Eutrope (Clermont), and three times made an army chaplain by the Ministry of War. After three years of laborious ministry I was very much worn out, all the more because I had to serve as superintendent over the construction of the beautiful church of Saint Eutrope at Clermont. For four years I looked after the workmen from ten o'clock in the morning, from the water in the foundation to the cross on the top of the steeple. I put the three last slates on the roof. Our professor, M. Vincent, in order to give me a change, made me come to Lyon, where I had never been. One of the first days I was there he said at breakfast: 'M. l'Abbé, will you accompany me? I am going to see our forests at Saint-Just-Doizieux.' I accepted his invitation. We started in a carriage. After having passed Saint-Paul-en-Jarret, I uttered an exclamation: 'Oh! but I know all this country!' and in fact I would have gone all over it without a guide. About a year before I had seen in my sleep all these little terraces made of yellow stone.

I returned to my diocese, but was sent to the mountains in the West to fulfill a difficult mission, which was too great for my strength. I was ill seven months at Clermont. At last, being on my legs again, they sent me to the Hospital of Saint-Ambert, to take the place of the Chaplain, who had had congestion of the brain. The railroad to Saint-Ambert was not then built, so I took my place in the coupe of the diligence which ran between Clermont and Ambert. After passing Billom, I looked to the right, and *recognized the little castle, with its avenue of willows, as well as if I had lived there.* I had seen it in my sleep as much as eighteen months before."

We were in *l'année terrible* [Franco-Prussian War, 1870]. My mother, who had seen the allies marching through the streets of Paris, is a widow. She claims me as the prop of her old age. They gave me a little parish near Yssoire. The first time I went to see a sick parishioner, I found myself in narrow lanes between high, dark walls, but I could perfectly find my way. I had, in my sleep, some months before, passed through this *network of dark alleys*.

Events, quite independent of my will, took me to Riom; there I presumed I should feel as if I were in a strange country. What was my surprise to find an old acquaintance in the chapel that my colleague, the Abbé Faure, had built for the soldiers. I had never seen it with my eyes, and had not even known that it existed ! I made a drawing of it, which I send you, as if I were still employed in superintending ecclesiastical architecture..

BERTHELAY,
Riom (Puy-de-Dôme)."

Enclosed with the letter above were four hand drawings of monuments seen in dreams.

It is likely that it was Father Berthelay's preoccupations that led to the disengagement of his spirit (an out-of-body experience), sending him in his sleep to the towns where he was to live later. When he woke up, these memories had faded away, but they resuscitated when he actually saw them.

HAUNTED BY THE LIVING

I will now borrow from one of Ernest Bozzano's fine books,[174] the following case along with his commentaries.

---

174 E. Bozzano, *Les Phénomènes de Hantise* (Paris: F. Alcan, 1920). [Trans. note: the actual original is from the *Annales de Sciences Psychiques*, vol, XXI, May 1–16, 1911, p. 144, given below in its English version].

"Case 1. In this first case the two hypotheses of telepathy and bilocation have an almost equal value, and the example shows a type of incident frequent in discussions of telepathy. Dr. Hodgson records the case in the *Proceedings of the S.P.R.*, Vol XL, page 445....

Mr. G. P. H., member of the French Society for Psychical Research, had sent an account of an important psychic case to *The Spectator*, and this was followed by the following letter of confirmation from the man who was interested (*Revue des Études Psychiques*, 1902, page 151):

To the Editor of *The Spectator*

SIR,—The letter which has been sent to you by Mr. G. P. H. and which you published in your last issue, June 1st, under the title 'House of Dreams', evidently refers to a dream of my wife, who is now dead. The account is precise on the main points although I am unable to recognize the identity of your correspondent. The same story has been reported less exactly in the diaries of Sir Mountstuart Grant Duff, quoted in your article of May 25th. It will not, therefore, be superfluous if I give a concise summary of the occurrence. Some years ago my wife dreamed on several occasions of a house of which she described the interior arrangements in every detail, although she had no idea of the locality in which the building was. Later in 1883, I rented from Lady B. for the autumn a house in the Scotch mountains surrounded by hunting land and fishing water. My son, who was then in Scotland, made the business arrangements without either my wife or myself seeing the property. When I went, without my wife, to sign the contract and to take possession, Lady B. was still living in the house. She told me that if I did not object she would give me the bedroom which she usually occupied, and which had been for some time past haunted by a little lady, who made frequent appearances. As I was somewhat of a skeptic in such matters, I replied that I should be delighted to make the acquaintance of the phantom visitor. I slept in this room but I was not visited by the phantom. Later when my wife arrived she was astonished to recognize in the house that of her dream. She went over it from top to bottom, and found that every detail corresponded with what she had .so often seen, but when she came back again into the drawing room she said: 'This cannot be the house of my dream, for the latter had on this side a series of rooms which are lacking here.' She was immediately told that there were really such rooms, but that they could not be reached from the drawing room. When they were shown to her she recognized each room perfectly. She said, however, that one of the bedrooms of this part of the house had not been a bedroom when she visited it in her dream. It happened, in fact, that the room in question had been quite recently converted into a bedroom. Two or three days later my wife and I visited Lady B.; as they had not yet met I presented the two ladies to each other. Lady B. cried out at once, 'You are the lady who used to haunt my bedroom.' I have no explanation to give of this occurrence. My wife has never during the remainder of her life had any adventure of this kind, which some people would call a remarkable coincidence, and the Scotch a case of double sight. My dear wife was certainly the last person in the world who would allow her imagination to run away with her. I can, then, guarantee, as can also other members of my family, that she has been able to give an exact and detailed description of a house which was arranged in rather a particular way, and that she did this before either she or the other members of the family knew that such a house existed. You can give my name to those people who are seriously interested in psychical research, and who desire to obtain further information. To this end I enclose my card. (Mr. G. P. H. gave also to the editor the full name of Lady B., who belonged to the British aristocracy.)"[175]

This example justifies the distinction I made between paramnesia and true reminiscence. Here Mrs. G. P. H.

---

175 [Trans. note] Excerpted from *Light*, vol. xxxi, July 22, 1911, p. 340.

remembers not only having visited this house, but she indicates the existence of a series of rooms which it was impossible for her to know, but were found to really exist.

If the memory of this dream had not been preserved, this recognition could have been attributed to paramnesia or a memory from a previous life, which would have been a double error, since the phenomenon at hand was due solely to clairvoyance alongside duplication on the part of the subject. So how can one distinguish a true memory of previous lives from lucidity during sleep or an anomaly of memory? Obviously it will be through the study of the circumstances that accompany the dream, old memories that must place it unmistakably in the past.

Here are two examples that will help you understand what I mean.

Poet Armand Silvestre[176] is walking in Moscow, where he has just arrived; what he sees and hears causes a strange feeling mixed with oppression in him. This atmosphere envelops him in something maternal. He feels, he says, his head bowing among all heads, his knees bend and prayers to him from lips whose words he cannot understand; and he wonders how to explain this phenomenon, in which situations are mysteriously regained, lands never seen before can still be recognized, feelings that come to your heart as if a grandparent, long asleep in a tomb whose place was unmarked, suddenly opened the arms out of the shroud.

This is no longer a question of paramnesia; these unknown prayers are so reminiscent of the past that Napoléon-Magloire Chauvet, resuming the hypothesis of Dr. Letourneau,[177] believes that they should be ascribed to ancestral memory. Indeed he says:

"Suppose that a man has seen a landscape or a city and that, for particular reasons, generally affective ones, has kept a

---

176 A. SILVESTRE, *La Russie* (Paris: G. Charpentier & E. Fasquelle, 1892).
177 Bulletin of the *Société d'Anthropologie de Paris*, cited by the *Annales des Sciences Psychiques*, July 1906.

mightily shaped memory of it. He could transmit it in power to some of his descendants who would bring it from birth buried in the depths of their unconscious. Should these be one day in presence of such a landscape or such a city, the ancestral memory would then be resuscitated: it would rise again and the illusion of déjà vu would thus emerge."

This hypothesis, which absolutely nothing can justify, is contrary to all that we know about heredity. Never has there been direct evidence of any physiological transmission of a memory from parents to their descendants. It is impossible to suppose that a definite mental impression remains latent through several generations, due to the incessant renewal of bodily matter. It is therefore useless to dwell longer in this strange hypothesis with no grounds of support whatsoever.

Let us now come to the study of cases where it seems that real reminiscences have occurred. We have seen that all the intellectual activity of our past lives lies in latent state in the perispirit. This immense storage of psychic materials constitutes the bedrock of our intellectual and moral individuality, forming this primeval frame of a richer or less rich intelligence on which each life embroiders new arabesques. But all these gains can be manifested only by those primeval tendencies which each of us brings upon being born, and which is called one's character. Therefore, the most perfect unconsciousness should be the rule, and that is precisely what happens, yet there are no rules without exceptions.

Just like some somnambulic subjects have observed the preservation of memory upon awakening, so can individuals who clearly remember having already lived; while in others the renovation takes a more vague and imprecise form, in a fugitive manner, under the influence of certain milieus or certain circumstances in which people are placed. This is the true reminiscence which differs from paramnesia in the knowledge of real things which the subject designates accurately without having seen them, before and without the reasoning of attributing this knowledge to clairvoyance.

The following cases seem to fall into this category.

LIKELY REMINISCENCES AMONG CHILDREN

It is quite natural to think that during the first years of their reincarnation some children can momentarily recover some memories, or at least reminiscences of their previous life. I received a number of letters from trustworthy persons telling me what they saw happen to their children.

LITTLE GIRL SPEAKING A SPECIAL IDIOM IN WHICH FRENCH WORDS ARE FOUND

I would like to quote first of all a note published by the *Revue Spirite* of December 1869, page 367:

"In 1868 French newspapers reported a strange phenomenon, according to an English medical journal, *The Quarterly Review*. It is a little girl whose physician, a Dr. Hun, narrates the astonishing story. Until the age of three, she remained silent and could only pronounce the words Mom and Dad. Then, suddenly, she began to speak with extraordinary fluency, but in an unknown language having nothing to do with [her native] English. What is most surprising is that she refuses to speak this language, the only one spoken to her, and obliges those with whom she lives, for example her elder brother, a little older than her, to learn hers instead, which contains some words in French, although, according to her parents, one has never uttered any word in French before her.

How can this be explained otherwise than by the recollection of a language that this child would have spoken in a previous existence? It is true that one may still deny it. But the little one exists. *The Quarterly Review* is a serious medical journal which is reporting it, so denial is but a convenient subterfuge, and may have been used a little too much. This attitude is in many ways an equivalent of the devil, a deus ex machina who always comes to explain everything, dispensing with research."

Here is a passage from Mrs. Panigot's letter to me with a confirmation from her daughter.

> "My daughter was barely walking, because she started to walk very late, at age of three: it is true that she walked on her toes and did not let go.
> We passed, my maid, she and I, by the cemetery of Préville; it was at the period of All Saints' Day. Suddenly the child stopped in front of a grave and with her little finger showed me white flowers. "You see, mom, here are the flowers as there were on the grave of my first mother."
> Stupefied, I said to my maid: "If I put her in a nanny's care, I think it would change that little one's behavior." Going home, I begged my darling girl to explain to me what she wanted to tell me. She gave me details of troubling facts. She told me that she had lost her mother, who was naughty and had a sister who was kind.
> I will pass her the pen now to finish this story.
>
> Panigot mère
>
> I am happy to complete a story that may be of interest to you. All that I am going to write is still very vivid in my memory, even though I am over thirty-two years of age.
> The one I call my first mother was tall, dark and thin; she was far from being kind. I often went near a big round tower and most often two greyhounds with very light beige fur accompanied me.
> These are all my precise memories. As for my sister, I have no memory of her. I will add two things to my story:
> 1) I do not remember growing up. Therefore I must have died young.

2) I learn English very easily and its pronunciation by intuition. Perhaps it is in England that I have already lived.

Sincerely yours,
Mrs. and Miss Panigot,
11, Dupont-des-Loges Street;
Nancy (France)."

Are these dormant memories roused?

At the time when this happened, Mrs. Panigot had nothing to do with Spiritism, and the child could not possibly have heard about successive lives. It cannot be assumed, therefore, that Mrs. Panigot had suffered from autosuggestion.

Would it be then, that the child had an intense dream which would have externalized in that manner? It is possible, since we do not have a positive demonstration of these remembrances of the past. The same considerations should also apply to the two following cases.

Mrs. Valpinçon reported to me a case related by one of her friends, a most intelligent woman who would like to remain anonymous.

"I am going to tell you a fact that was often recounted to me by my mother, because then I was five or six years old. I loved dolls very much and took my duties as their 'mother' very seriously. They had complete trousseaus which I washed and ironed myself. One morning, after a very heavy washing of these tiny objects, I came across my mother, telling me to come and take a rest near her. Not wanting to interrupt her reading, I sat quietly beside her in my little chair, looking at my hands and especially, insistently at the tips of my fingers. Suddenly, showing them to my mother, I cried out as if coming out of a dream:
'Mother, see, I have my hands all wrinkled as when I was old.'
'What do you mean, my child?'

'Oh! That was not long ago, you know, mom.'
Very frightened, my mother scolded me for talking nonsense. This was the subject of many reflections; silence was made over it, and it was only after my marriage that mother dared to speak to me about that raving outburst."

The following, on the other hand, is an account that comes from Italy, and whose narrator does not want to be named. His story is corroborated by the testimony of his mother and a friend.

"I am very interested in psychical studies, but when I was a child neither I nor those around me had any notion of reincarnation, and yet I always said that I was once a knight of the Middle Ages, and I was quite convinced of that, and I complained that I was a girl when I wanted to be a man to fight and die for the homeland. Many years later, I was living in Naples at the Commander's Palace with my husband, an army officer, when one day I was with a gentleman at a window overlooking the inner courtyard of the Palace, where the corps commander of the army with his suite of staff officers stood at the head of the cortège and went out through the great gate that overlooks the Plebiscite Square, when I felt myself shaken and in spite of myself I exclaimed: 'But what am I doing here, while I have to ride my horse and put myself at the head of the procession!' But suddenly I remembered that I was Mrs. X. and that for me there was nothing else to do but to look. However, at that moment I had the precise recollection of having been a military commander and of being at the head of the troops. I also think I was forced to enter a convent, because I remember how much I cried and shouted as a child if my hair was cut off. One day the scene was very tragic, I threw myself on the ground sobbing on my hair which had been cut, I put it back on my head. Another time, I was about fourteen years old, I was at the window with relatives and friends to see parading tanks, and while all laughed and joked, me, at the sight of a tank where there were Garibaldians in red shirt, who were massacring priests, those pretending to be priests, felt such an emotion that I burst into bitter complaints at the great excitement of all those present. I must say that during my current life I have not had to deal with priests or religious people; nevertheless, I feel for them a real repulsion and my heart tightens when I see them. Since I was a little girl and at any time, at will, I can completely get out of myself, asking myself, like Rudyard Kipling's Kim, who am I? I would like to add that I am a healthy and well-balanced woman, and even that I refuse to talk about these things with anyone to avoid being labeled as peculiar by those who are not interested in such studies.

A. M. L. M.
May 29, 1922, Milan (Italy)"

Following are the testimonies of the mother and a friend of Mrs. A. M. L. M. If these stories are not due to the imagination of the narrator, they would seem to indicate true reminiscences relating to various past lives. To finish this short review, here is a letter that was still addressed to me from Nancy:

"In October 1921, as a result of the housing crisis, we were forced to put our furniture in a furniture deposit until March 1922, and to ask for hospitality at one of my sisters in Lunéville. My sister had at that time one of her grandchildren, Georges, aged four and nine months, whom we all loved very much.

One afternoon, while George was having fun, he spontaneously spoke the following: "Auntie Adine, you will become old, very old, you will die, you will become very small, you will grow up and we will play together." Another time, eight days apart, he said to me:

'Auntie Adine, is it true that we will become very small, very small, we will grow up and love each other very much?'

Adeline MULLER,

55 Félix-Faure Avenue, Nancy (Meurthe-et-Moselle)."

One of my friends, Mr. C.,[178] chatting with his little girl aged between three and four, was surprised to hear that she was Polish, her parents being from French Switzerland. Surprised at this answer, for the little girl had never heard of Poland and Poles, they pointed out to her that she was French, since they themselves were French. The logic of this reasoning could not convince the child.

> "'No,' she said, 'I'm Polish and I remember very well when mom died.'
> 'You do not know what you say,' said the mother, 'you see, I'm not dead because I'm talking to you.'
> 'There is no question of you,' said the child, 'I mean my other mother, the Polonaise. This is how she was always called; when she died, they put a nice dress on her, and then put her amidst a quantity of burning candles in the middle of a large, beautiful salon. Priests came and sang all day long. One day, she was put in a big coffin and carried her away. My other mother was rich; we had very large living quarters; we also had horses and carriages.'
> 'Who told you this story?'
> 'Oh! Nobody told it to me; I remember it very well, for I was big then.'"

At several different times, Mr. and Mrs. C. questioned their daughter and always received the same answer. Today she is a girl between the age of ten and twelve years, and she now cannot remember anything.

The cases I have just reported are not entirely demonstrative, because no verification is possible. If I have cited them, it is because, as I will later show, in other children, memories of previous lives were presented with enough clarity so that we could control (i.e., verify) their reality. Thus, these <u>can be considered as</u> a first sketch of the reconstitution of

[178] [Trans. note] Here a mistaken footnote pointing to a book (and page) by Léon DENIS was omitted in the current translation.

integral memory being translated fleetingly by vague reminiscences in subjects whose organism did not lend itself to a full awakening.

Reminiscences which seem induced by the sight of certain places

We know that there are subjects called psychometers, who have the ability to reconstruct scenes from the past through psychometry, when we put in their hands any object that would have been associated with these events. For example, a stone from an Egyptian sarcophagus evokes the idea of Egypt and the funerary scenes that took place there. It seems that, under certain specific conditions, when people suddenly recognize cities or countries they have never seen, these new places exert on them an action analogous to that experienced by psychometers, but with a difference, namely, that these are inner memories that are evoked in them, and that these reminiscences are absolutely personal to them. This is a peculiar form of resuscitation of the past, which presents itself frequently enough, so it deserves serious attention.

Here are some interesting examples that relate directly to our study. First, I quote the story of Major Wellesley Tudor Pole.[179]

Retrospective visions

Major Wellesley Tudor Pole recounts the deep impression he felt when visiting the temple of Karnak, in Egypt. It seemed to him to be saturated with a mystical atmosphere and magnetic fluids. It was, he adds, as if diving into the sea where one is surrounded by different currents of various colors, lifting the soul and the imagination outside the current of

---

179 See the August 1919 issue of *Pearson Magazine*, which published a collection of psychic cases related to world War I. The editor is astonished that there are so many people with the sixth sense.

present time and placing it in the same conditions that it was three thousand years ago.

He saw before his eyes an ancient procession of the high priests of Amon-Ra. "One in particular," he says, "caught my attention; he was blond with blue eyes and differed profoundly from all his companions."

This individual seemed familiar to the major. "I do not know why," he said, "I watched the procession turn around the broken pillar on which we were placed; my eyes were always drawn to the priest with blond hair. When he was in front of me, he extended his arms in my direction and I had the impression that he was myself. I was certain of it and I became unaware of what was going on around me." The rest of the vision is no longer of interest to us.

It would seem from this account that Major Wellesley had a kind of retrospective hallucination which allowed him to recognize himself as one of the temple's former priests. The psychometric action of the environment here appears very probable. This may also have happened in the two following cases.[180]

A CLERGYMAN

"Some ten years ago I paid my first visit to Rome. Again and again within the city there came these flashes of recognition. The Baths of Caracalla, the Appian Way, the Catacombs of St. Calixtus, the Colosseum — all seemed familiar to me. The reason appeared obvious. I was renewing my acquaintance with what I had seen in pictures and photographs. That might explain the buildings, but not the dark underground windings of the Catacombs. A few days later I was out at Tivoli.

The whole place and countryside were as familiar as my own parish. I found myself struggling with a torrent of

---

[180] ROCHAS D'AIGLUN, *Les Vies Successives*, p. 314.

words, describing what it was like in the olden days. I had read nothing of Tivoli, and seen no views; yet here I was acting as guide and historian to a party of friends who concluded that I had made a special study of the place; then the vision in my mind began to fade. I stopped like a man who has forgotten his part, and I could say no more. It was as if a mosaic had dropped to pieces, leaving only a few remaining fragments still in situ, and presently these receded from my grasp. On another occasion I was with a companion in the neighborhood of Leatherhead, where I had never been before. The country was quite new to me and to my friend. In the course of conversation he remarked: 'They say there is part of an old Roman road somewhere round here, but I don't know whether it is on this side of Leatherhead or the other.' At once I said, 'I know', and led the way with certainty in my mind that I knew where we should find it, which we did; and there was the feeling that I had been on that road before riding, and that I had worn armor. Such incidents have caused me from time to time to pursue this subject among my friends, and quite a number of them can quote similar experiences. To the west, 3 ½ miles from where I live, is a Roman fortress in an almost perfect state of preservation.

A clergyman called upon me one day and asked me to accompany him there for an examination of the ruins. He told me he had a distinct recollection of living there, and that he held some office of a priestly nature in the days of the Roman occupation. One fact struck me as significant. He insisted on examining a ruined tower which had been bodily overturned, and said: 'There used to be a socket in the top of it, in which we used to plant a mast, and archers used to be hauled to the top in a basket protected with leather from which they picked off the leaders among the ancient Gorlestonians.' We found the socket he had indicated."[181]

---

181 [Trans. note] ROCHAS D'AIGLUN had quoted a French translation of the original article by Rev. Forbes PHILLIPS, "Ancestral Memory," published

Curious coincidence

In the November 18, 1916 issue of *Light*, page 374, we read the following account, as provided by the editor of a London monthly magazine. The latter declares that this story is firsthand and authentic:

> "'A——' is a well-known artist, who at the time spoken of was working in London. He is a Romanian of very old family and held a post of some importance at his own Legation. He joined one of our Yeomanry regiments, and one day was out on maneuvers in Berkshire, and was riding alongside his captain. They were ascending a fairly steep ridge, tie contour of which struck him as vaguely familiar. He mention this to the officer.
> 'Oh, you know the country hereabouts, then?' said the latter.
> 'No, sir,' said A——; 'I've never been in Berkshire before in my life, but somehow I seem to know this hill, and, what's more, beyond it is another steep ridge – rather conical in shape, with a clump of trees on the top, after which the ground slope sharply to a stretch of flat level land.'
> 'That's right,' said the captain, who was a Berkshire man. 'But you can see nothing of all that from here, so how you can tell me that if you're strange to this bit of county, beats me.'
> There the matter dropped for the time being, and A—— gradually forgot all about it, until a little more than a year afterwards some excavations were being made on the summit of the ridge up which A—— had been riding, and a large stone monument was unearthed. On it was inscribed 'To the memory of the fallen of the tenth Dacian Legion' (the Dacians as they were then – or the Romanians as they are now – when legionaries of the Roman Empire at the time when Rome held sway over England).
> Beneath the inscription there were, carved in the stone, fit names of the fallen men, and amongst them was the name

---

in *The Nineteenth Century and After*, London, vol. 59, no. 352, June 1906, pp. 977–983, which has been faithfully restored above.

of a famous ancestor of A——'s, spelled after the Roman fashion, of course, for the whole inscription was in Latin. Whether it was mere coincidence that the unknown scene was so familiar to A—— at a glance that he was even able to describe accurately the contours of the unseen country beyond or whether it was some process of a mental throw back across the centuries – a process of the laws of which we know little or nothing – is for the reader to decide. I have given the bald facts accurately, only suppressing the actual names.

C. H."

Reminiscence or clairvoyance[182]

Following an investigation I undertook, I received from Mrs. Mathilda de Krapkoff, whom I have the pleasure of knowing personally, the following story:

"During the delightful spring of 1898, my husband and I landed in Yalta, Crimea, to go to Livaldia, where the Russian court was staying. We went to my brother-in-law's, who held a post with the Emperor. I had, a few days before, crossed for the first time the Russian frontier at one *volost*. I had just married, a little against the will of my mother, who was sorry to see me go so far, into a young Russian noble's family, and I felt inexplicably attracted to this distant Russia, so different from my birthplace. I had read all that I could find to learn about it, and I lived with the heroines of Tolstoy and Ivan Turgenev, rapturing over what they were called with their surname added to their first name. I said to myself: "There, I will be named Mathilda Iossifova. How sweet too when I met the man who was to be my husband and that he named me so! I realized that my destiny was fulfilled and I was intoxicated with the happiness of finally going to the enchanted country of my dreams.

---

182 [Trans. note] See footnote 20 above.

As my heart beat faster as I approached the border post that marked the threshold of a much desired existence, the sad black and white colors seemed to radiate more brilliant rays, and when everyone around me spoke the sweet Russian language, my ear thought to recognize it. I eagerly asked for the meaning of every word that I seemed to relearn so easily. Arriving at Odessa, nothing surprised me, I felt at home, and when landing in Yalta I was not a French woman eager for novelties, but a local citizen happy to have finally returned to spend a few days on the beautiful shores of Crimea. My brother-in-law, to make me recognize the immense forests of the inner lands, organized a little cavalcade. The day before the departure, I could not sit still, all my being was as if projected outside me, toward this countryside that I was going to visit. It was a strange feeling other than the one I had felt since I arrived in Russia, more irresistible and more powerful. Besides, from the very first hours, my eyes had been invincibly drawn toward the dark mass of the woods as if by some magical magnet.

The night seemed endless. At last dawn rose radiant and our caravan set out on its journey, accompanied by two Tartar guides who knew the region well.

For hours we wandered beneath those majestic forests, sometimes towering over vast panoramas of verdant oceans, sometimes plunged into darkened valleys where the trees stood higher, interweaving their mighty antlers. We had several stops, but as evening approached, horses and riders were tired and we obediently followed the guides on the way back. This day was ineffable. My heart was overflowing with a thousand confused feelings, my mind seemed to be running forward toward new paths, toward the unknown. We were still going, but the guides were beginning to worry, searching right and left, inspecting the thickets. Here they stop us and tell us that they have lost the road. The paths become more and more confused; they do not know which way to take. General consternation, fury of some. It's already late; how to move at night in these dark forests that seem to have no bounds? My husband wants to reassure me, but I am very quiet; I feel that I know where we are. It seems to me that another complementary being has come into me and that this double knows the region and this place precisely. I calmly declare that we must be reassured, that we are not lost, since we only have to take the path to the left and follow it, that it will lead us to a wider path, leading in turn to a clearing, and at the bottom, behind a curtain of trees, there lies a village half Tartar, half Russian. I see it, this village, its houses rise around a quadrangle square; at the bottom there is a portico supported by elegant Byzantine columns. Under this portico a pretty marble fountain, and behind the portico the steps of an old house with small windows with braces; all that, charming, old-fashioned and so harmonious ... I stop, I spoke without hesitation, very quickly, with confidence; the vision is in me so clear, so precise! It seems to me I have seen all this already so often. All surround me and look at me with amazement; what a singular joke! It seems to them very inappropriate, but these French (they think) ... I must be very pale; I am cold; my husband examines me with anxiety, but I repeat shouting: 'Yes, yes, yes, all that is right, you will see.' And I jerk the bridle to the left path. Since I am treated like a spoiled child and the burdened guides are sitting on the ground, they follow me a little mechanically, not realizing what is going on. The scene is always in me, I see, I am calm and assured. My husband, very much troubled, said to his brother, 'After all, my wife may have a gift of second sight, and since we are lost, let's go with her; there or elsewhere, what does it matter?' With his approval, I stir the horse forward through the coppice which became more and more sparse. I cut through the woods, so impatient I am to arrive. No one is speaking; the mist rises and no sign of a clearing, but I know it is there, right in front of us and I continue my way. Finally I stretch my arm and my whip indicate the clearing, magic word. We exclaim, we run, yes, it is a clearing longer than wide. All see it in the dark, Its bottom is lost in the mist, but the horses, too, seem to feel that we have arrived, they gallop and we reach the big trees under which we enter. I am out of myself, projected toward what I want to see. A last veil is torn. Here is a dim light, and at the same time a voice murmurs not in my ear, but in my heart: "Marina, O Marina, here you are, you've come back. Your fountain murmurs again. Your house is still there. Be welcome, dearest, dearest Marina." Ah! What an emotion, what superhuman joy! Everything is there in front of me, the portico, the fountain, the house. It is too much, I stagger and fall, but my husband has already seized me and drops me gently on this earth that is mine, near my sweet fountain. How to describe my ecstasy? I am overwhelmed with emotion, I burst into tears; people's shadows are hastened, surrounding me; we speak Russian, Tartar. They bring me to the house; my shaky legs go up the stairs. My heart seems to be crushing over the threshold. Then, suddenly, fiction gives way to reality; I see an unknown room, strange objects, the shadow of Marina fades away; I will never know who she was or when she lived, but I know she was here, that she died there very young; I feel it, I'm sure of it ...

My husband makes me drink hot tea, all my companions sit around me, exclaim, want to know how I guessed, how I saw, but I explain nothing to anyone, except to my companion. Nobody will know the secret of Marina and I feel so well in this sweet home where I breathe an air of another world. I have never felt such well being; I feel so light, so happy. We settle down as best we can for the night. But I sit on the doorstep and ask my husband to question and ask who this house belongs to, who lived there. We do not know much; the house belonged to a Polish descendant, he said, of an exiled family. The elders remember him; he died very old and alone. A relative has come. The very dilapidated house has been sold; the heir is gone again. We have repaired it somehow and it is now the village chief, the *staroste*, who lives with his family and I will know nothing more, but what I do know is that, me, Marina, I have lived here; my eyes have gazed upon this curtain of beautiful trees, the murmur of the fountain rocked my reveries; this sweet house once sheltered me ... The perfumes of the warm spring night seem to envelop me entirely, and I listen intensely, with ecstasy, to this divine elegy, the murmur of the fountain, the chant of the nightingale, the sweet murmur of the breeze in the branches. To this celestial harmony, my heart splits with ecstasy and deep in my self a very distant voice, very soft and weak but penetrating, repeats: 'Marina!'

Many years have passed since this radiant journey; I lived them in Russia, in this country of my dreams which did not disappoint me, for I was very happy there and I always knew how to feel at home. I learned with surprising ease the Russian language and also Polish. Every time I came back to France, I was on vacation, but when I found the customs unbearable, the gendarmes suspicious, and the gentle Slavic speaking, I went home, to my country. I must add that nowhere in Russia has anything happened to me like the story I have just told in all sincerity and from which I have always kept the most vivid and most delicious memory. I have studied since; I now know that I was not mistaken, and that Marina and I were the one and only Mathilda de Krapkoff.

Paris, July 2, 1922."

This narrative places us in presence of one of those ambiguous cases where one hesitates to decide categorically on an explanation whether as clairvoyance or as memories of an earlier life. However, since this last interpretation seems to be the more likely one, I decided to reproduce herein Mrs. Mathilda de Krapkoff's report.

Now for another example of recognizing places where it is likely that the narrator lived previously; for there is no reason to suppose that these extremely clear visions that he had during his childhood were reminiscences of a clairvoyant sight which no cause could have determined.

"In early childhood I was much given to day dreams, as many only children of active imaginations are. Two scenes have haunted me many hundred times, I am sure, though as I attained manhood they faded and were only recollected as childhood's dreams. I will describe each of them. They were two of my dominant scenes to the inner visual organs in childhood.

1. A large village lying northward, with heaving plain and woodlands in the back. In front there is a little stream crossed by a small bridge. It is looked at from a hill. There is one church in that village, and a road going north, and a park to the east. I have thought of that village a hundred times and peopled it with imaginary people and quaint adventures, as children will. Now when I was an undergraduate in Oxford my mother suggested my going to visit Adderbury, which had been connected with our family since 1800, and where she had spelled some of her childhood, staying with her uncle who dwelt there. She intended going herself there, but was prevented. Still she told me to go there and see the old place, full of her childhood's memories. I did so one winter's day. I came to a low hill and there before me was almost exactly the scene of my childhood's dreams-the large village, the little stream, the park, the woodlands, and the church. Now my mother had never described to me Adderbury. It is curious I should have thought of it, for, spending my childhood in Devon, I had conceived a typical Oxfordshire village, totally unlike any place I had seen in childhood.

2. Another scene was more curious and more persistent. It was a large village near the sea facing eastwards. The hill is very steep-so steep that you must descend part of the way by steps. The houses are in terraces one over the other. Above there is a woodland. I always thought I dwelt there and had a house on the north side. Hundreds of day dreams had I of that village and its steps and terraces, and blue sea, but my home was always on the north side and a little inland. Till last July, I never in all my journeys had seen any place

like that scene of my day dreams. I was then asked to visit Clovelly in North Devon, where my maternal ancestor (my great-grandmother was a Cary) had long lived. To my astonishment there were the terraces, the steep hill, the steps down to the sea facing eastward, and, to the north, Cary Court, where for ages our people had lived. I saw in the church seven of the Cary tombs. Clovelly is described in *Westward Ho*, which I only read some years ago for the first time, and the resemblance never struck me." [183]

In the following chapter we will find stories in which reminiscence is accompanied by circumstances that seem to indicate that we are now in presence of real memories of past lives.

---

[183] *Journal of the Society for Psychical Research*, vol. IV, no. 68, March 1890, pp. 230–231.

RECOLLECTIONS OF PREVIOUS LIVES

A SURE REMINISCENCE OF THE 18TH CENTURY · AWAKENING RECOLLECTIONS OF MRS. KATHERINE BATES · THE CASE OF LAURE RAYNAUD

THE SECRETARY of the Society for Psychical Research wrote:[184]

"The account was sent to us by an Associate of the Society, Mrs. Stapleton, of 46 Montagu Square, London, W. The writer is, she tells us, a person of strongly developed artistic sensibilities, and in particular a remarkably gifted musician. The name was given to us in confidence, and Mrs. Stapleton, who has known her intimately for many years, believes that this report of her experiences is a literally accurate one. It is of course probable that the apparently veridical features of the visions were derived from pictures or descriptions seen or heard and afterwards forgotten....

'I was born in Petersburg, of Russian parents, though from my father's side of mixed nationality, his mother having been French, a Parisian. I was a nervous, highly-strung child and up to about twelve years of age suffered from an almost continuous high temperature.

My earliest recollections were of a strange nature: every night, after I had been put to bed, I saw the door open and a strange woman come in, who glided up to my bedside and sat down on a chair, bending over to look at me. She had masses of gray hair, done up in a fashion quite unlike to the people I was accustomed to see, as was also her dress, of brown color with a flowery design, and around her neck and shoulders there was a white fichu, the ends of which

---

[184] *Journal of the Society for Psychical Research*, vol. XIII, no. 240, June 1907, pp. 90–96.

hung down in front. At first this apparition almost threw me into convulsions of terror, which were not lessened by any caresses bestowed upon me, and the assurance of my mother and nurse that ' there was no such woman ' as I described....

As my people appeared to me so unsympathetic about her, I finished by never mentioning her again, and tried not to betray even by a movement when she entered the room. But this only helped to strengthen the secret bond there was between us – or so it appeared to me. When I was about six years old an incident took place which threw me into a great agitation. My mother went to a fancy dress ball, and I entered her room just as she was dressed. I rushed forward with a shout of joy on seeing her: it was the dress of my silent friend ! I may mention here that she did not always appear in the same dress, but sometimes in a very beautiful blue or white one with gold and silver worked all over it. My mother wore the dress of the Louis XVI period. She seemed surprised at my appearing to recognize this dress, which certainly I could never have seen before; but being very anxious not to encourage what she termed my nervous fancy, she tried to make light of it, and not to refer to it again afterwards.

Thus, this apparition visited me daily till I was nearly ten years old. Sometimes she also came by day and watched me playing.

There was another curious fact of my early childhood: I had a great fancy for drawing, and being a very reticent, silent child, used to amuse myself for hours by inventing stories and illustrating them as I went along....

But all my figures wore knee breeches, long coats, buckled shoes, and wore their hair gathered at the back with a ribbon; and the ladies had enormous mountains of hair upon their heads, and wore dresses of the Louis XVI period. Yet I had never seen any pictures of this period....

Of course, every child, and even most grown-up people, may have a special sympathy for some figure in history, but mine was more than an ordinary sympathy, it was a cult, an obsession. I spent hours at the South Kensington Museum gazing at Marie-Antoinette's bust, examining her toilet-table with its little rouge pots, etc. I can honestly say that my happiest hours were spent in contemplating these treasures, though it was always with an emotion bordering on tears that I faced the bust of the queen.

However, life went on, I became very active, had many various interests, and the image of the queen faded a little out of my busy life; though when I did think of her, it was with an extraordinary affection; I felt that she was dearer to me than any one in the world. I very frequently dreamed of her, and though my dreams generally were very disconnected and intangible, whenever I dreamt of her it was in a most logical sequence, and, contrary to most dreams, I remembered every detail of it in the morning. These dreams represented a routine of daily life at some palace – always the same palace – but one I had never seen in reality.

About five years ago I was staying in a doctor's family at Margate. We were a very cheery party, and there certainly was nothing to suggest 'ghosts' in the house. One day, however, on entering my bedroom, I saw the same figure – Marie-Antoinette – standing by a small, rough deal table (there was no such table in my room); she supported herself with one hand against this table and looked up at me as I entered. It was the same face, yet a horrible change had taken place: it looked haggard and agonized, and her eyes, no longer radiant, fixed me with a strange, glassy look. Her hair, almost white, was parted in the center, and it was flat now, not as she wore it before. This time I could not restrain myself, I rushed forward with a sob, and, extending my arms, gasped: 'Marie-Antoinette!' But as I moved the apparition was gone. A year after this I went to Paris for the first time, and among other places, went to the Musée Grevin. I received a real shock on seeing there the exact reproduction of my vision at Margate, with every detail. It represented the Queen at the Conciergerie, only the wax face was unlike the one I had seen; it did not express any of the agony I noticed....

After this incident there was a period of constant dreams: the same palace or else a park; Marie-Antoinette playing billiards; Marie Antoinette playing cards with Louis XVI, Madame Elizabeth and myself; my playing on a spinet in a salon full of people, and Marie-Antoinette standing near, signing to the crowd to be silent, and so on. The odd part about these dreams was that I always saw myself in them as a boy, never as a girl.

This last summer I was staying at a small village not far from Versailles. The country of that part ought to have appeared quite new to me, as I had never been on the outskirts of Paris. But wherever I walked, St. Cloud, Marly, Versailles, I was haunted by the sensation that I had looked on all this scenery before. The very first time I went to Versailles I was accompanied by a servant who had to do her shopping there. When she had done all her commissions I suggested our looking at the Palace. When we got there the place was already shut. We walked round the outside of the palace, and, though I had not seen any plan of it, I found myself pointing out to the servant where used to be the king's apartments, where the queen's, etc. She asked me whether I knew the palace well. 'Oh, no,' I said, 'I have never been here before, and I don't know how I know all this, but I know!' In walking through the park the place was so familiar to me and seemed so full of some vague memories which no sooner I seemed to elucidate than they evaded me, that I trembled from emotion, feeling a horrible choking sensation at my throat....

The first thing I verified on entering was that I had perfectly correctly located the different wings of apartments inhabited formerly by Louis XVI and Marie-Antoinette. We wandered through endless suites of rooms, all more or less alike, and as nothing was written up anywhere to indicate any special room, it was impossible to find out anything except from the guide book. However, before my friends had been able to form any idea from the guide book, I stopped them in one particular room, seized by that same choking emotion as the day before, and I went straight to a little door which, being in a panel of the wall, would be hardly noticeable to any one not knowing it was there. 'There are rooms beyond, I must go in there !' I said. Just then one of the guides came up to us: 'Do you wish to see the petits appartements de Marie Antoinette?' and he unlocked the door for us. My friends were perfectly astounded at my knowledge of the place, and I found myself acting as guide to them better than the official guide, who only shows the public what is cataloged in the book, whereas I found doors leading to passages, leading to other rooms, without being able to explain how I knew. Even the guide was astonished, and thought I must have made extensive historical researches ! The place was just as I knew, as I expected it to be, and yet very much changed. I believe if I were left alone in those rooms and had my eyes shut, I could reconstruct on paper the exact disposition of the rooms as they were formerly furnished....'"

Trianon

"Trianon seemed to me even more familiar, though I missed a great many objects which I fancied should be there. The music room was the identical one I had seen in my dream when playing before the queen, only the chairs ought to have been placed in a different position. One other curious fact in connection with Trianon is this : I had often designed the monogram 'M.A.' underneath portraits of Marie-Antoinette, and as every one will see, there are many different ways [in which] this monogram can be drawn. But my monogram was always the same, and I found it to be the facsimile of the iron-wrought monogram on the staircase at Trianon. But what disturbed me frightfully in seeing Trianon is the crowd among which one is driven through the apartments by the guide. I feel almost certain that if I could pass a day or a night alone in those apartments, I should see people and scenes which have passed there before.

Of course many people have the sensation, on seeing a new place for the first time, that they have seen it before. There may even be a simple scientific explanation for this. But I not only remember these places, but before turning a corner I can tell what is beyond in absolute detail. For instance, of the Château at Marly little remains but ruins, and no guide book makes even mention of it. On going there for the first time I described to a friend what we should find around a bend in the road, and this was quite accurate.

In Paris itself I found less that seemed familiar to me, except that I can never pass through the Rue St. Honoré without a cold shudder down my back, and nothing could induce me to walk over a certain spot on the Place de la Concorde,—I always describe a circle round it, and have a horrible sensation of fear and horror of the entire square. One night, while sleeping at a hotel at the corner of the Rue St. Honoré, I had a horrible nightmare. I heard the savage howling of a mob, and on looking out of the window saw Marie-Antoinette pass in the tumbril, and myself in the crowd, struggling frantically to push my way through and shouting incessantly : 'The queen ! Let me get to the queen ! I must get to the queen ! ' And again I was under the scaffold, stabbing furiously at the legs of the executioner to prevent him from doing his gruesome work, while the crowd jostled me back. Then I gave a horrible shriek ... and that was the end of my dream. While staying near Versailles I several times saw Marie-Antoinette sit on a chair by my bed, and even a fortnight ago, now I am in England, I saw her sitting in a dejected attitude at my writing-desk in broad daylight. The vision lasted only some seconds.

I have tried to find some explanation, some solution to this mystery which has haunted me since my earliest childhood, but there seems no plausible explanation. I seemed on the point of reconstructing a consecutive remembrance of some former existence while in France, but no sooner do I seem to hold the thread [than] I lose it, which is a very painful sensation. But I have not yet lost hope that, on returning to France, I shall get nearer the solution of this haunting mystery."[185]

This narrative presents characteristics which make it possible to place it among those which offers proof of an earlier life. It is very remarkable that from her earliest youth the witness drew human characters, men or women, of the late 18th century, when she had never ever had a model before her. There is more than the feeling of déjà vu in the descriptions of the Palace of Versailles, since this lady knew in advance where were the apartments of Marie-Antoinette and, in Trianon, she recognized the room where, in a dream, she played the harpsichord. It is probable that it is not by means of clear-sightedness that she acquired this knowledge, because she also possesses it for the castle of Marly, of which there remain only ruins. This vision, almost constant from an early age, of Marie-Antoinette, suggests that there existed between this lady and the Queen of France previous rapports. Therefore I think this case deserves the most serious attention.

Awakening of recollections

Mrs. Emily Katherine Bates recounts the following case:[186]

"I must begin by confessing that I have for many years had a vague, floating impression, that a closer tie than usual binds me to an ancestor of my own – to be quite honest, I have sometimes thought that I might be carrying on his life at the present moment. I have absolutely no ground for such an assumption except an extraordinary feeling of affinity with a man who died many years before my birth and of whom (through force of circumstances) nobody has ever spoken to me. So far the matter is very plain sailing

---

185 *Op. cit., ibid.*, pp. 95–96.
186 E. K. Bates, *Do the Dead Depart?* (New York: Dodge Publishing Co., 1908), pp. 153–157; 159–151.

– simply a case of imagination, strengthening as years have passed and fully accounting for a curious coincidence in an experience I had once with a clairvoyant, whom I visited for the first time, when I was quite unknown in English psychic circles. Some letters written by this ancestor when a young and dashing Life Guardsman, more than a hundred years ago, had been unearthed in our solicitor's office and I had been allowed a sight of them. The morning they arrived I was visiting this clairvoyant and thought I would take one of the old-fashioned large squares of discolored ancient letter paper and see what came of it through psychometry.... Naturally I expected that these would at once and obviously, refer to the age of the letter and to the opening years of the nineteenth century. Nothing of the kind occurred. The character of the writer was the only fact demonstrated or apparently observed by the psychometrist, who evidently realized that the writer was not alive but made no special point of this fact until she said at the end of her character reading, *'This was a crowning incarnation, I think.'*[187] ...

'I was mistaken in saying about the other spirit that it was a crowning incarnation. They tell me that spirit is incarnated again here in the writer of this note, and that this is a far more favorable incarnation.'

'Far less favorable,' I said, 'so far as money and position are concerned.'

'Bah! what do we think or care about that?" she answered, evidently under some control [i.e., spirit guide]; 'it is far more favorable for spiritual development — that is the only thing that really matters." ...

Now it will be naturally and quite reasonably suggested that this clairvoyant (Mrs. Howarth) read my own impression and was reproducing it in a slightly dramatic form. Granted—but I have something further to tell, which happened several years later and does not admit of the same interpretation ..."

---

187 We thus see that the idea of reincarnation is not so unknown in England as it has often been asserted in France.

Mrs. Bates recounts that she had promised one of her friends, Mrs. Bigelow, to visit Broadway during her vacation. She was completely unaware of this village in Worcestershire, and even said she had never heard the name. However, with one of her cousins, she went there, and this is what she felt. But here let her resume the story:

> "It seemed to me as though I knew the place just as well as if I had been born there and had come back to revisit the scenes of my childhood. Several times before rounding a corner I said quite naturally, 'Oh, I know what there is here. It is only some farm buildings or an old barn (as the case might be). It is no use going on here. Let us turn back.' ...
> It was only when three or four times my remarks had proved true that either she or I recognized there was anything odd about them. It all seemed so natural to me and so fanciful to her, even when she was forced to admit that it was *'rather queer.'* There was not a shadow of doubt that I had never been in the place before, nor even heard of it, and *she knew it no better than I did, except by name.*
> Now I must mention that in my ancestor's old-fashioned letters, written in his youth and some of them from Worcester where he had been sent with a sergeant as a recruiting-officer in those past days, there had been several mentions of General Lygon who commanded the Second Life Guards at the time. I think he may have been Colonel Lygon then and he had doubtless taken a fancy to the handsome young officer under his command, who was asked in consequence to balls and other festivities. *'Just been staying with my colonel for a few days'* was a fairly constant remark in his letters; but there was no mention of the special locality and as I knew this General Lygon had later become the first Lord Beauchamp, I naturally concluded that these visits were paid to Madresfield Court, the Beauchamp property in the neighborhood of Malvern."

Mrs. Bates assumes that the deceased ancestor with whom she sympathized could have sent her all information about

Broadway by suggestion, but she insinuates that she is also inclined to admit that these are personal memories awaken in her when she visited the village of Broadway, England.

This theory of reincarnation, she says, is not illogical, since it makes it possible to understand individual progress through successive lifetimes.

It seems that we are in presence of two kinds of phenomena which confirm the theory of evolution, since a psychometrist detects in the two different written texts submitted to her the same spiritual author; and that afterwards, Mrs. Bates recognizes herself in the Broadway village, where her ancestor had come so often to Colonel Lygon's home, before he lived in Madresfield Court.

The case of Laure Raynaud

The interesting story about the reincarnation case of Mrs. Laure Raynaud was very well observed and described by Dr. Gaston Durville.

This research was published for the first time in the French journal *Psychic Magazine* of January 1914, and later reproduced by the *Le Fraterniste*. The following are its essential parts in condensed form, since the lack of space does not allow me to reproduce it in full.

Laure Raynaud died at the age of forty-five. Thanks to her remarkable power, she had cured a crowd of disinherited people. The healed sick, who are legion, keep an eternal gratitude to her. Here is what Dr. Durville, who knew Raynaud particularly well, since she was employed by his clinic and a former student of the Hector Durville School of Magnetism in Paris, tells us about her:

> "The story I am about to tell here may seem strange to many people unfamiliar with our psychical studies. To the psychists themselves, or at least to some of them, it will not fail to seem very delicate to interpret. In any case, I hope that

it will be seen as the result of an impartial study, and that it will at least have the merit of being the faithful report of facts lived in my immediate surroundings.

Strange as it is, this is the story of the unforeseen facts that built it and, in terms of its interpretation, it poses a whole philosophical problem. Since facts of this kind are exceptional at first, and then those which have already been recounted are sometimes too hastily reported and insufficiently complete, I wished to set forth this curious case in detail: I have endeavored to report as much as possible the exact words of the witnesses and, to give the readers maximum guarantees, I quoted in full the name and address of these witnesses. I sincerely hope that this method becomes widespread, we are no longer at the time when we had to hide in order to deal with psychism.

Only one of the actors of the story preferred to be designated only by his initial; I graciously acceded to his wish, regretting, however, his reserve. I will call him Mr. G. I regret even more not to mention his name as it is one of the most famous and most considered personalities of Genoa, Italy. Finally, as this narrative does not have the pretension to lead to a scientific proof of what it advances, and as it is, in short, only a series of coincidences, I did not want to mention either in full the name of the family where Mrs. Raynaud's personality had lived in a previous life, and I will name her by her first name and the first letter of her surname Giovanna S. The family F. lives, indeed, whatever we say, in Genoa. I do not know them, I have nothing to do with them; they could therefore be aghast at seeing their family name mingled with a story of reincarnation. I want to point out to readers that the ideas that follow are not mine; by telling them I will set aside my own personality and my scientific and philosophical conceptions. I wanted to act as a passive data recorder that takes notes and transcribes facts. I hope to have reached my goal. I have similarly sought to be impartial. As for the interpretation of the facts, I attempted to give support to every valid materialistic motive, whether as illusions or transmissions of thought. As for the materialistic explanation of theories of reincarnation, and the spiritualistic explanation, I will consider these hypotheses by discussing them. Besides, I have neither the intention nor the foolish pretension of wanting to settle the issue. I leave this study to my fellow psychists, should they want to delve into it and tell me what they think.

When she was still very young, it seems that Laure was not like all the children of her age. Her mother, a brave woman who was in her fifties, was kind enough to come to see me in Paris and told me, 'My daughter Laure had ideas in her early years that we did not understand, that she made herself without being taught them. She often bothered us with her stories, and I told her she would go crazy if she kept thinking that way.' She knew that the precepts taught by the priests at the church were untrue and her ideas were so obstinate, so decided, that she stubbornly refused to go to Mass with her family on Sunday. 'To lead her to Mass,' continues her old mother, 'it took a good hiding.' And the 'good hiding' (i.e., the whip) would not prevail over the child's ideas. The village priest was interested in Laure, because she was clever and he liked to come to see her and talk to her. Little Laure denied the existence of paradise, purgatory and hell, and told him that the spirit after death returns to earth in another body. Then the priest became angry and murmured between his teeth: 'Strange child! Mysterious little girl!' And went away musing without ever getting the child to repent, but instead exclaim with a big pout, 'Fair enough, I won't say anything anymore.'

This priest exercises his ministry at Auront, in the Somme (France), native homeland of Laure Raynaud. He is an old man of seventy-two years, called Géimbard. The 'weird' ideas of little Laure did not go away as she grew older. When language allowed her to express them better, they became more precise. At the age of seventeen, she came to Ariens. There, she was haunted by the idea of touching the sick to heal them, and to her inner circle, to her neighbors, she expounded, at the hours of confidences spent together, her conceptions of survival. I will not tell anything else about this period, and instead move on to 1904, the year she got married.

It was easy for me to reconstruct the ideas of Laure Raynaud from that moment on, thanks to her friends that I could find. Laure Raynaud knew that humans have an immaterial spiritual principle that survives death. But this survival does not happen in a distant paradise or hell; it is on earth that the soul returns to reincarnate, having lived for years a celestial life. Laure Raynaud knew all this; she remembered having already lived and she enjoyed talking about her previous life. Her memory was not complete, she knew only a few passages, some circumstances of that existence, but these passages, these circumstances, had for her an unparalleled clarity.

The house where she had lived, or rather the outside of it, the surrounding park, the surroundings, the azure blue sky, all this was present in her mind like a shiny photographic print. She said that she could recognize her home as easily as a lover of paintings would recognize a canvas of their liking. She saw herself in this previous existence, but she knew nothing of the minute details of her life; she saw herself at twenty-five years of age and gave a precise description of herself at that time. As for her family, she did not remember them.

Her husband, Mr. Pierre Raynaud, who lives in at Petrarque Street, in Paris, expressed to me his memories of his wife's feelings and ideas:

'You know how very skeptical I am regarding many psychical phenomena. Well, even so I have to admit that there are some very odd things in my wife's reincarnation story. As far as I am concerned personally, I can assure you that Mrs. Raynaud told me since the beginning of our relationship the facts relating to a life she had previously lived. I do not remember exactly what she told me; nevertheless, I know that she often spoke of a sort of photographic projection she had of herself. She saw herself young and sick in her chest, wandering in a large park, in a country which she could not name, but whose sky was pure and clear, a country in the South of Europe, no doubt. If you bear in mind that Mrs. Raynaud, although born in the North, has a distinctly southern type, a dull skin, very brown hair, you would say like those who see her for the first time that she comes from the South. My wife gives the following explanation for this: her type comes from her previous life. I remember perfectly well that she was thinking of one day finding her country. Now, in what she has discovered on her trip to Genoa, there are things that strangely coincide with what she told me in the past'

An old friend of Mrs. Raynaud, Mrs. Dutilleu, who lives at 2, Dammartin Street, at Amiens, mentioned to me a story analogous to that which Mrs. Raynaud have narrated to me. Moreover, I have found some new details in it.

'It was during the long evenings that we spent together', she told me, 'that my friend detailed her other life to me, passed away so quickly under a sky which was more hospitable than ours. She complained of the cold weather of the North: her country had a different, warmer, happier sun.' The years went by, and Laure Raynaud finally fulfilled her childhood dream of touching the sick to heal them – and she got remarkable healings. Word of her cures spread like wildfire. Both rich and poor were piling up in her living room on Enguerrand Street, in Amiens, to find relief for their illnesses. The most prominent people in the region, judges, lawyers, even doctors, came to consult with her. But soon Mrs. Raynaud, no longer pleased at staying in Amiens, wished to come to Paris; and then, at the very moment of her greatest success, at the time when her supporters worshiped her like a goddess, she abruptly left her clients. We contacted her in Paris ... she came! It was to perfect her healer's knowledge that she moved to the French capital. She enrolled in the practical school of magnetism – that is where I met her. I quickly noticed her remarkable healing faculties; so in 1911 I offered her the direction of my health center, which she accepted.

What Mrs. Raynaud told Mr. Durville in 1911

Since 1911 I have worked alongside Mrs. Raynaud; therefore I was able to follow her daily routine and study at length her curious faculties and original ideas. I can say that she is in perfectly balanced mental state. She is not a psychopath; she has no hallucinations, no morbid ideas; she is a calm and reasonable person; she has great faith in the therapeutic power of her hands. But the results that I saw her get at my health center allowed her to increase her self-confidence. She is also wonderfully intuitive, and has predicted in advance many events in my life that nothing could have anticipated. In spite of this I admit I am not convinced of everything she says, especially her statements about successive lives. I would need strong evidence and what I have collected cannot be considered to be more than a series of interesting coincidences, in my hitherto unexpressed opinion. Mrs. Raynaud spoke to me many times about her last previous life, but I attached little importance to these stories, since I did not see the possibility of any verification. Mrs. Raynaud told me that she had already lived before. She had certainly lived in a country in the South; her house was large, very large, much larger than ordinary houses, with a terrace on the front, a large terrace; the windows were wide, numerous, and arched at the top; there were two floors and another terrace upstairs.

It was on this terrace that she loved to walk, a young, dark woman, with very black, big eyes. She felt sad because she was very seriously ill. She was coughing and was about to die from a lung and chest condition. Her character was proud, haughty, severe, almost wicked; the disease had no doubt embittered her. She was nonchalant and liked to wander, idly, in the private park. This park was planted with old trees; she went uphill; behind and on the sides: there were some small houses inhabited by a group of workers. Death surprised her soon, maybe at twenty-five years of age. She was waning thin, pale and exhausted. More than half a century passed during which she lived beyond the earth. Then she reincarnated in the village of Aumont, in the Somme, France. That is what I heard from her many times.

The testimony of Princess Fazyl

In June 1912, Princess Fazyl (or Fazil), who lives in Paris, at 116 Rue de la Faisanderie, was at home tired. She had stretched out on a bed. Madame Raynaud kept her company. Then the princess began to evoke memories of childhood, Egypt with the sky of fire, with its mimosa woods, its tamarisks, its pomegranates, its fig trees, its palms; and the Nile, the beneficent Nile with the green or red waters that the black-headed ibis comes to visit. And by the river, the big house of her family, white, with its garden going down up to the water. 'And I too,' added Mrs. Raynaud, 'have known a country full of sun, but not in this existence.' And she told the princess her memories of her previous life, of herself, of her house, of her country.

'I don't know if it was in Egypt that I lived. Yet no, I don't remember a big river; it would be Italy instead; besides, I always knew that I would one day return to this country and I know that I will recognize it, so much the images that I have in my mind are clear before my eyes.' And the princess smiled at hearing this, not of incredulity, but of surprise.

How Mrs. Raynaud found her house

Things went no further and months passed away. I was always in accord with Mrs. Raynaud's ideas regarding her previous life insofar as the relative value of her dream could have granted, until an unforeseen circumstance occurred. At the beginning of March 1913, I received a letter from Genoa (Italy), requesting my presence by the side of a lady belonging to the Genoese aristocracy. At that time we were in the middle of the second International Congress of Experimental Psychology, and I was very busy chairing my commission and following a contest. I could not leave Paris. Fortunately, the patient in question was very fond of Mrs. Raynaud. She had already been magnetized by her at my health center in Paris. So I asked Mrs. Raynaud to go to Italy. The trip must have been filled with curious surprises. Arriving at Turin, Mrs. Raynaud had the vague impression that the country was not unknown to her. It seemed to her that she had already seen sites like those unfolding before her eyes. Yet she had never been to Italy, nor had she read any books about this country, nor did she believe that she had seen pictures of it; and the express train kept rolling on. It finally arrived at Genoa. There, what hitherto had been for Mrs. Raynaud only an impression became a certainty. She really knew this country: it was there that she had lived in a previous existence. When she arrived at her host's, she told them about her thoughts and her desire to go in search of her house.

The excellent Mr. C., a scholarly psychist and convinced spiritualist, immediately offered to help Mrs. Raynaud in her quest. Knowing Genoa thoroughly, he asked Mrs. Raynaud to give him all description of her house that she could; and to repeat to him her story already mentioned above.

'There is, not in Genoa itself,' said Mr. C, 'but nearby, a large house, which seems to me to correspond to the shape, the location, and the architecture that you have just described. Let us go there.' And Mr. C. asked Mrs. Raynaud to come with him. They got into a car and crossed Genoa. Soon the car stopped in front of a big white house. 'No, not that one,' said Mrs. Raynaud, 'but I know this place very well and my home is not far from here. Let's go, we will find, by turning on the left, a road that goes up, and from this road we will see through the trees what we are looking for.' The car advanced according to the indications given by Mrs. Raynaud, and indeed, they found a road on the left spreading in a rather steep slope until a beautiful white house which corresponded to the given description, with a big quadrilateral building with a large terrace down below, another terrace above, and numerous, wide and arched windows at the top, of Italian Renaissance style. There was an uncultivated park ahead, descending backward: 'Ah!' said Mr. C. 'this is the family S.'s house, a very well-known family in Genoa.' 'That's where I lived,' added Mrs. Raynaud, 'it is there, on that terrace, that I walked feeble, sick of the chest – I was very ill, I was sad. It is there that I died in the flower of my age, a century ago.' Then the car took away Mr. C . and Mrs. Raynaud satisfied with their discovery. Now they were going to look for documentary evidence."

IN GENOA A DEATH CERTIFICATE IS FOUND WHICH WOULD BE THAT OF MRS. RAYNAUD

"Back at our friends' house, at dinner. Mrs. Raynaud gave details of her find and spoke with pleasure of some memories of her previous existence, then adding, 'I know that I am not buried like everyone else in the cemetery; I am convinced that my body rests in a church.' Everyone was completely baffled.

But time was pressing. Mrs. Raynaud had completed her mission in Genoa; it was necessary for her to come back to France. I was in great need of her to magnetize my patients, and she, for her part, wished to come back before the end of the International Congress of Experimental Psychism. She returned. Then I was informed of all the surprising events that her trip had in store for her, and I immediately decided to take notes, as far as possible, for the control of everything my colleague was reporting to me. There were several interesting points to verify.

First of all:

– Had there ever been in the house in question, in Genoa, a lady who could be identified with the hypothetical one of Mrs. Raynaud, a brown-haired woman, chronically sick, who had died from her chest about a century ago?

Figure 6. LAURE RAYNAUD

Figure 7. GIOVANNA SPONTINI'S HOUSE RECOGNIZED BY RAYNAUD

– If this person did exist, where is her grave?

Equipped with these questions, my friends conducted long researches in Genoa, which resulted in very strange corroborations. The church of San Francesco d'Albaro, in Genoa, keeps in its records the death certificates of the persons who died in the house indicated by Mrs. Raynaud as once being her own. In these minutes, my friend discovered a death certificate of which he sent me a copy and which I reproduce in full, except for the surname which I designate by the letter D. In it, we can read:

1st) That it refers to a woman who was always sickly, which is consistent with what Mrs. Raynaud had said;

2nd) That this woman seemed to have died from a chest condition, since it is said that she died of a cold; the expression dying of cold was usually synonymous with dying of pulmonary tuberculosis. This is also in accordance with Mrs. Raynaud's statements;

3rd) That the death goes back about a century, exactly on October 23, 1809. This is also consistent;

4th) That the body of the deceased is buried in a church; which is also consistent.

Finally, note that nothing in the certificate contradicts what Mrs Raynaud had affirmed."

Excerpt from the death certificate of the parish of San Francesco d'Albaro, Genoa

"On October 23, 1809, the lady Giovanna S., widow of B.,[188] for several years living in her residence, chronically ill, and whose health condition had deteriorated in recent days as a result of a strong chill caught in cold weather, died on the 21st, having received the sacraments of the Church, and today, on our written permission and, with permission of the

---

188 [Trans. note] Giovanna Spontini, widow of Benjamino Spontini.

Mayor also in writing, her body has been transported with a private service into the church of the Madonna del Monti. (*The undersigned*)."

One of Dr. Durville's subjects, Mrs. d'Elphes, completes the evidence given by Mrs. Raynaud

"When I received from Genoa the death certificate which would be that of Mrs. Raynaud's previous life, it was about 9 o'clock in the morning; I was at the table and I was having breakfast. I was particularly late that day for my daily activities. Several patients were waiting for me. In hastily swallowing the contents of my cup of milk, I also hastily opened my mail, just taking a look at the length, the writing, the nature and the signature of the correspondence, I would leave the details for later. The death certificate had the same fate as the other letters; the letter with the Italian stamps and the handwriting of my friend from Genoa indicated to me the origin of the document and its nature. I saw the header, a few words of the text, then the signatures, nothing else. I closed the document and threw it on the table with the other correspondence, so I could see my patients. During the course of the morning, the idea of the death certificate came back to my mind. I mentioned it to a friend who asked me for details. I told him something like this: 'I did not read the document, I only know that it comes from Genoa, it's an excerpt from a parish, but I don't know which one, only the first name of the deceased (who would have been Mrs. Raynaud), which is Giovanna, I also believe that the name of the family begins with D, That's all I know.'

Then the idea came to my mind of sending the Genoese certificate to one of my subjects who had clear-sightedess to check if it could reveal some interesting facts, but to avoid as much as possible the transmission of thought – this big pitfall of clairvoyance – I wanted to make sure that nobody around me could read the content of the document. By knowing the certificate, it would have been possible, who knows how, to act telepathically on the subject magnetically asleep, and perhaps to interfere in the nature of the result. So I took the letter and, without throwing my eyes on the writing again, I put it inside the envelope and then sealed it. I alone had seen it in Paris, and from it I only knew the few words we read before. I was just going to receive one of my subjects, Mrs. d'Elphes, who lived at 49, Falguière Street, in Paris, to put her into magnetic sleep and give her the document, without saying a word about what I wanted her to do.

Sitting of May 28, 1913. — I put Mrs. d'Elphes into magnetic sleep, and without having told her a single word about what I wish to know, I give her the sealed envelope which contains the death certificate. I sit at my desk, take my pen and write down everything the subject says, without saying yes or no, or if it is wrong or right. I transcribe here my notes as I read them on my notebook of experiments: 'This letter comes from far away ... Wait till I orient myself ... Let's see, it is by there ...' (she points to the South). Yes, But, oh, it's far; I leave France, but without crossing the sea ... Ah! I am there now: it is Italy, there is the sea nearby, a port, it is Genoa. (Since I started experimenting with asleep subjects, this is only the second time a subject can tell me the exact name of a city. In another series of experiments, this same subject told me that a letter I had handed her was from Grenoble, and it was right.)

(Silence) ... 'Here! Here I am in a big house; what a beautiful house; it is white, tall, without being too large, but what is this style? I see large windows and above smaller ones, which are arched (up to here everything rigorously coincides with the statements made by Mrs. Raynaud ...) To the left, looking at the facade, I see a round tower (this is inaccurate) ... It is accessed by several steps in a large paved hall. The house is on a slope, the garden goes up behind, everything around the house looks down' (all this is very accurate on the photograph I published of the house, we do not see the main facade, so not the steps, we could not do it otherwise). 'But what should I find in this house?' Mrs. d'Elphes asks me, 'I see a lot of people there—' Look for,' I say, 'a lady who is mentioned in the paper that you hold. 'A lady ... Ah! Yes, I see her, but she's dead, that lady.' 'Could you tell me her name?' A name, now, that is very difficult. (She searches, sighs, and then) 'I don't know if I'm wrong, I see Giovanna.' 'And the Family name?' 'Wait, I have several (Sic"), Broglio, I find that this name is related to what interests us; I can't look for it with my eyes, I can still see two that start with an M. would it be Modena? Medici? (All this is wrong). Here, I now see an S. and a seven-letter name, the second letter might be an A, and I see two F's in the middle of the name. (Fairly accurate.). Then the subject gets tired, and I wake her up.

Sitting of June 4, 1913. — I put Mrs. d'Elphes into magnetic sleep; when she is in somnambulic state, I give her the same sealed envelope that contains the death certificate and say only, 'Well, resume your story where you left it in the previous sitting.' Then Mrs. d'Elphes says, after a few moments, 'Ah! I'm there again, I see Giovanna there in the big house at Genoa. Here, but how sick she is ... She coughs ... And she is not very sweet in character ... She has a haughty character, but I do not see her living for much longer, I see her dead.' ... (silence) ... 'So who do I see?' (All so far is in accordance with the description Mrs. Raynaud had given me of herself.) 'Go on,' said I, 'to see the lady Giovanna.' 'What do you want me to see in her? Ah! Wait, but it seems to me that she is not buried like everyone else in a graveyard.' 'Not in a graveyard! So where can she be buried?' 'But, doctor, I do not know if I am mistaken, yet it seems to me that I see her in a church.' (I think it is interesting to note that until then my subject had only told me things known to me. Here is where the real revelations begin.)

In a church? "Yes," continues Madame d'Elphes, "the church is rectangular, almost square, with columns at the entrance, and pillars further on. The lady Jeanne is there in a tomb; the tomb is very near the altar, it is rather modest; the stone is not horizontal, it is vertical, and behind it I see seven coffins. They contain people from Jeanne's family and her casket at her is located quite left against the wall ... That's all I see, I'm tired. Ah! I have an idea! Does not this lady Jeanne have descendants in France ... in the South ... I see many of them. I do not know anything about it (the meeting was long, I wake up Madame d'Elphes.)

Mrs. Raynaud had never told me that after her short life she had been buried in a church. So I wanted to find out if the somnambulic subject was right. I unsealed the envelope containing the death certificate of Giovanna S. and read: 'Her body has been transported with a private service into the church of the Madonna del Monti.' Had I read the certificate unconsciously before sealing it in the envelope, and was the revelation provided by my subject just a reading phenomenon of my thoughts deep in my brain? Who knows? In any case, what concerns the description of the church was certainly not read by Mrs. d'Elphes in my subconscious, since I could not possibly know it. I did not know how the church of the Madonna del Monti was built or looked like, because I have never been to Genoa.

To check if my somnambulic subject's vision was right, I wrote to my Genoese friend, sending him a copy of the story told by her, and asking him to see for himself what was true in these revelations. A few days later I received a letter from which I will now quote the following passage:

> *'Dear friend and doctor,*
>
> I went Sunday morning to the church you mentioned; it is located at a certain distance from Genoa. The surroundings are not of easy access. I could not conduct all necessary investigations, the church being busy in the service of masses. I searched in vain for the tomb in question, near the high altar located in the crypt which was crowded with people at the time. The church is indeed rectangular, almost square, with columns at the entrance and pillars

afterwards. I'm going back there one day next week and make an inquiry of the same person who assisted me in my first search.'

Therefore the story of my subject seemed to contain an inaccuracy (the place of the tomb). The rest was exact.

A few days later I received new information from Genoa. My friend C. had gone back to the church outside the hours of religious service. Here is a passage from his letter:

'Please find attached a photograph of the church; I could not get it otherwise because of the topographic location of the building. There is indeed, as your seeing subject told you, a tomb; it belongs to the S[pontini] family. It is not located next to the altar, it is located beneath it. It is accessed by a staircase.'

This letter corrected part of the previous one. There was indeed a tomb in the church. The location alone was inaccurate. I could not find out the number of deceased persons buried in this tomb, nor the place occupied by Giovanna's remains. That was very regrettable.

Writing again to my Genoese friend, I specifically requested him to inquire whether the family S. had descendants in the South of France. After several weeks, he replied:

'There is no member of the S. family in the South of France; but there are some in the Principality of Monaco, which is not far from the South of France.' (Indeed.)

Sitting of June 11, 1913. — Subject: Mrs. d'Elphes. Experimenter: Dr. Gaston Durville. Witnesses: André Durville, Mrs. Raynaud.

I put Mrs. d'Elphes into magnetic sleep. As before, when she enters the somnambulic state, I ask her to return to Genoa. Then, spontaneously, she says:

'But Giovanna is now reincarnated, I feel attracted to the North of France, in a land of plains; it is a very small village, a country, but very near a big town. Why do I see this village? I see as a rainbow that unites the church where Giovanna's body rests to the village.'

'But what's the meaning of this rainbow?' I ask.

'It means that there is a close relation between the two countries it touches. Yes, it is in this village that the lady Giovanna has reincarnated.'

'But how do you expect me to recognize a village in the north of France with the description you gave me of it?'

'Wait, in the big town I see a rather important river, and then a beautiful church. Ah! It is so beautiful that church. I see a big Gothic cathedral.' (Silence.) 'But I know it, this cathedral is the cathedral of Amiens. Then Giovanna is reincarnated in a small village near Amiens. Yes, definitely.'

'Could you describe her house?'

'Wait, I'm looking for it! Ah! Here it is, how odd it is, it has nothing beautiful in this house; you know, what a difference with that of Genoa, it's a very, very simple little house.'

'Enter the house and tell me what you can see.'

'I'm entering a large room directly after climbing two or three straight steps; I can see another room and, in front, a wooden staircase leading to the attic.' (There is in this statement an inaccuracy, we will see it later.) 'In the house I see a little girl; it is she who interests me, it is she who is Giovanna reincarnated; but why did she reincarnate in such a modest house? I see her parents, they are good simple peasants. Well, but what do I see now? Suddenly, I've just seen the little girl turn all blue.' (I do not understand anything about this episode.)

'*All blue*, what does it mean? Is her body blue?'

'No, I mean she's all dressed in blue; she's in blue clothes, blue stockings. But whatever that means, no doubt it's a symbol.

'I don't think so. That's not a symbol, it means only that the child is dressed in blue.'

'Have you ever seen children dressed in blue?'

'Of course. In the countryside, children are frequently dressed in blue; and thus dressed until the age of nine.'

(Surprised at what I have just heard, I glance at Mrs. Raynaud who is sitting behind me in an armchair; she beckons to me silently that what the seeing subject has said is very accurate and that I must let her proceed.)

'Then explain to me why this little girl is wearing blue.'

'Now I see the child grew older; she is dressed like everyone else. I see her leaving her native homeland early. She goes to the nearby town, no doubt, but she does not stay there either; I see her now ... Ah! ...' (The subject is astonished and continues ...) 'Hey, who's coming in here?' (No one has come in with us, it is my brother André Durville who made a noise while stirring.)

'No, no, I don't say someone has come in here with us. It's the lady.'

'The lady? What lady? the reincarnate Giovanna?'

'Yes, precisely ... she is here, I can see her. Ah! But –' (she goes toward Mrs. Raynaud) Oh! But – is this possible? – she's blended with her!'

'What do you mean? You're hallucinating.'

'No, I assure you: I'm made to understand that Giovanna and Mrs. Raynaud are the same person.'

'What do you mean the same person?'

'Perfectly so, can't you see? Ah! I understand now. Tell me, was not Mrs. Raynaud born near Amiens? So, that's it, it's good of you that it was like that. Were you dressed in blue when you were a child?'

'Yes, indeed,' answers Mrs. Raynaud. (At this point the subject is tired, so I wake her up.)"

Curious statements

"The sittings of May 28 and June 4 had been very curious. Mrs. d'Elphes, without knowing anything of the history of Mrs. Raynaud, had made an interesting description of the places she would have inhabited. Then she had indicated the existence in this place of a lady, Giovanna, who coincided with the report given by Mrs. Raynaud. She then revealed that this lady, Giovanna, was buried in a church.

In the sitting of June 11, Mrs. d'Elphes informed us that Giovanna had reincarnated in a village near Amiens, gave us a description of the birthplace, affirmed that Giovanna, now reincarnated as a child, was dressed in blue, and finally concluded: Giovanna reincarnated and is now Mrs. Raynaud. Let me talk about this last sitting. The subject tells us that Giovanna is reincarnated in a small village near Amiens. Well, Mrs. Raynaud was actually born in Aumont, twenty-five miles from Amiens; the subject could not know this detail beforehand. As for the description of the birthplace, the subject said things that correspond to the place where Mrs. Raynaud was born ... I was able to verify it thereafter by going to Aumont. The house has, indeed, a very modest aspect. We enter straight into the main room where we can see another room on the right – but the staircase indicated by the seeing subject does not exist. Also, there is only one step at the door instead of two or three."

Dr. Gaston Durville, having inquired Mrs. Raynaud's mother, learned that Laure Raynaud had been devoted to wearing blue after a novena which had coincided with her recovery.

The critical remarks with which Dr. Gaston Durville followed the story of Mrs. Laure Raynaud does not seem to me sufficient to completely eliminate the hypothesis of a previous life of the subject. Indeed, it is hardly possible to reject the testimony of Laure Raynaud's mother, when she asserts that her daughter spoke to the priest about her past existence. We have already found that some children have the intuition of having lived before, and we will see that there are others who have retained indisputable memories of their past lives. Therefore, the objection that claims that an ignorant child would be able to formulate such complicated thinking is hardly sound or valid.

There is a possibility that when she heard people say that she had a southern type, Laure Raynaud imagined that she was born in a country in the South of France, under the beautiful blue sky of Italy. It could still be, and this is the most serious objection, that during her sleep she has by clairvoyance visited the country of her dreams, and that she has accidentally stopped in the neighborhood of Genoa, in front of the house of which she gives, before having seen it, so exact a description. Even so, this would already be a curious case of lucidity, but this hypothesis is far from accounting for all the circumstances. In fact, it does not explain Laure Raynaud's knowledge that a lady of the beginning of the 19th century would have died of a chest illness in this house, or that she was buried in a church, let alone the certainty that Mrs. Raynaud had during her childhood of having lived previously.

From the examination of the facts, it seems to follow that the most probable hypothesis – because it is the one which best explains all the incidents of this remarkable case – is that of Laure Raynaud's preexistence.

Dr. Gaston Durville is not systematically hostile to this, since he says in closing his study: "So, is this a case of reincarnation? I admit that I do not know, but I find that the reincarnationist hypothesis is not in this case more absurd than any other. Illusion, autosuggestion, lucidity, clairvoyance, do not explain everything. Maybe they have been used to explain too many things. There is room for other hypotheses; that of reincarnation is in their number."

Yes, indeed, dear doctor; and it is indisputably the best of all theories.

11

OTHER FACTS INVOLVING REMEMBRANCE OF PAST LIVES

GREAT PERSONAGES WHO REMEMBER HAVING LIVED PREVIOUSLY · JULIAN THE APOSTATE · EMPEDOCLES - LAMARTINE - PONSON DU TERRAIL - JOSEPH GRATRY · JOSEPH MÉRY · PROFESSOR DAMIANI AND OTHERS · THE CASE OF NELLIE FOSTER · INNATE KNOWLEDGE OF A FOREIGN COUNTRY · THE RANGOON CASE OF MAUNG KAN · CASES TAKEN FROM DR. CALDERONE'S INQUIRY ON REINCARNATIONS IN INDIA · DR. MOUTIN'S CONFIRMATORY SURVEY · PROFESSOR TUMMOLO · THE TUCKER CASES · LE MESSAGER OF LIÈGE · BLANCHE COURTAIN · THE CASE OF HAVANA · ESPLUGAS CABRERA · SUMMARY

I WILL REPRODUCE BELOW facts that I have assembled in the memoir on successive lives presented at the London Congress of 1898. Then, I will have them followed by observations collected ever since.

Roman emperor Julian the Apostate remembered having been Alexander the Great. Greek philosopher Empedocles also said that he remembered being a boy and a girl. But since we know nothing about the circumstances which could determine these affirmations, we shall move on to the writers of our day and age, who relate facts of the same order.

Among modern names, the great poet Lamartine claims, in his book *Travels in the East*,[189] to have had very clear reminiscences. Here is his testimony:

"I had neither the Bible nor any book of travels in my hand, nor any person to give me an account of the place, and the ancient name of valley and the mountains; but my boyish

---

189 [Trans. note] A. de LAMARTINE, *Travels in the East* (New trans. Edinburgh: William & Robert Chambers, 1839), p. 77.

imagination had so vividly and with such truth conceived the form of the localities, the physical aspect of the scenes of the Old and the New Testament, from the descriptions in the holy books, that I recognized, at a glance, the valley of turpentines, and the battle field of Saul. When we got to the convent, I had only to hear the exactitude of my ideas confirmed by the fathers. My fellow-travelers could not believe it. The same thing had occurred to me at Sephora, in the midst of the hills of Galilee. I had pointed out with my finger, and called by its name, a hill surmounted by a ruined castle as the probable place of the Virgin's birth. On the following day, the same was repeated with respect to the residence of the Maccabees at Modin ... Except the valleys of Lebanon, the ruins of Baalbek, the shores of the Bosporus at Constantinople, and the first view of Damascus from the heights of Anti-Lebanon, I have never encountered a scene the first glance at which was more a recollection! Have we lived twice or a thousand times? Is our memory but a dulled mirror, which the breath of God makes bright?"

These reminiscences cannot be due to reminders coming from readings, because the Bible does not give the exact description of the landscapes where the historical scenes take place, it simply recounts the events. Can we attribute these intuitions, so clear and so precise, to clairvoyance during sleep? It is by no means demonstrated that Mr. Lamartine was an entranced somnambulist, but if we raise this hypothesis, how would one have done to know the exact names of each of these places? If it is the spirits that told them, why do such persons only remember those landscapes and not their invisible instructors? We must not bring in spirits to this argument until their presence is demonstrated and it seems to me that the following is such a case. In the newspaper *La Presse* of September 20, 1868, a popular novelist, Ponson du Terrail – albeit an enemy, of Spiritism – wrote that he remembered having lived under Henry III and Henry IV, and in his memory the great king was nothing like the one his parents described to him. I could also point out that Théophile Gautier and Alexandre Dumas have repeatedly asserted their belief based on inner memories of past lives,[190] but I prefer to move on immediately to the stories that bear in themselves the proofs of their authenticity. I am grateful to Mr. Edmond Bernus for the following information concerning Joseph Gratry. This is what he writes in "Souvenirs de ma jeunesse" ["Memories of My Youth"]:[191]

> I had just started studying Latin. I will never forget that one night, in an instant, the sense of the nature and character of Latin language was given to me. Reflecting on a Latin phrase, I suddenly understood the spirit of that language. And indeed, my progress was singular. I learned Latin inside out; it seems to me that I pulled it from the bottom of my mind where it was inoculated. For several years I thought in Latin. It has happened to me to dream in Latin, to hold dreams in Latin verses which I remembered on waking and which were grammatically correct.
> I was able to express, more easily and with far more clarity, the least of my thoughts in this language than I could in my native French."

Mr. Bernus pointed out that Gratry did not know any reincarnationist theories, which gives a lot of value to this passage of his memoirs. Now, here is yet another case where reminiscence occurs by means of the Latin language. In a biographical article on Méry, published during his lifetime in the *Journal Littéraire* of September 25, 1864, the author states that this writer firmly believed that he had already lived several times; that he remembered the slightest circumstances of his preceding existences, and that he detailed them with a force of certainty which inspired belief. Thus,

---

190 See *Le Spiritisme à Lyon* [*Spiritism in Lyon*], no. 40, "The Pioneers of Light." The same newspaper, no. 72, quotes an article of the Gazette de Paris, April 19, 1872, containing a conversation between Alexandre Dumas and Méry, where both claim to have lived several times.
191 *Grande Édition*, Pierre TRÉGUIER, 1917, pp.13–14

says the biographer, he claims to have fought the Gallic Wars, and fought in Germany with Germanicus. He has repeatedly recognized sites where he once camped and, in certain valleys, the battlefields where he fought in ancient times. He was then called Minius. Here is an episode that seems to establish that these memories are not just mirages of his imagination. I quote it textually.

> "One day in his current life, he was in Rome visiting the Vatican Library. He was received by two young men, novices wearing long brown robes, who began to speak to him in the purest Latin. Méry was a good Latinist in everything that was related to theory and written things, but he had not yet tried to talk colloquially in the language of Juvenal. On hearing these Romans today, admiring this magnificent language so well harmonized with the monuments, with the mores of the period in which it was in use, it seemed to him that a veil fell from his eyes; it seemed to him that he himself had conversed at other times with friends who used this divine language. Spoken, irreproachable phrases fell from his lips; he immediately found elegance and correctness; he spoke Latin at last, just as he speaks his native French. All this could not be done without an apprenticeship, and if he had not been a subject of Augustus, if he had not crossed that century of all splendors, he could not possibly have improvised a proficiency which is quite impossible to acquire in a few hours."

The author is right. This fact must be carefully distinguished from the hyperesthesia of memory seen many times during somnambulism and illness. In these special states, the subject sometimes repeats whole tirades heard once in the theater or read previously but deeply forgotten in the normal state. But a sustained conversation in an unusual language, without hesitation, without seeking for words, while in full control of one's normal faculties, obviously presupposes for the pronunciation and the translation of ideas, the setting in motion of a mechanism which had long been inactive, but which awakes at an auspicious moment. One cannot improvise speaking a language, even though one knows the words and the grammatical rules. It remains the most difficult part: the enunciation of ideas depends on the muscles of the larynx and locations in the brain, and can only be acquired through practice. If this mnemonic resurrection joins the precise memories of places once inhabited and recognized, these are very strong grounds for admitting the possibility of multiple lives as the most logical explanation for these phenomena. Such cases are also less rare than we would like to believe. Next, I will also mention some examples taken from the collection published by the Revue Spirite.

A pioneering Spiritist, Professor G. Damiani, on November 1, 1878, sent a letter to the publisher of the American journal *Banner of Light* in Boston, in response to controversies about reincarnation; from which I excerpted the following passage:

> "Let me give ... the reasons why I think I was not and am not mistaken in what I saw with my spiritual vision. Long, long before (mark this well) I became a reincarnationist, and when indeed I was as opposed to that theory ... I was told (mark this also) in different parts of Europe, and by several clairvoyants unknown to each other, the story of my several incarnations, at which I heartily laughed.... Years after, and when I had entirely forgotten the circumstance, the gift of spiritual vision came to me, when I saw myself in the midst of the families of my long past existences, decked in the costume of the times and the peoples of the world described by the other seers. For me, therefore, *seeing must be believing*."[192]

This statement seems convincing to me, since it comes from a skeptical observer who himself was only convinced through his personal control. What cause could produce the concordant affirmations coming from mediums unknown to one another, but which are nonetheless in agreement, all <u>relating the same facts</u>?

192 [Trans. note] *Banner of Light*, vol. XLIV, December 21, 1878, p. 2.

If past lives leave traces in us, if it is possible for certain subjects to read these cryptic inscriptions, these venerable ruins written in a language that only the psychometric faculty allows to decipher, must be similar to descriptions given by seers, since they rely on actual documents. Hence, probably, this unanimity that Professor Damiani finds and that he could verify when this power developed in him.

The Spiritist Review[193] of 1860 contains a letter from a naval officer who remembers having lived and died, murdered at the massacre of St. Bartholomew in 1572. The circumstances of this existence became deeply engraved in his being and he tells us facts which show that these reminiscences are not due to a whim of his spirit.

> "If I told you that when I was seven years old I had a dream like this: I was twenty years old, a seemingly wealthy young man. I saw myself in a duel, losing my life. If I told you that I did the military greeting typically done with the sword, before saluting, the first time I had a sword in my hand; if I told you that I knew beforehand every detail taught about the art of war, before my formal education with the weaponry ... Sometimes it seems that a flash of light trespasses the mist and I have the conviction that the memory of the past comes back to me."

In another letter addressed to *La Revue Spirite* of 1880 (page 361), Mr. Lagrange tells that he met at Vera-Cruz a seven-year-old child named Jules-Alphonse who healed by the imposition of his little hands, or with the help of medicinal plants that he prescribed. When asked where he learned all that, he replied that when he was tall he was a doctor. This extraordinary faculty was revealed at the age of four, and many skeptics later became convinced.

It can be argued here that the child was simply a medium. Indeed, he could hear spirits, but he could perfectly distinguish what was revealed to him from what he could

---

[193] [Trans. note] *The Spiritist Review*, year 1860 (Trans. L. A. V. Cheim. New York: USSC/USSF, 2016), "Memory of a Previous Life," p. 368.

find by his own means, with this certainty that he had been a physician before. This idea was not inculcated by his spirit guides; it was innate.

Mr. Bouvéry[194] quotes from the French journal *Le Lotus Bleu* the case of Mr. Isaac G. Foster, whose child named Maria died at eleven years of age, in Effingham County (Illinois, USA).

A few years later, he had a second daughter who was born in Dakota, where he came to live after Maria's death. The new girl was called Nellie, but she stubbornly continued to call herself Maria, saying that it was the real name by which she was formerly called.

On a trip with her father, she recognized the old house and many people she had never seen, but the first girl Maria did know very well.

> "One mile from our old home, says Mr. Foster, is the school house Maria attended; Nellie, who had never seen it, made an exact description of it and expressed a desire to see it again. She asked to go to the schoolhouse which her sister used to attend, and when she entered the schoolroom she went to the desk which her sister had occupied and said: 'This is mine.' It seems as if a dead person came back from the tomb, adds the father, it is the exact expression to describe it, because even if one would imagine that in somnambulism the child had somehow come to this place, no one could have indicated to her the persons that Maria knew, and yet Nellie was never mistaken, being able to name them exactly."

If reincarnation is a true fact, it is quite logical that the memories that refer to a previous life wake up, as I have already said many times before, even more willingly in children, since the perispirit before puberty still has a vibrational movement which, under special circumstances, can acquire

---

194 [Trans. note]J. BOUVÉRY, *Le Spiritisme et l'Anarchie devant la Science et la Philosophie* (Paris: Chamuel, 1897), p. 140. For the original American story, see *Banner of Light*, Boston, vol. 72, no. 6, October 15, 1892, p. 8.

enough intensity to resuscitate each of the memories of a previous existence.

We will see several more examples; the first one is due to the kindness of my good friend, Major Mantin.

> "My mother had kept with a friend of the convent constant correspondence, from which I extracted what you are going to read. This lady had with her in Bordeaux a little niece, daughter of a sister married in Spain, in Valladolid. After several repeated requests to bring her or to send her her child, my mother's friend wrote to us that she decided to entrust the little girl, whom she had taken to Hondarribia, to honest Spanish travelers who were going to Segovia via Valladolid. At that time the railroads were scarcely built in Spain; from Hondarribia to Irun, San Sebastián, and Valladolid, the journey was by stagecoach and lasted several days. After kissing her niece and recommending her to her traveling companions again, the amiable aunt saw the school kid leave her, and she did not take her eyes off her until she had disappeared at the turn of a road.
> The girl settled on the bench in front of one of the windows, to contemplate the landscape. She seemed amazed, laughing, babbling by herself. Then, as if she was crossing a well-known and already seen land, she began to say the names of the villages where the stagecoach was going to stop. The attention of the travelers was suddenly awakened by the exact remarks of the child. They questioned her, and feeling marveled by the memory of such a little girl, they asked her if it had been a long time since she had made this trip. Attentive only to all that she seemed to know and see again, she replied with a laugh: 'But I've never been here,' and the Spaniards, amused, left her yo her babble, more and more surprised by her memory.
> The cute traveler announced everywhere in advance all that should be beautiful and interesting there under the eyes of her companions. She showed that she had already come to San Sebastián. Before reaching Burgos, where they spent

the night, the child announced that they were going to see the most beautiful church in Spain.

And so it was until Valladolid, where the stagecoach arrived on the fourth day: the mother waited impatiently for her dear daughter.

After having tenderly caressed her, she thanked the travelers with sentiments of the most ardent gratitude for the care they had had for her child.

It was then that they praised her prodigious memory which had so much astonished them in such a little girl, and that they told her mother how she had so wonderfully remembered all that she had learned from her previous journey. But they did not hide from her how surprised they were with the little being untruthful when telling them that she was coming to Spain for the first time.

The mother, utterly surprised, told her daughter's traveling companions that she had not lied, because it was indeed the first time she ever came from France, where she had been entrusted her to her aunt, until that the mother and her husband had time to settle in Valladolid.

Perceiving that the Spaniards seemed to doubt the assertions of her mother herself, started to sob, saying: 'I did not lie, I don't remember having made the first trip; but what I do know is that I had already seen all that.'

A few days later, one of the little girl's companions came to give her mother the curious story which he had thought fit to be written down, and which he had entitled: 'Truthful dreams of a waking little girl.' It is this story, recopied by one of his friends who then sent it to my mother, that allows me to assure you of its authenticity, and I would like to add that this story dates from 1848.

Major MANTIN."

Here again any other interpretation than that of memories from an earlier life cannot explain knowledge of facts as numerous and precise as the girl displayed.

In children, the phenomenon of remembering their past life is not peculiar to an epoch or a country; examples are found everywhere. The following are two accounts which prove that whether in Asia or America, as well as in Europe, resuscitation of memory is found in all walks of society.

Le Journal, September 19, 1907:
THE ENGLISH POPULATION OF RANGOON IS IN COMMOTION BECAUSE OF A CHILD'S REVELATIONS

London, September 17 (By special wire)
"The overseas press reports a so-called reincarnation case that occurred in Rangoon.[195] Near this city, Major Welsh died in 1903. In recent times a three-year-old child astonished his parents by gravely announcing to them that he was the major in question, and the toddler described in great detail the habitation of the deceased officer. He went as far as giving an account of his occupations and the number of his ponies. Further still, he recounted how Major Welsh had died during an excursion on Lake Meiktila with two other people. The child's parents are absolutely upset, their son having never known anything about the major and his family.

Such a bizarre case has caused a great stir in English scientific circles and comments are building up fast."

Next, an excerpt added after Dr. Heinrich Hensoldt's account of his visit to the Dalai Lama in Lhasa, by Rochas d'Aiglun:[196]

"Fifty years ago, two children were born in a village called Okshitgon in Burma, a boy and a girl. They came to the world the same day, in neighboring houses, grew up together, played together, and loved each other. So they married and started a family, farming together for survival in the arid fields surrounding Okshitgon. They were known for their

---

195 [Trans. note] Rangoon, nowadays called Yangon, is the huge capital of the Yangon Region and commercial capital of Myanmar (also known as Burma).]

196 ROCHAS D'AIGLUN, *Les Vies Successives*, p. 311.

deep attachment to each other, and died as they had lived: together. The same death took them away the same day, they were buried outside the village, and then they were forgotten because the weather was hard. It was the year after the taking of Mandalay and the whole Burma had raised; the country was full of armed men, the roads were dangerous and the nights were lit by the flames that devoured the hamlets. Sad times for peaceful men, and many of them, fleeing their homes, took refuge in places more inhabited and closer to the administration centers. Okshitgon was in the middle of one of the worst-hit districts and many of its people fled, including a man named Maung Kan and his young wife. They settled in Kachin. Maung Kan's wife had given him two twin sons born in Okshitgon shortly before the flight of the household. The eldest was named Maung Nge, that is, Big Brother. The children grew up in Kabo and soon began to talk. But their parents remarked with astonishment that their names were not Maung Gyi and Maung Nge, but Maung San Nyein and Ma Giroin; this last name being a woman's name. Maung Kan and his wife remembered that these names were those of the dead couple at Okshitgon, around the time when the children were born.

So they thought that the souls of this man and this woman had entered the bodies of their children and took them to Okshitgon to test them. The children knew everything about Okshitgon, roads, houses and people, and even recognized the clothes they had worn in their previous lives. There was no doubt about it. One of them, the youngest, also remembered that he had borrowed two rupees from a certain Mrs. Thet without her husband knowing, while he was the woman Ma Gyroin, and that this debt had not been paid. Mrs. Thet was still alive; she was interrogated and she remembered that she had lent the money. I did not hear that the father of the children reimbursed the two rupees. I saw them shortly after this occurrence. They are now six years old. The eldest, in whose body the soul of the man entered, is a fat, plump little fellow, but the younger twin is less strong and he has a curious dreamy expression, rather that of a girl. They told me many things about their past life. They said that after their death they lived for a time without a body, wandering in the air and hiding in the trees, because of their sins, and a few months later they were born again as twins.

'The past was so clear," said the elder. 'I could remember everything, then it became more and more effaced. Now I can't remember it as before.'"

The first of the two cases above has an anecdotal character that may lend itself to criticism. "Travelers have the privilege of lying," says an old proverb that is often right.

However, if I reported this story, it is because when an audit could be done in other circumstances, the witnesses' story was found to be accurate. The following are, in fact, two cases published by Dr. Moutin in the "Inquiry on Reincarnation" promoted by Dr. Calderone.

Excerpt of an inquiry by Dr. Calderone, reported by Dr. Moutin

"Around the year 1906, the *Paisa Akhabar* newspaper in Lahore reported the story of a girl of about seven years of age, born in a village in Punjab and belonging to a Muslim family, who suddenly became serious and circumspect and spoke like a matron. She declared that she had had a previous existence and that she now remembered all the details of the life in question. She had been the wife of a Hindu, she used a rather aggressive language and insisted that she be taken immediately to her former husband with whom she had to settle an important issue. At first she was not given any attention, but as she was very obstinate, her parents took her to the place indicated, partly giving in to the importunities and threats of the child, and partly because of their own curiosity.

As soon as she arrived on the spot, she went straight to the house she had talked about, behaving as if she had known it very well. When she found herself before her so-called husband, she said a great many things which surprised this man, and finally asked him to marry her. To prove that she had been his old wife, she had an old trunk brought to her which had belonged to her and which had remained closed since the day of her death. She indicated exactly what it contained; when we opened it, we found that she was absolutely right. Her former husband and the girl's parents were not prepared for the new marriage because she was Muslim and the alleged husband was a Brahmanic Hindu; therefore, the child was forcibly brought back to the paternal home.

On receiving this information, we [Dr. Moutin] at once wrote to the director of the Lahore newspaper, asking him to inform us whether this story had reached him from a worthy source; we asked him at the same time for new details and what had transpired since about this case. The director kindly replied that he was absolutely sure of the facts which his newspaper had reported, and that he would not fail to send us new information as soon as he finished making a thorough investigation of it.

After some time we wrote to him again; we were only told that the director had made repeated attempts to elucidate the facts, but that the persons in question had suddenly become silent about them, declaring that the publication of the story had already created quite a few embarrassments to them, having scandalized their friends. If we continued to advertise this event, it would not be easy to marry the girl when she became old enough.

Another fact of the same kind that came to our [Dr. Moutin's] attention after 1906 is a story that was published in all major Bengali newspapers about two years ago. We give here a literal translation.

Ramshadon Guin, forty-five years old, of the Bratyks Hateria caste, is a resident of Krolberia, in the jurisdiction of Bhangore, in 24 Parganas district, India. His wife Manmohini Dassi died of cholera twelve years ago. His father was a Dipchand Mandal from the village of Baota. After Manmohini's death, her maternal aunt, who lives in Bahalgarth, had a daughter. Last August, when this girl went to visit Bamon Mollar with her mother, she happened by chance to pass through Krolberia, and showing the house of Ramshadhon, she declared that this building with the garden and the basin therein is belonged to her husband during her previous life. Mother and the little girl then entered this house. The child, after greeting an elderly woman who was there, said: 'She was my mother-in-law in my previous life. This room was mine; these young persons were my children.'
[Slightly rephrased continuation:]
The girl then told Ramshadon that he had been her husband and insisted that he marry her, otherwise she would commit suicide. Ramshadon then asked the girl to provide some proof of what she was claiming. She said, 'At the moment of my death, we sewed six rupees in the stuff of my dress; you have withdrawn that money and you can remember that on my death bed I asked some money and some ornaments for my eldest son. I also left a red vase and some ribbons for the hair on the wall and two hairpins in a trunk. Look for them and you will find them.'
Ramshadon discovered, in fact, these pins covered in dust. The girl then told him to look in the trunk to see if her silk dress was there: he actually found it, but torn in two places. The girl asked for explanations, the dress having only one tear when she wore it. They inquired and learned that Ramshadon's daughter-in-law had worn the robe and tore it up elsewhere. She then recognized her sons and other relatives whose names she said. A woman who was present asked her to tell her who she was. The girl replied: 'One day, as you were going to die of hunger, you came to ask me a

little food; I gave you a bowl of rice; you then called me your godmother; can you recognize me now?'

Ramshadon Guin told the girl that he did not want to marry her again, now that he was forty-five when she was just eleven years old. But the girl insisted, saying that after her departure her children would side with her. She did not want to go back to her parents, whom she called her uncle and aunt. They brought her back by force, but some time later Ramshadon agreed to marry her.

Krolberia is at a distance of only ten miles from Calcutta, under the jurisdiction of Sealdah for all matters relating to civil status. Babu Taraknath Riswas, who heads the Swaldah office and is well known in the country, was responsible for ensuring the authenticity of this story. On the 17th of the last month of Baisakh, Ramshadon, with some other inhabitants of Krolberia, went to Sealdah to register some documents. Babu Taraknath took the opportunity to ask him for information. Ramshadon declared that all that the newspapers had published was absolutely truthful and that other inhabitants of the village were able to attest to it as he did. He confirmed that the girl had recognized all the inhabitants of the village with whom she had been in contact during her previous life.

Since Ramshadon had said he could not marry her, she often cried. Ramshadon and the village notables received letters from different corners daily, asking for clarification about the case. As they could not answer individually, they asked Babu Taraknath to find some way to satisfy the authors of these letters. The Hindu thus undertook to inform the public of the authenticity of the fact, which could serve as a subject of study on the part of Western scholars. The published certificate is signed:

AMBIKA CHARAN GUPTA"[197]

In the same inquiry, Prof. Vincenzo Tummolo wrote:

---

197 [Trans. note] *Annales de Sciences Psychiques*, vol. XXII, y. 1912, p. 118.

"Mr. Romolo Ponzoni, from Rome, is one of my friends whom other occultists also know as a person of absolute good faith. He is an intelligent Spiritist, although he has not published anything on such subjects. Now, Mr. Ponzoni and his wife, dead since then, often told me that, having adopted a little girl, she suddenly, from time to time, told about a life she had spent in the midst of savages. She described their manners marvelously, giving the most perfect illusion of having lived as a savage as well."

Also in Italy, the periodical *Ultra*, in 1908, mentions the following case of reincarnation. So here is what the *Rivista Teosofica Ultra*, of Rome, reproduced on this subject:

"A police inspector of Pegu [Bago in Burmese, a port city of Myanmar] named Tucker, while pursuing bandits, was killed by a shot at close range. About the same time, in another part of the district, a woman of humble condition gave birth to a son. So far, nothing remarkable. But the marvelous event began when the four-year-old child said that he was the new incarnation of Inspector Tucker, whom had never been mentioned to him before. Moreover, he told a number of episodes of the life of the same inspector with such precision that the parents of the deceased, who were at that time in the country, were amazed and affirmed it to be perfectly accurate. These known facts have attracted a crowd of curious people who come to listen to the extraordinary speeches of this toddler."[198]

Le Messager of Liège, Belgium, published in its 1910 issue an interesting article by Mr. Henrion containing the curious details reproduced below, about the memory resuscitation of a seven-year-old girl:

"The fact that will be narrated only came to our knowledge on January 16. It was told to us by Mr. P. Courtain, a retired train operator of the State railway.

---

198 [Trans. note] *Cf. The Daily Mail*, London, Tuesday, July 7, 1903, p. 5.

Mr. Courtain's family knew absolutely nothing about Spiritism at the time of the events in question, and it was only later and as a result of the fact that will be reported that it was brought to their beliefs.

This most estimable family lived at Pont-à-Celles and counted among its children a young person of seven years of age, and a girl named Blanche, aged five at that time. The latter, being rather delicate, said from time to time to her parents that she saw spirits; she made descriptions of her maternal and paternal grandparents, who died more than fifteen years before the birth of their granddaughter. The parents, attributing these visions to Blanche's sickly state, led her one day to Dr. Roels at Gouy-lez-Piétons, and the latter, after questioning and examining the child, prescribed some potion. The visit and the potion cost 7.50 francs. The next day, in need of green fodder for their cattle, they went to their meadow; little Blanche leading the wheelbarrow ran in front of her parents. Upon arriving at a considerable distance from her father and mother, the child stopped to wait until they had rejoined her. When all was done, she said to them solemnly: 'I will not take the bottle of medicine that the doctor prescribed.' 'And why, may I ask?' said her father, 'so you want us to throw 7.50 francs in the bin? You have to take this medicine.' 'I will not take it,' replied Blanche. 'There is a man near me saying that he will heal me without it. Besides, I know what I have to do. Once I was a pharmacist too.' 'Oh, have you been a pharmacist?' And the parents looked at each other in amazement, wondering if Blanche had lost her mind. 'Yes, I was a pharmacist in Brussels, at number ... in ... street. If you do not believe me, go see it for yourselves. It's still a pharmacist who lives there and the door of his pharmacy is all white.'

The parents were dumbfounded and did not know what to say or what to do, and for a while there was no more talk about the subject, but one day the eldest daughter having to go to the capital, they proposed to Blanche to accompany her sister. 'Yes,' she said, 'I will go and lead my sister where I told you.' 'But you've never been to Brussels.' 'That doesn't matter. When I'm there, I'll be guiding my sister.' The journey went on as it had been arranged, but when she arrived at the station, the eldest said to Blanche, 'Now guide me.' 'Yes, come, it's right here,' and after walking for some time she said, 'There's the street, look. That's the house, you see, it's a pharmacist.' The elder, stupefied, found that all was exactly as Blanche had described: street, house, number, color of the door; there was no detail out of place.

Since then, the parents knew Spiritism and Blanche's mediumship flourished and developed. She was a medium of physical effects, psychophony, viewing and hearing mediumship, until her death, which came after an accident followed by sufferings that lasted two and a half years. Let us add that she herself had predicted the duration of such sufferings to which she succumbed."

To end this list, here is a story published by most journals in South America.[199]

Memory of a previous life

"Several Latin American Spiritist journals, such as *Fiat Lux* of Ponce (Puerto Rico), *Constancia* of Buenos Aires, *O Reformador* of Rio de Janeiro, etc., report a fact that is all the more interesting for leaving no other explanation other than by admitting the hypothesis of reincarnation. This, of course, if the case was in fact exactly and faithfully reported.[200] It is truly deplorable that there is no one in the world with the means to study a case such as this one by serious, competent people with the scientific authority to have the results of their research accepted.

---

[199] *Revue Scientifique et Morale du Spiritisme*, March 1907. Case borrowed from the *Annales des Sciences Psychiques*.

[200] Mr. Quintin Lopez, director of the newspaper *Lumen* of Terrassa, Spain, assures me that according to his investigation the case is quite authentic.

In the city of Havana (Cuba) lived the spouses Esplugas Cabrera, who had a son, the little Eduardo, now four years old, very loquacious, and endowed with a very bright intelligence. The residence of the Esplugas Cabrera family has always been the house located at no. 44 San José Street in Havana, where Mr. Torquato Esplugas is in charge of a typo-lithographic company of which he is the co-owner. This is where little Eduardo was born.

The child, while talking to his mother, Mrs. Cecilia Cabrera, told her already a while ago: 'Mom, I had a house different from this one before, I lived in a yellow house at no. 69 Campanario Street. I remember it perfectly.' Mrs. Cabrera, at that moment, did not attach much importance to the thing. But as the child insisted from time to time in his statements, his parents ended up paying attention to him, and after having asked a series of pertinent questions, decided to follow the indications obtained from the little boy.

'When I lived at 69 Campanario Street, my father's name was Antonio Seco and my mother Amparo. I remember that I had two little siblings with whom I always played and who were called Mercedes and Juan. The last time I came out of the yellow house was Sunday, February 28, 1903, and my other mother was crying a lot as I walked away from home that day. This other mother was very white in complexion and had black hair; she worked on making hats. I was then thirteen years old and I bought medicines at the American pharmacy, because they were cheaper there. I left my bicycle in the downstairs room when I came back from my errands, and I was not called Eduardo then, but Pancho.

'This is the house where I lived,' he shouted.

'Then, go in,' said the father, 'if it's true you recognize it.' The child ran in, went to the stairs, went up to the first floor, entered the apartments of the house as if he had known it, and immediately went down very sad to find no parents there, but other people he did not know. He did not find again the toys with which he said he had so much fun with his little siblings then, Mercedes and Juan.

The spouses Esplugas Cabrera, considering the successful result of the first attempt, continued the necessary research to obtain definitive proofs and finally arrived at the following conclusions with the help of official data: '1. The house no. 69 of the Campanario street was occupied until shortly after February 1903 by Antonio Seco, now away from Havana; 2. the wife of Mr. Seco was called Amparo, and from their marriage three children were born, named Mercedes, Juan, and Pancho; 3. in the month of February, the latter died, after which the family of Mr. Seco left the house; 4. near the house in question, there is the pharmacy where little Eduardo assures that he used to go to at the time.'

By carefully examining the facts reported in this chapter, it seems impossible to explain them logically, as a whole, by any other hypothesis than that of reincarnation. We have actually seen that physiological heredity does not exist when it comes to intellectual phenomena, not only because most often individuals of genius come from the least educated circles, but also because their descendants do not inherit their talents and faculties.

There is a law of *innateness*, as Dr. Prosper Lucas stated in the 19th century. It is because the reincarnating spirit brings in itself, in latent state, the result of its previous studies, which, when circumstances allow it, are shown from the tenderest age in some children with incredible abilities for the acquisition of knowledge and skills which would require from other human beings years and years of study and practice. However, all forms of human activity, whether artistic, literary, scientific, etc., have shown themselves so precociously among child prodigies, that it is really impossible to ascribe these astonishing manifestations to anything but reminiscences. Alone, the barely formed brain in these little beings would be incapable of storing, retaining, let alone coordinating, the multiple and varied notions and skills indispensable for performing these arts or sciences, which reveal them to be, right from the first time, infinitely superior to the average human being.

There is no doubt child prodigies are exceptions, but I have shown by examples that I could have multiplied again and again, that memories relating to an earlier life are frequently exhibited in children with such an abundance of precise details that we cannot attribute them to a play of their imagination.

In most cases, clairvoyance (clear viewing or remote viewing), albeit a factor whose importance should not be denied, cannot be invoked to explain these phenomena, because in order for lucidity to be brought into play, it is generally necessary to establish a cause that establishes a relation between the seer (the viewing subject) and the scene described. However, in the examples cited, this rapport does not exist.

Even among grown-ups, the phenomenon of the re-suscitation of memory sometimes presents itself with an accumulation of circumstances independent from one another that do not allow us to attribute this memory to some clear viewing or remote viewing on the part of the subject. Most cases of remembrance, are no longer about a feeling of déjà vu, because the subject knows in advance and describes exactly what lies within the reach of his/her gaze; the subject has the very clear notion of having once known those scenes he sees for the first time.

And when we can verify, as was the case of Laure Raynaud, of the children cited by Dr. Moutin, and others, there can no longer be any doubt that we are really in presence of memories of a past life .

Undoubtedly, more of these testimonies will be needed for this particular kind of phenomenon to definitely enter the field of science. The facts are already numerous enough that they cannot be neglected, and should be considered as the first foundations of a scientific demonstration of the reality of successive lives.

I shall now move on to another order of facts that may confirm the great law of spiritual evolution, which is gradually emerging from the darkness in which it was confined, to shine through for all those intelligent beings who have freed themselves from the shackles of materialistic and religious dogmas.

12

CASES OF REINCARNATION ANNOUNCED IN ADVANCE

THERE ARE CASES WHERE REINCARNATION HAS BEEN PREDICTED WITH ENOUGH ACCURACY TO ALLOW CHECKING ITS REALITY · THE CLAIRVOYANCE OF A MEDIUM IS NOT ENOUGH TO EXPLAIN SUCH PREMONITION · EXAMPLES OF YOUNG CHILDREN WHO TELL THEIR MOTHER THAT THEY WILL COME BACK · UPCOMING REINCARNATION ANNOUNCED TWICE IN ADVANCE· MEMORY OF A SONG LEARNED IN A PREVIOUS LIFE · A VERY PERSONAL CASE · A REPORT FROM LYON'S NAZARETH GROUP · THE CASE OF MR. ENGEL · TWO CASES REPORTED BY MR. BOUVIER · THE CASE OF MR. DE REYLE · THE JAFFEUX CASE · STORY OF LITTLE ALEXANDRIA REPORTED BY DR. SAMONA

WE HAVE SEEN IN the preceding chapters that the law of successive lives no longer presents itself as a mere philosophical theory, since it can be based on experimental facts such as those obtained by producing in appropriate subjects a regression of memory pushed back beyond the current birth. This latent memory that rests in the subconscious can sometimes re-emerge in normal consciousness and produce those flashes of reminiscence that uncover a corner of the panorama of the past. In child prodigies, the resurrection of previous knowledge is so radiant that it is impossible not to see in it the reawakening of prenatal knowledge.

I have discussed the logical hypotheses that could be used to explain these cases without involving reincarnation. I showed that they were insufficient. I now wish to review a number of narratives in which the spirits who are to return here have made known in advance and in different ways their intention to take back an earthly body.

Sometimes these assertions have been accompanied by precise details about the gender and the circumstances in which the return of these beings to Earth would occur.

I will examine whether all these stories can be attributed to mere premonitions or whether, on the contrary, we must see the intervention of spirit entities independent of the mediums.

This proof will result in certain cases from the existing conformity between a spirit's prediction of its coming back among us and, once the rebirth has taken place, the memory which this spirit retains of its previous life.

Therefore, it is these different aspects of the phenomenon that I will now review. I will start this study by reproducing an article published in the *Revue Spirite* of 1875, page 330.

The evident sincerity of the narrator already compels me to take into account his testimony, for it is regrettable that the mother did not make herself known and that we are not informed whether she is a Spiritist. Anyway, here is the story:

A NEW PROOF OF REINCARNATION

August 27, 1873

"Mr. Leymarie,

It is with satisfaction that I bring to your attention a new proof, quite evident, of the sublime law of reincarnation. On Monday the 23rd, I was on the bus that rides from the Chaussée du Maine to Ménilmontant, with Mrs. Fagard. Her husband, who is our friend, could only find a seat on the upper deck. A young and distinguished lady was sitting near us; she held on her knees a charming little girl, fifteen months old, joyful and very playful, who held out her beautiful little pink arms. I hesitated to take her, for I was afraid of displeasing the young mother, but, seeing her approving smile, I took the charming little girl.

She was kind and graceful; at this age the children are adorable, and this one, especially, was so playful, so kind, that one felt disposed to like her. I said to this lady: 'It would be an insult to ask if you adore her; there can be no doubt in this respect.'

'Yes, sir, I love her tenderly, she is sweet and amiable; then she is doubly entitled to my affection ... You would be astonished if I told you that this is the second time that I am a mother of the same child; my strange words are only the expression of the truth, for I am neither crazy nor hallucinating, Nothing I say is without proof. I will explain myself and you will judge if my saying is wrong. I had a delightful little girl who was taken away by death at the age of five and a half. In her last moments, this little angel, seeing my tears, my deep distress, said to me these remarkable words: "Sweet mommy, do not be sorry for yourself, take courage, I'm not going away forever, I'll be back in the month of April, on a Sunday." So there; in the month of April and on a Sunday, I gave birth to this little Ninnie whom you are kindly cuddling now. All who knew the first Ninnie recognize her in the second. She still says only two words, Dad and Mom, and yet, last week – you can imagine my joy and my utter surprise – I was kissing her, thinking of the other, I said, 'Oh! I would that you were really Ninnie!' To which she replied, 'It's me ...' I ask you, sir, may I doubt it?'

'No, madam, one would have to be biased not to understand that it is the same spirit that has returned in this little charming baby. God was good enough to teach you that, that's all. If we, human beings, studied harder, we would understand these quite natural facts and their undeniable value.'

I could not give this lady any other explanation, for she was getting out of the bus at the Buci junction; I deeply regret not having asked her name and address. Let us hope that these few lines will come to her attention somehow and that she will show up to confirm my words, which on my honor I affirm to be nothing but the truth.

Mrs. FAGARD at Plailly (Oise)
Floux Mary, 5, Rue Vauvilliers, Paris."

It is remarkable, if this account is absolutely precise, that the child before dying had the exact premonition of the day when she would come back again to her dear mother.

Now let us see other examples where a reincarnation is announced in advance to two different people.

Here is a case which has been pointed out to me by Mr. Warcollier,[201] and which I have published in my periodical, *Revue Scientifique et Morale du Spiritisme*.

Upcoming reincarnation announced twice in advance

Reported by Mrs. B. directly to Mr. Warcollier in July 1919:

"Mrs. B. lost during the war a son, whom she loved particularly, and her husband a few months later. There are still other children, including a married young man – that will also be discussed in this story. Still under the influence of these successive bereavements, she told me a curious case of reincarnation that followed, with all the accents of the most obvious sincerity. 'My son,' said Mrs. B., 'was a man of rare intelligence already manifest in all his activities since the young age of eighteen. In the political arena, he worked in the newspapers of his party and had become a prominent figure.

A volunteer at the beginning of the war, he quickly earned the ranks of second lieutenant and distinguished himself during an attack; he was mortally wounded in it and died in a hinterland village to where he had been transported. A week or so later, I received a letter from one of his comrades announcing that his body had been put in a coffin and buried in the cemetery of said village, where it would be easy for me to find him when a permit was granted for me to go there. I wrote a letter to the priest of this village and received a reply, confirming that my son had died as a Christian, that he had received the last sacraments, and that

---

[201] R. Warcollier, author of the book *La Télépathie*.

he (the priest) would surely come to see me when he had the opportunity to come to Paris. A few days later, I dreamed (Mrs B. is subject since her youth to supernormal dreams) of a road, an embankment of entirely sandy railway. There, I rushed to the ground, and, digging the ground with my hands, I discovered not a coffin, but the legs of a soldier. Gradually, I scavenged the sand and detached it from the body up to his head, but when I reached the face, a thick and clumpy layer prevented me from recognizing it; yet I knew it was my son. He was not buried in a cemetery, I had been lied to.

The priest later paid me a visit, but to me he seemed financially motivated and I suspected his good faith, because he could not advance any specific information about my son, that I did not formerly give him myself. He even told me things that were completely false. So I took numerous steps next to the authorities to obtain a permit to go into the army zone. Finally, at the end of a year, I was able to travel to the village where I had to find my son. He was not at the cemetery, but I soon recognized the entirely sandy railway embankment of my dream. With the aid of two gravediggers, I had to dig at the place of my vision. First the legs were discovered, then the whole body was cleared from the sand. Finally the unrecognizable face under his sand mask.

I relived my dreadful nightmare. The identity was easily established by the personal items I found on the corpse. I had it put in a coffin and buried in the village cemetery. A few months later, I dreamed of my son.

He said to me: 'Mom, do not cry, I'll come back, not to your house, but to my sister's.' I did not understand at first what he meant. My daughter, who had been married for several years, had never had a child and was very sorry about it. I did not think about reincarnation. Two or three days after this dream (I could not figure exactly from Mrs B., but it was probably not on the same day), my daughter came one evening and told me an extraordinary dream in which she had seen her brother become a kid and play with toys in her room!

Soon after that she got pregnant! Many times, in a dream, my son spoke to me of his upcoming return, which I could not believe. Finally, one day, I dreamed of him one last time. He gave me the vision of a newborn baby with black hair, whose features were quite distinct. We were waiting for the birth to happen any day now: but it was precisely that day that the child, the baby of my dream, was born in my hands. I recognized him without a doubt. I will not add comments to this story, because I only wanted to record a really curious case, so that it is not lost.'

However Mrs. B.'s impressions are worth noting. She believes that her grandson shows some particular traits and skills; his keen intelligence, the ease with which he spells out the headlines of the newspapers, lead her to believe that he is her reincarnated son.

I asked this lady many questions about whether she had previously been a reincarnationist. She says no; she added that she was a Catholic by birth and rank! But while sympathizing with the clergy and the Catholic world, she was absolutely skeptical, perhaps even an atheist. She told me her case in hopes that I could provide some clarification on the subject reincarnation, a troubling conception for her.

R. WARCOLLIER,
Chemical Engineer,
79 Avenue de la République, Courbevoie."

In more ways than one, the preceding story is quite interesting. First, because it comes from someone who says she does not believe in reincarnation, which removes the hypothesis of autosuggestion regarding this viewpoint.

Secondly, it is more than probable that the clear case of clairvoyance, which allowed Mrs. B. to find the body of her son in circumstances identical to those of her dream, was produced by mediumistic action. Moreover, Mrs. B.'s daughter saw her brother come back in the form of a little child, while she was sorry that she had never been a mother, and nothing could have made her foresee motherhood.

Finally, on several occasions, the mother had the dream vision of a baby with brown hair, as he came into the world. It seems to me that this set of circumstances demonstrates the action of the spirit of Mrs. B.'s son, who warned his mother and sister of his new arrival here below.

Now here is a report from an officer of the Italian army, not a Spiritist either, who started believing in the return of the soul to Earth only after having found it in his own family. I have copied textually the story contained in the *Annales des Sciences Psychiques* of February 1912, page 60.

Recalling a song as learned in a previous life

"The Theosophical journal Ultra, of Rome, published in its 1912 issue the following communication of Captain F. Battista, whose seriousness and respectability is said to be known by the periodical's directors. This case is similar to that of Dr. Carmelo Samona....

'In August 1905, my wife, of whom we shall speak later, who was three months pregnant, witnessed, while lying in bed *but well awake*,[202] an apparition which impressed her deeply. A girl whom we had lost three years earlier suddenly presented herself before her, in a joyful and childish aspect, pronouncing in a sweet voice these words, 'Mommy, I'm coming back'; and before my wife had recovered from her surprise, the vision disappeared. When I returned home, and my wife, still deeply moved, told me the story of the strange event, I had the impression that it had been a hallucination; but I did not wish to deprive her of the conviction that it was an act of Providence, and I immediately agreed to her desire to give our future daughter the name of our deceased little daughter, Bianca. At that time, not only did I have no

---

202 My emphasis.

knowledge of what I later learned – very late – from Theosophy, but I would have called reincarnation a mad person's idea, convinced that, once dead, no one is born again.

Six months later, in February 1906, my wife happily gave birth to a girl who, in all respects, resembles her little dead sister, having like her large, very dark eyes, and abundant, curly hair. This coincidence did not shake my materialistic convictions; but my wife, filled with joy by the grace received, was convinced all the more that a miracle had been accomplished and that she had given birth to the same little being twice. This child is now about six years old and, like her deceased little sister, there was an early development of her person and intelligence. Both of them, at the age of only seven months, pronounced the word mommy distinctly, while my other children, also intelligent, had to wait until they were twelve months to do the same.

To make the following event better understood, I must add that, during the life of the first little Bianca, we had a certain Marie as a nanny, a Swiss woman who spoke only French. She had imported from her native mountains a cantilena, a sort of lullaby, which must have sprung from Morpheus's own head, so much did its soothing virtue instantly acted upon my little girl when Marie sang it to her. After my first Bianca's death, Marie returned to her homeland, and the lullaby, which reminded us too much of the lost child, was relegated in our house to a complete ostracism. Nine years have passed since then and the famous lullaby had completely disappeared from our memory, when a truly extraordinary fact occurred, which reminded us of it. A week ago I was in the workroom adjoining the bedroom, with my wife, when we both heard, like a distant echo, the famous lullaby, and the voice came from the bedroom where we had left our little girl asleep. At first sight, deeply moved and stupefied, we had not distinguished in this song the voice of our child; but having approached the room from which the voice came, we found the child sitting on her bed, singing with a very pronounced French accent the lullaby which none of us had taught her. My wife, without showing too much amazement, asked her what she was singing. With astonishing promptness, she replied that she was singing a French song, although she knew only a few words from her sisters in that language. 'Who taught you this pretty song?' I asked her. 'No one, I learned it alone,' replied the child, and she continued cheerfully, with the air of someone who has never sung anything else in her life.

I leave the readers to their our conclusion about these facts which I have faithfully narrated and personally witnessed. But as far as I am concerned, the conclusion is this: The dead are coming back.

Captain Florindo BATTISTA,
32 Via dello Statuto, Rome."

The very precise recollection of the song that put the first Blanche to sleep reemerged in the second one so perfectly that it is impossible to explain this reminiscence by anything but a real memory, on the part of the little girl, of a circumstance of her previous life.

The captain even specifies that for nine years this lullaby had not been sung or heard anywhere in the house, so there could not have been any case of suggestion by the parents or the little girl's siblings, a proof that the former Bianca had indeed resumed her place in the household by reincarnating through the same parents.

REINCARNATIONS ANNOUNCED IN SPIRITIST SEANCES

An almost personal case

I have before me a venerable notebook describing spirit communications obtained in the middle of the 19th century by Mr. Page, an excellent friend of my father and mine. This precious collection contains the history of seances held in a Spiritist group that was organized in Tours, France, in 1860.

One notices a religious character which gives these notes a moral value of the highest order.

From the first seances a spirit called Francis appeared; he was irresponsible and still attached to material things.

Little by little, under the influence of the good counseling given by the sitters, he became more attentive, and his communications progressively denoted a very marked moral evolution. Francis had a true individuality independent of that of the medium, Miss Marie Olivier, for he often manifested himself in other towns with a character identical to that which he showed at Tours.

Mr. Page married Miss Marie Olivier in 1865. I now transcribe, textually, the notes of his notebook:

> "The affection that our friend Francis had for us, mainly for my wife, who had the privilege to be his medium, made him manifest, in order to accomplish progress more quickly and for atoning for faults committed in former existences, a desire and the need to reincarnate. He therefore chose for his family that which he had adopted in the state of spirit, that is to say, two Spiritists of the group he was fond of. He announced his plans on April 24, 1865, in presence of our good friend Alexandre Delanne[203] who was passing by our town. He tells us that he had chosen to reincarnate through Miss Marie, my fiancée at the time, and me, and that, at the same time, he chose his godfather and his godmother; he then named our good friend Rebondin, of Tours, as godfather and our good friend Mrs. Delanne as godmother. Mr. A. Delanne replied that if his predictions really came to fruition, Mrs. Delanne would gladly accept the title of godmother – the spirit does not say whether he would be reincarnated as a boy or a girl. The conversation with our friend Francis stopped there.
>
> Our wedding took place on May 5, 1865. So it happened a month before Francis had chosen both his parents and his godparents.

---

203 [Trans. note] Alexandre Delanne was the author's father.

A year later Francis came to bid us farewell, telling us that the moment had arrived to begin a new life; afterwards he was mentioned at Tours, Clisson, Halut, and Paris, where he had already manifested himself before, but he never communicated again; no doubt, Francis had reincarnated."

On January 29, 1867, we had the great joy of gaining a daughter to whom we gave the name of Angèle Marie Francoise; Francoise as a souvenir of our good friend; Angèle as a remembrance of the name of the protective spirit of our maid of honor, who will also be the invisible protector of our dear daughter, and Marie in memory of her mother's name.

The baptism took place on February 27th of the same year and the godfather and godmother appointed by the spirit François held the baby on the baptismal font."[204]

I will now reproduce some examples I cited in 1898 in a memoir presented at International Spiritual Congress in London.

Here is a report elaborated in Lyons, according to which an "incorporation" (i.e., psychophonic) medium predicted the birth of a female child who, owing to circumstances in her past life, would bear a scar on her forehead. She was actually born a girl with said birthmark.

I had received from Lyon the following minutes which I am now pleased to publish, knowing the author personally:

"Nazareth Spiritist Group, 6 Terraille Street, Lyon, France.

Thursday, October 8, 1896; at 8:30 p.m., the seance begins. Present at the meeting:

Mrs. Vernay, notions dealer, Rue de Seze, in Lyon; Mr. and Mrs. Valette, locksmith, 34 Tronchet Street, in Lyon; Mrs, Guerin, 34 Tronchet Street, in Lyon; Mrs and Miss Pisenti, 62 Grillon Street, in Lyon; Miss Mourlin, midwife, 95 Rue de Seze, in Lyon; Mrs. Vanel, grocer, 17 Sébastien-Gryphe

---

[204] [Trans. note] Individual sacraments such as baptism were still practiced by Spiritists in predominantly Catholic France in the 19th century.

Street, in Lyon; Mr. and Mrs. Toupet, magnetizer, 6 Terraille Street, in Lyon.

Formerly, the seance was not to take place, for my wife was plagued by labor pains; but as the midwife told us that there was still some long time for the birth to take place, we started the sitting anyway. We began with a mediumistic writing seance, then the medium Mrs. Vernay was led into trance by a spirit who was seeking his brother to bring him back to his mother.

'Oh God, maybe they killed him too,' he said. We asked him if it was a crime. 'No,' he tells us, 'it was during the battle of Reichshoffen that my brother disappeared.'

We made him recognize the state in which he was now, that is to say, his soul had left his body; and then we sent him for his brother; he saw two corpses, his own and that of his brother, Alfred. 'The wretches,' he cried, 'they hit him with a bullet in the middle of his forehead.'

At this moment the medium woke up.

Suddenly the medium fell into ecstasy: 'My friends,' said she, 'I am the mother of these two brothers dead at Reichshoffen, one of whom, Alfred will reincarnate in your household, and I will be the spirit guide of this child who will be born.' I thanked that spirit, and told her that I would do my best to make a man of him. 'No,' she said to me, 'not a man.'

Then the medium wakes up abruptly, saying: 'I have the word girl which does not want to leave my brain. The next day, October 9th, at seven o'clock in the morning, my wife gave birth to a child of the female sex, to whom we gave the name of Emilie. She had in the middle of her forehead a scar in relief the size of a grain of wheat.

That is the fact exactly as it happened.

Here are the reminiscences observed on the child in her youth. Up to three months old, whenever I imitated the trumpet of cavalry, she began to cry inconsolably; while having fun, she always sits as if on horseback, imitating the movement of a rider on the move.

She is now seventeen months old, and her favorite toy is the wooden horse, which she prefers to dolls, but in the

street she cannot be approached by a horse; she screams with terror.
The undersigned:
Mrs. Vesnay; Mrs. Pisenti; Miss Pisenti; J.-M. Valette; G. Toupet; Miss Mourtin; Mrs. Valette; Mrs. Guérin; Mrs. Vanel; Mrs. Toupet."

The *Progrès Spirite*, in its issue of March 20, 1898, page 45, published a letter of Mr. Engel which I reproduce in full:

"Dear Sir and fellow Spiritist,
I have the honor to give you some details about a reincarnation announced by the spirit itself, with circumstances preceding the incarnation and disincarnation. In a period of four years, all this was accomplished, down to the minimum details as predicted, first by my eldest son, who died in 1874, and then by my daughter, who died in 1878, after four years of suffering, ending in a veritable martyrdom. The motives that motivated this reincarnation are the following: during her lifetime, she had an implacable hatred against another brother who had offended her with his language, and she died with that dark grudge in her heart; despite her efforts, she could not drive it away. Seeing the deep error of her resentment and wanting to progress at all costs, she sought a reincarnation in the body of a child who was to be born from this brother, now a family father. God permitted it, allowing the progress of that spirit to be restored as a repentant spirit, and the child was born in the hated brother's family near the end of the year 1879
One day, as my wife and I were sitting together, talking about that prediction made by my son who had died four years earlier, namely, that his sister Marie was to be reborn soon, and that we would recognize this reincarnation because, on such day, at such time (5 p.m.), Marie's new mother would come, without greeting, to our house, and that her first words would be: 'Godmother, here is your godson (a boy);' and that the child would utter a loud shout, when placed on the lap of his first mother.

What was said did occur: it was also predicted by my deceased son, that his soulmate, Marie, would live only four years (a little longer) and that in her last moments she would experience terrible suffering; that my wife alone could calm her through magnetizing passes and praying. Extraordinary thing: my wife was often with the child to calm her suffering, and as soon as my wife appeared on the doorstep, all cries stopped and a filial smile accompanied the extended arms of the child who wanted to be held by her. For several consecutive hours, the child no longer cried, but as soon as my wife came out of the house the child's cries began again.

The father, a good and powerful Spiritist magnetizer, and who has done wonders in many circumstances, was unable to calm her sufferings. As for me, I produced the same effects as my wife on this little cherub. We were again warned of the child's pending disincarnation by my son, and she, his sister, came herself two or three days later to say that the toddler Pierre Yerly, 'the one who once was your daughter Marie,' is free again, but now also freed from this terrible hatred nurtured against his current father, former brother. The result of her communication urged us not to harbor any hatred, for, she said, 'hatred is the greatest misfortune that can happen to a soul because, with it, there is no forgiveness,' etc., etc.

As for my deceased son Pierre and my deceased daughter Marie, they were two deep and sincere followers of Spiritism. Other facts, no less conclusive, on the existence of lives prior to this last incarnation are known to me. My late son and daughter were so friendly that one could not stay away from the other. When my son was studying, his sister had to be at his side. No fruit or other sweeties were eaten by one without a portion being kept in reserve for the other, if absent at a given moment. After their deaths, we knew from powerful mediums that, an incalculable number of years had united them as twin souls, and that, because of our knowledge of Spiritism, we ought to understand the main reason for this close friendship, etc ... Finally, as a conclusion, I can assert that many of the predictions did consistently occur, which is also a proof that spirits do watch over us, and that God does not separate what love has united (loving hearts), and that our universal Parent never abandons those who trust in It.

Sincerely yours,
Pierre ENGEL
President of the Spiritist Group of Liège."

This story shows that spirits return to Earth to improve themselves. It is no longer a case of entranced somnambulists, but rather typtology and writing mediums; therefore also excluding clairvoyance as an explanation, unless it came from the discarnate spirits themselves. But then, another difficulty crops up: could it be that these invisible beings deceive us voluntarily, that they knowingly lie to support errors? This conjecture seems totally unreasonable to me, when it refers to spirits that have shown, in many circumstances, high moral qualities; and I would rather accept what they announce and what turns out to be true, rather than believe in some improbable universal subterfuge.

I got the following two facts from Mr. Bouvier, an excellent magnetizer, director of the journal *La Paix Universelle*, published in Lyon.[205] A subject he used to put into magnetic asleep, and who, when in this state, enjoyed the faculty of seeing spirits, said to him one day, spontaneously, that the soul of a nun wished to speak to him. Mr. Bouvier asked her who she was and what she wanted. She gave her name, indicated the convent situated at Rouen, in which she lived, and said that she would come back after her death, which would be soon. The entranced subject, as well as Mr. Bouvier, were absolutely ignorant of the existence of this religious establishment and had never even heard of it. Some

---

205 See my memoir presented at the London Congress of 1898.

time later, the same nun manifested herself and said that she had left her earthly body, which was later recognized as accurate, but that she would come back to incarnate in the subject's sister, as she would still be a female, and that she would live only three months. All these events have occurred exactly as predicted.

A second case of incarnation was predicted to Mr. Bouvier, announcing that the spirit would be embodied in the feminine gender, in a family well known to the director of *La Paix Universelle*, and that had no plans of having another child, who was not wanted in any way. The spirit said that it would be miserable because no one would love it. All this unfortunately took place under the conditions predicted. The magnetically-induced clairvoyance of Mr. Bouvier's subject cannot account for the appearance of this nun whom he never knew on earth, for the exercise of this faculty always has its raison d'être in a certain relation between the interested parties. Even if we admitted that the entranced subject's sister would be the indirect cause of the reincarnation prediction, the intervention of the nun would still be inexplicable, if not by her intention to take back an earthly body. In the second example, there is absolutely no connection between the somnambulist and the parents of the child; the spirit that is reincarnating is indeed the author of the phenomenon, because the subject was not a Spiritist and could not fall prey of any autosuggestion on this matter, nor could he have received a suggestion from Mr. Bouvier who was far from expecting any such manifestations.

Among the many letters I received in reply to my request for reincarnation cases, this is from one of my former colleagues at the journal *Le Spiritisme*. It is quite interesting in more than one way:

"Dear friend, Gabriel Delanne,
You have asked to be informed of facts tending to prove reincarnation. These facts should not be trivial, that is why I hereby communicate to you one which, although not

offering anything transcendent, is however rather characteristic of its kind.

In August 1886, we performed a seance of evocation, during which we first had typtology [i.e., spirit-rapping], then, upon our wishes, mediumistic writing. A child lost at an early age by my parents (or at least an entity presenting itself as the child's soul) assures that it is waiting for the birth of my first child to reincarnate, even specifying that it will be a baby boy, who would come in about eighteen months.

Please remember this number of months, which clearly excludes the idea of second sight or suggestion, since at the time there could still be no plans of a child to come. My mother, my two sisters, one of whom was a medium, my young wife and myself, were present at this sitting.

This communication was differently appreciated by the sitters, minutes were taken down and kept, and soon the episode was forgotten.

But in February 1888, our first son was born, who received among other names that of Allan, in tribute to the pioneer of Spiritism, on the scheduled date, a male as predicted, providing evidence, or at least an assumption, in favor of reincarnation.

You know that since then our firstborn has fallen gloriously to the invasion during the war. I am certain that he was suddenly winged high in the highest regions of spiritual life, because of his voluntary sacrifice; but I do not know anything specific about it, because we only received very vague messages from him, which we cannot be certain about the authenticity.

I am happy to establish this fleeting contact with you, my old comrade of struggles during the beautiful time of our exuberant youth.

      Sending you my fraternal embrace and affection,

E. B. H. REYLE,
2 Levrier Alley,
Le Vésinet (Seine-et-Oise)."

Here is another example again borrowed from the fine book of Léon Denis, *The Problem of Life and Destiny*.[206] The circumstances in which reincarnation must have taken place are sufficiently precise to deserve our full attention.

> "Mr. T. Jaffeux, a lawyer at the Court of Appeal of Paris, France, communicated the following fact to me (March 5, 1911):
> 'Since the beginning of 1908, I had as my guide a woman whom I had known in my childhood, and whose spirit communications all had a character of rare precision: names, addresses, medical care, family predictions, etc. In the month of June, 1909, I transmitted to this Entity, on behalf of Fr. Henry, who was the director of the mediumistic group, the advice not to prolong indefinitely a stationary stay on the spiritual plane. The Entity replied to me at that time: 'I intend to reincarnate; I will successively have three very brief incarnations.' Around October 1909, she told me spontaneously that she was going to reincarnate in my family, and she indicated to me the place of this reincarnation: a village in the department of Eure-et-Loir (France). I had, indeed, a cousin who was pregnant at that time. I asked the spirit the following question: 'By what sign can you be recognized?' Answer: 'I'll have a 2-centimeter scar on the right side of my head.' On November 15, the same Entity told me it would stop coming in the following January, and that she would be replaced by another spirit. I thought from that moment on to give that proof all its significance, and nothing would have seemed easier for me to do, after making the spirit prediction officially known, than to have a medical certificate written at the birth of the child. Unfortunately, I found myself in the presence of a family that displayed a fierce hostility against Spiritism; which left me totally disarmed. In January 1910, the child was born with a 2-centimeter scar on the right side of the head. That happened exactly 14 months ago.'"

---

206 L. Denis, *The Problem of Life and Destiny* (Trans. H. M. Monteiro. New York: USSF, October 2018), pp. 261–262.

The Twin Girls of Dr. Samona

I come now to an entirely remarkable fact, not only in the number of testimonies that confirmed it, but also in the circumstances that preceded the reincarnation of the young Alexandrina and by those who followed her second earthly birth.

Dr. Samona is well-known in the scientific circles of Italy, and the report he sent to his friend Dr. Calderone appeared in the inquiry published by him. It is a model of precision and conscientious analysis of all the circumstances that concern this truthful story.

I will use all the documents published on this subject in the book of Rochas d'Aiglun, *Les Vies Successives* [*Successive Lives*], page 337 *et seq.*, in my *Revue Scientifique et Morale du Spiritisme* of October 1913 and 1917, and in the recent book of Mr. Lancelin, *La Vie Posthume* [*Posthumous Life*], pages 307 *et seq.*, where this latter author, with his customary erudition, carefully gathers all that relates to this sensational case.

First of all, here is Dr. Samona's story in a letter to the director of *Filosofia della Scienza*, Dr. Innocenzo Calderone.

> "My dear Calderone,
> In spite of the very intimate character of the facts which preceded the birth of my two daughters I do not hesitate to give them publicity in the interests of science through the agency of your estimable and well-known review, without concealing the names of the various persons who have had knowledge of them, as and when they occurred. If I abstain from discussing them myself, I think it useful to divulge them, in order that others may do so.
> No science can progress if it remains in ignorance of the facts. If, in the sphere of metapsychics, through fear of ridicule or for other reasons of the same order, everyone keeps to himself these kinds of more or less rare cases which may happen, then farewell the hope of progress ! I send you an absolutely faithful and synthetic account of the facts as they occurred, without the least discussion on my part relative

to the interesting problems to which they give rise, namely, premonitory dreams, mediumistic personalities, etc.

The present case is favorably presented, I believe, from the scientific point of view, since the persons who, from the beginning, were au courant with the various successive details, and who observed them with great interest, enjoy general esteem for their integrity and intelligence. Besides the narration of the facts I send you the declarations of certain of these persons which confirm my statements, and I am ready to furnish other evidence of the like nature and all the information which might be deemed useful for scientific investigation

With the high esteem of your affectionate friend,

Carmelo SAMONA."[207]

Synthetic Statement of the Facts

"On March 15th, of the year 1910, after a very grave illness (meningitis) there died, aged about five, [my] adored little daughter, named Alexandrina. My grief and that of my wife who was nearly driven insane, were profound. Three days after the death of my little girl my wife dreamed of her; she seemed to see her as she was when living, and heard her say, 'Mamma! do not cry any more. I have not left you; I am only removed from you. See now! I shall return as small as that.' And she showed her at the same time what seemed like a complete little embryo; then she added: 'You are about to begin suffering again for me.' Three days afterwards the same dream was reproduced. Having heard of this, a friend of my wife's, either through conviction or with the object of consoling her, told her that such a dream might be a warning from her little girl, who was perhaps, preparing to be re-born in her, and to better persuade her of the possibility of such a fact brought her a book by Leon Denis, dealing with the question of reincarnation. But neither the dreams nor this explanation nor the reading of Denis's

---

[207] [Trans. note] See *Psychic Science*, vol. IX, no. 2, London, July 1930, G. Delanne, trans. E. W. Duxbury, pp. 109–110.

work succeeded in assuaging her grief. She remained equally incredulous about the possibility of a fresh maternity the more so from having had a miscarriage which necessitated an operation (November 21st, 1909) and being followed by frequent attacks of hemorrhage, she was almost certain that she would no more become *enceinte* [i.e., pregnant]. Early one morning, a few days after the death of her little girl, when crying as usual, and still skeptical, she said to me: 'I see only the atrocious reality of the loss of my dear little angel ; this loss is too great and too cruel for me to snatch a thread of hope from simple dreams such as I have had, and believe in an event so improbable as the re-birth into life of my adored little girl, through my agency, especially when I take into account my present physical condition.' Suddenly, whilst she was lamenting in so bitter and despairing a manner that I did my utmost to console her, three sharp, clear raps, as though struck with the knuckles by someone wishing to announce himself before entering, were heard at the door of the room in which we were and which opens into a small hall. These raps were at the same time heard by our three little boys who were with us in this room. Thinking that it was one of my sisters who was accustomed to call at such a time, they immediately opened the door, crying 'Come in, Aunt Caterina!' But great was their surprise and ours when we saw no one, and, looking into the adjoining room, plunged in shadow, realized that no one had entered. This incident impressed us greatly, so much the more than the raps were struck at the very moment of the supreme discouragement of my wife. Could they have had, by any chance, a metapsychic cause and some relation with her deep depression?

The evening of the same day we decided to begin some typtological mediumistic sittings, which we continued methodically for at least three months, and in which my wife, my mother-in-law, myself, and sometimes the two oldest of my boys took part.

From the first sitting two entities presented themselves, one representing herself as my little daughter, and the other as a sister of mine, who died a long time ago at the age of about 15, and who, as she said, appeared as the guide of the little Alexandrina.

The last named Alexandrina expressed herself in the same childish language which she used when still living; the other used an educated and correct speech, and usually did the talking, either in order to explain some sentences of the little entity who sometimes could not make herself properly understood, or in order to make my wife believe the affirmations of the little girl.

In the first sitting Alexandrina, after having said that it was herself who had appeared in a dream to her mother, and that the raps heard the other morning had been struck in order to indicate her presence and to try and comfort her mother by more impressive means added, "My little mother, do not cry any more, because I shall be re-born through your agency and before Christmas I shall be with you." She continued, "papa, I shall come back; little brothers, I shall come back; grandmother, I shall come back. Tell the other relatives and Aunt Catherine that before Christmas I shall have returned," and so on for all the other relatives and acquaintances with whom the little Alexandrina had the best relations during her brief existence.

It would be idle to transcribe all the communications obtained during about three months, because, apart from the variation of a few tender phrases with regard to persons who were most dear to her, they are almost always a constant and monotonous repetition announcing her return before Christmas, specified as at the first sitting, to each of her relatives and acquaintances. Many times we tried to stop so prolix a repetition, assuring the little Entity of our care in communicating to all her return, or rather her re-birth, without forgetting anyone; but it was useless, as she persisted in not being interrupted until she had exhausted the names of all her acquaintances. This fact was strange enough; one might have said that the announcing of this return constituted a kind of monoideism on the part of the little Entity. The communications almost always ended with these words: "Now I leave you, Aunt Jeanne wants me to go to sleep." And, from the beginning, she announced that she would only be able to communicate with us for about three months, because afterwards she would be more and more attached to matter, and would go to sleep therein completely. On April 10th, my wife had the first suspicions of pregnancy. On May 4th, there was a fresh warning of her coming from the little Entity (we were then at Venetico in the province of Messina): 'Mamma,' she said, 'within you there is another.' As we did not understand this sentence and supposed that she had made a mistake the other Entity (Aunt Jeanne) intervened saying, 'The little girl is not mistaken, but she has not expressed herself very well; she means that another being is hovering about you, my dear Adele; it wishes to return to this earth.'

From that day Alexandrina, in each of her communications constantly and obstinately affirmed that she would return accompanied by a little sister and, from the fashion in which she said it, she seemed to rejoice at it. This, instead of encouraging and consoling my wife, only increased her doubts and uncertainty; after this new and curious message it appeared to her that everything must end in a great deception. Too many facts, in truth, would have to be realized after these announcements, to permit the communications to be veridical; it was necessary, in fact, first, that my wife should really become enceinte, secondly, that given her recent suffering she should have no miscarriage, as had happened previously, thirdly, that she should bring into the world two beings, which appeared still more difficult, such a case having had no precedent either in her own case, or in that of her ancestors or of mine, fourthly, that she should be confined of two beings who would be neither two males, nor a male and a female, but two females. It was truly still more difficult to add faith in the prediction of such a complex assembly of facts, against which arose a series of contrary probabilities.

My wife, in spite of all these fine predictions, until the fifth month still lived in tears, skeptical and with an anguished soul, although in her last communications the little Entity had besought her to show more contentment, saying: 'You will see, mamma, that if you continue to yield to sad thoughts you will end by giving us very indifferent constitutions.' In one of the last sittings my wife having expressed the difficulty she would have in believing in the return of Alexandrina, because it would be difficult for the body of the coming child to resemble that of the child she had lost, the Entity Jeanne hastened to reply: 'On this point, Adele, you will be satisfied; it will be re-born quite similar to the first, and, if not much, at least a little more beautiful.'

On the fifth month, which coincided with the month of August, we were at Spadafora; my wife was examined by an able accoucheur [a male midwife], Dr. Vincent Cordaro, who afterwards said spontaneously: 'I shall refrain from giving any definite opinion, for at this period of pregnancy it is not possible to state it with certainty, but all the facts incline me to diagnose a pregnancy with twins.'

These words had on my wife the effect of balm; a glimmer of hope began to shine in her sorrowful and afflicted soul, which was ere long to be tormented anew by an event which occurred. She had hardly entered on the seventh month when an unexpected and tragic piece of news shocked and impressed her so greatly that she was suddenly seized with internal pains; other symptoms which transpired for nearly five days rendered us anxious and in dread, from one moment to another of a premature confinement, which would render the creature or creatures, brought to light incapable of life, seven months not having elapsed. I leave you to guess the physical sufferings of my wife, and the anguish which rent her heart from this thought alone, after the hope which she had begun to conceive. And this state of mind still further aggravated her condition. On this occasion she was attended by Dr. Cordaro; happily, and contrary to all expectation, every danger was dispelled. My wife having completely recovered, and now having the assurance that the seven months had elapsed we returned to Palermo, Sicily, where she was examined by the celebrated obstetrical physician Giglio, who diagnosed a pregnancy with twins; thus one part, already very interesting, of the communications, was confirmed. There still remained many other facts as important to be verified specifically, the sex, the birth of two daughters, and the specified detail that there was to be a physical and moral resemblance between one of them and the deceased Alexandrina. The sex was confirmed on the morning of November 22nd, on which day my wife gave birth to little daughters. As to the recognition of possible physical and moral resemblance, these certainly demand time, and can only be verified in due course, as when the little girls grow up. It nevertheless seems strange that already from the physical point of view, certain characteristics are manifest which would confirm the prediction, encourage the continuance of observation, and authorize us to think that, in this same respect the communications would be literally verified. The two little girls[208] at the present time do not resemble each other; thus, they differ very perceptibly from each other in height, complexion, and figure; the smaller seems a faithful copy of the deceased, that is to say, Alexandrina, at the moment when she was born; an extraordinary thing is that she has in common with her the three following peculiarities, hyperemia in the left eye, a slight running in the right ear, and a slight irregularity of face quite identical with that which Alexandrina presented at the time of her birth.

Dr. Carmelo SAMONA."[209]

Let me add that Alexandrina's twin sister came into the world first, which, according to generally accepted ideas, would indicate that she was conceived second. Finally, the nine normal months, which would have ended at Christmas, were not over, because double confinements are always a little earlier.

---

208 The two twins.
209 [Trans. note] *Psychic Science*, vol. IX, no. 2, July 1930, pp. 110–113.

The following are the documents relating to this story, published by the *Filosofia della Scienza* of January 15, 1911.

A.—Declaration of Caterina Samona Gardini, Sister of Dr. Carmelo Samona:

"From regard for truth I can attest that my brother's account in the matter of the two dreams experienced at three days' interval from each other, by my sister-in-law, is in perfect conformity with reality, both as regards date and statement. These dreams were personally related to me by my sister-in-law a few moments after their occurrence, as soon as she awoke, since I was accustomed to go and see her every morning early. On one of these morning visits, still in the month of March, the little children who came to meet me related that a few moments earlier they had heard three sharp raps on the door, and, believing that they came from me, had opened it but without finding anyone outside the door. This was confirmed by my brother and sister-in-law, who were still feeling impressed by so strange a phenomenon. I had never taken part in the mediumistic sittings which my brother and sister-in-law conducted at home, but, and quite before they left Palermo to go to Venetico, which occurred in the early part of April, my sister-in-law related to me that in these sittings two Entities had presented themselves, calling themselves the little Alexandrina and my sister Jeannette; these Entities had said that in the dreams it was really the little girl who had appeared, and that it was she who had made the raps on the door, and, finally, they had announced that before Christmas the little girl would have resumed her place in the family with the help of her mother.

When my brother returned, in May, from Venetico to Palermo he told me nothing on this head [sic!], and it was the children who, coming to see me at Palermo, where they passed an examination in June, related to me this fact. They told me that for a long time their little sister, Alexandrina had announced, by means of the table, that she would not return alone, but accompanied by a little sister.

I can affirm that the two little girls, since born, have no resemblance to each other. One, of short stature, has a perfect resemblance to the little Alexandrina (the one who died), when she came into the world. I can attest this from having been present at her birth, and from having always had her under my eyes from her first day until her death. I can also corroborate that the little girl who has just been born presents the same physical peculiarities as the little dead girl, in the eye, in the ear, and on one side of the face, the peculiarities mentioned by my brother.

Caterina SAMONA, Gardini's widow.
Palermo, Villa Amata,
January 1st, 1911."

Declaration of Adelia Mercantini, daughter of the eminent Professor Mercantini.

"Towards the end of March of last year, 1910, Mrs. Adelia Samona related to me the dream which she had had, then again, a second time, immediately after the death of her dear little girl, and it was only in June that I learned that in several mediumistic sittings the birth of twins had been announced, in conformity with what Dr. Carmelo Samona reports on this point.

Adelia Mercantini
Palermo, January 2, 1911"

Letter from Professor Raphael Wigley, evangelical pastor, to Dr. Carmelo Samona.

"My very dear friend,
On May 5th, of this concluding year you were returning to Palermo from Venetico, where business had retained you some days; there was no carriage at the station, seeing that they were all taken on account of a display of airplanes. You therefore made the journey on foot from the station to the Villa Amata, in order to rejoin your relatives. We met each other at the Place Verdi and walked together on the road to the Villa, about two kilometers.

On the way you related to me the two dreams your wife had, one three days after the death of the dear Alexandrina and the other three days later. You spoke to me of the three raps struck very distinctly on the door of your room whilst your wife was in despair from the loss of her child, and unable to believe in the dream which promised its return, the more so as, in her opinion, certain reasons precluded even the material possibility of it. You finally spoke to me of the mediumistic sittings, in the course of which the little girl had twice announced her return, and you added that, according to the last sitting, she would not return alone, but with a little sister.

The testimony which I here give you may confirm the sincerity of the case.'

Kindly accept my deep esteem and affection.
Devotedly yours,
Raphael Wigley.'
Palermo.
December, 31st, 1910"

Letter from the Marquis Joseph Natoli, a well-known personality in literary and artistic circles, addressed to Dr. Carmelo Samona.

"Very dear friend,

I also declare how marvelous, in my opinion, from the metapsychic point of view, is the fact which is affirmed in your home. During the course of last August, the Princess de Formosa, your mother-in-law, revealed to me that your wife, after the loss of her adored little girl had seen her in a dream predict her return to this world, and that this dream had been confirmed by several mediumistic sittings in the course of which the deceased little girl announced her return, accompanied by a little sister. ·

I embrace and salute you.

Yours affectionately,
G. Natoli.
Palermo, January 1st, 1911."

Letter from the Princess de Niscemi, mother of the honorable Duke of Arenella, deputy in the Italian Parliament, to Dr. Carmelo Samona:

"Very dear friend,
I have participated in the consolation of Adele and yourself by the birth of the little girls, and I attest that before their coming into the world I had been informed of the mother's dream and the prophecies which had been made to her; these are truly marvelous things.
Remember me affectionately I pray you, to our dear Adele, and accept my sentiments of esteem.

N. de Niscemi.
Villa Niscemi,
December 28, 1910."

Declaration of Count Ferdinand Monroy de Ranchibile of Palermo, an eminent personality of the political and literary society, to Dr. Calderone:

"Very dear friend,
Speaking of the facts which are well known to you, and which Dr. Carmelo Samona made known to you in writing, I can assure you that last year, at the end of May, his wife, Adele Monroy, daughter of my regretted brother Albert, Prince de Formosa, thought that she was 'enceinte' and was to give birth to twin children of feminine sex. Her manner of predicting to me the early birth of the two children brought to my lips a smile of incredulity; however, she hastened to declare to me that she had dreamed of her beloved daughter Alexandrina, whom a cruel illness had snatched from her a few days earlier during March; the little girl had announced to her that she would return to earth; Adele added that she knew, I am ignorant how, however, that the little girl would return with a little sister.
Such assurances, many times repeated by the dear woman, were greeted by me with manifest incredulity. Great was my surprise, therefore, to see the happy presage verified, and what is more, to remark that one of the twins is the exact image of the dead little girl.

I do not intend to discuss the phenomenon, distrusting my knowledge in this matter, but I affirm, nevertheless, that the fact is simply marvelous. .

You may make what use you like of this letter, if you deem it useful in the interests of your studies.

Fraternal greetings from your

Ferdinand Monroy de Ranchibile."

Palermo, January 4th, 1911."

The preceding attestations affirm the authenticity of the facts and permit us to observe that it is not a matter here of a series of more or less fortuitous coincidences, since from the beginning, the phenomena follow and connect with each other with a logical sequence which forbids every explanation by chance, pure and simple.

This being established, can we suppose that by a phenomenon of autosuggestion Mrs. Samona could have been the author of the dream in which she saw the little Alexandrina tell her that she would return?

I do not hesitate to declare that this supposition is improbable, not only because the doctor's wife was not acquainted at this period with the theory of reincarnation, but also because she was absolutely persuaded that the state of her health forbade the hope of her again being a mother. This would confer on the sub-conscious a role which is without justification, whilst the intervention of Alexandrina as the producer of the phenomenon is the most probable explanation, for it is justified by her physical action by means of raps, unexpectedly in broad daylight, in order to affirm her presence in an indubitable manner. From this time, in every sitting she continues to predict her return and, better still, announces that she will return, accompanied by another spirit which will be of feminine sex. This appears so improbable to the poor mother that she is plunged again into all her perplexities, which only ceased when she was certain that the pregnancy was one with twins.

Here again, the intervention of the subconscious is quite improbable, and if there has been clairvoyance the phenomena do not remain less extraordinary, for the ulterior facts have ensued with a mathematical exactitude, and the previous knowledge of these facts does not demonstrate in any way that the little Alexandrina was not the author of them.

We have seen that after her reincarnation the new Alexandrina has presented the same physical aspect as during her former life; irregularity of the face, hyperemia of the left eye, and a slight running in the right ear; she is indeed, as her father said, a faithful copy of the first Alexandrina.

Bah! will say the skeptics, it is the subconscious of the mother which has modeled this second figure in the image of the first; it is a caprice of heredity. Although we do not possess many examples of a second child being the faithful copy of a first one, which has died and been deeply regretted, let us admit for a moment this ideoplastic hypothesis; we shall see that it does not suffice to account for the intellectual similarities which exist between the two Alexandrinas. Here is, in fact, another letter from Dr. Samona, published in June, 1913, in the *Filosofia della Scienza*, the translation of which I borrow from Mr. Lancelin's book, *La Vie Posthume*:

> "The case or my two twin girls, previously published in the *Filosofia de la Scienza*, no. 1, January 15th, 1911, and reproduced by various reviews and in several works, foreign as well as Italian, has aroused the interest of a large part of the intellectual world, as appears from many letters received, both by the editorship and by myself personally.
>
> On this account I assume a certain responsibility in continuing to spread the knowledge of it, for I do not presume to possess the whole faculty of observation which would be necessary to fathom the study of a case which is important to the point of seeming of general interest.
>
> I fear, however, that I have not noted certain details worthy, perhaps, of special attention, and that I have, on the contrary, inscribed others which merit none. But my qualification as a

father, by putting me in a position to have constantly under my eyes my little daughters and to know the peculiarities relative to the little dead girl has made of me the unique observer and the only possible witness.

Nevertheless, I hasten to insist on this fact, that my qualification as a father has not troubled in any way, as some might be led to suppose, the serenity of my observations; also, and for that very reason, I have sought to maintain an objective attitude, without letting myself be led away by preconceived theories a priori or simply sentimental.

As I have said in the above-mentioned issue of the *Filosofia della Scienza*, it was necessary in a case of this kind to allow some time to elapse in order to be able to collect usefully certain observations, if ever the opportunity should present itself, and in fact, now that two years and seven months have elapsed since the birth of the twins, it has been possible for me to note a few which merit a certain attention

Let no one expect, however, sensational facts; there has occurred, at least up till now, nothing of that nature, and yet what I have gathered merits a few reflections.

From the physical point of view the dissimilarity between the two twin-girls has been constantly maintained, and now this dissimilarity is not only physical, as could be observed from the start, but it also exists from the moral point of view. I wish to emphasize this difference; in fact, although at the first glance it does not seem to have any importance in the matter, it has, however, its proper value, which is this: It makes still more evident, on the one hand, the resemblance of the present Alexandrina with the previous Alexandrina, and tends, on the other hand, to eliminate the idea of the possibility of a suggestive influence on the mother's part, in the material and moral development of the present Alexandrina. In any case, in accordance with the decision I made when I published this case, I shall abstain from any personal opinion or interpretation, limiting myself to the simple exposition of the observations made, and leaving each to draw therefrom the conclusions he wishes.

CASES OF REINCARNATION ANNOUNCED IN ADVANCE

Figure 8. ALEXANDRINA 1
aged three

Figure 9. ALEXANDRINA 2
aged two

Figure 10. ALEXANDRINA AND MARIA-PACE
the twins aged two

The present Alexandrina continues to show a perfect resemblance to the other, who is dead. This cannot be clearly seen in the photographs which I publish, either because they do not reproduce identical poses, which are difficult to obtain, or perhaps and still more so because the photographs of the little dead girl represent her at a more advanced age than at that of the present Alexandrina. At all events, I can affirm in an absolute manner that, apart from the hair and the eyes which are at present a little lighter than those of the first Alexandrina at the same age, the resemblance continues to be perfect. But, much more than from the physical point of view, the totality of the psychological manifestations gradually developed in the child give to the case in question a new interest still greater. As soon as the life of the two little twin-girls began to enter into relations with the outer world it soon proceeded in two different directions, to the point that we can already recognize in them two natures absolutely distinct.

I omit to speak in any special way of the characteristics of Maria-Pace, because the knowledge of her psychology and its differences from that of Alexandrina has interest only for myself and does not present any for the reader. I approach as soon as possible what constitutes the interest of the problem, the study of the psychology of Alexandrina. I shall first indicate various details of her nature which will strike the note of her affectionate character and of her intellectuality.

She is generally calm, contrary to her sister, and this tranquility extends even to the manifestations of her affection, which is neither less tender nor less caressing. One of her chief characteristics is her way of passing the day; if she happens to be within reach of linen or clothing she will spend whole hours in folding and smoothing them with her little hands and in putting them in order according to her own idea, on a chair or chest. If she cannot apply herself to this pleasure, her favorite pastime is to remain leaning against a chair on which she places the object of her choice, which acts as a plaything; from time to time she talks alone and half-aloud, and can even remain a long time at this occupation without being tired. It will be readily understood that being self-sufficient in a way, she gives little trouble; it is the opposite with her sister Maria-Pace who, very lively and always active, can only remain a few minutes in the same occupation and needs the company of some one to amuse her. Now this calmness and these special occupations, which were particularly characteristic of the dead Alexandrina, have therefore attracted our attention. Undoubtedly the twin-girl, Maria-Pace, tenderly loves her mother, and often comes to her to caress her and cover her with kisses; but these manifestations, performed tumultuously, are of short duration, and she feels the need of returning to her games. Alexandrina, on the contrary, who equally seeks her mother is, as I have said, calmer in her affectionate manifestations, much calmer but not, on that account, colder. Her caresses are delicate, her manners are gentle, and, when she is on her mother's knee, she no longer wishes to leave her; this makes the sole exception to the tendency which she shows of being self-sufficient, and when her mother wishes to free herself to betake herself to her occupation, it is difficult for her to do so without exciting cries and tears.

Then it is a charming spectacle to see how differently the two little girls behave in society, when they are admitted to the drawing room. Maria-Pace advances quickly without hesitation, and gives her little hand to everybody, whilst Alexandrina goes first of all to hide her face and her tears in her mother's bosom. But in a few moments the scene changes. Maria-Pace, tired of society, wishes to leave the drawing room, whilst Alexandrina, familiarized with the new faces, no longer wants to go away and remains on her mother's knee, as attentive as if she were taking an interest in the conversation. Again in all this (I am speaking of her way of showing her affection and of her bearing during conversation) Alexandrina is the faithful reproduction of the one who has preceded her.

I am now going to cite a few more special details of the

child's character, which will contribute towards showing a perfect similarity to the habits and impressions of the first Alexandrina.

A great silence prevails around the villa in which we live, which is far from the town, so that the noise of a passing carriage in the neighborhood is clearly heard. Now this racket greatly troubles the mind of Alexandrina who, every time that it occurs when she is not absent-minded, hides in her mother's bosom saying: 'Alexandrina *si spaventa*' ('Alexandrina is afraid'). All this, in precisely the same words and the use of the third person, recalls the manner of acting and speaking of the first Alexandrina in a similar case. Like her also, she has a great terror of the hair-dresser every time she sees him coming to the house. It is needless to say that Maria-Pace does not suffer from such fears. Alexandrina has little love for dolls and prefers children of her own age, a preference which was also remarked in the other Alexandrina. Like her again, she always wants her little hands to be clean, and demands persistently for them to be washed, as soon as she sees them a little dirty. Again, like the other, she experiences repugnance for cheese and refuses her soup, however little it may contain, even when disguised.

The first Alexandrina died without being able to free herself completely from the defect of being left-handed,[210] in spite of our constant efforts to try and correct it; today the present Alexandrina has already shown herself obstinately left-handed, and naturally we have recommenced with her the same efforts to correct it. No other of my children, including Maria-Pace, has ever shown such a tendency.

In her brothers' room there is a little cupboard in which shoes are put away. When she can enter this room and open the cupboard it is a great diversion for her to pull out the shoes and play with them. This was a passion of the other Alexandria, but what has most impressed us is that the

---

210 [Trans. note] At the time (and even today), left-handed taboo or superstition still existed and was considered a "defect" to be corrected.

present one, like the other, always wants to cover one of her little feet with one of these shoes, naturally too big for her, and walk thus across the room.

Finally, another peculiarity is worthy of note because it was very characteristic of the other Alexandrina, and my sister, to whom it specially relates, concealed it as an evidential criterion, and awaited its realization in the child as a heart-secret, without speaking of it to anyone, for fear that the child might be led by suggestion to repeat it. The first Alexandrina, at the age of about two years, began through caprice, to change names; for example, of Angelina she made Caterana or Caterona, and came thereby, still through caprice to call her constantly 'Aunt Caterana.' None of us had then remarked this detail, and it was my sister herself who verified the fact in question at the same age in the new Alexandrina; she reminded us of this peculiarity which astonished us all.

It is needless to say that none of these characteristics has been manifested in Maria-Pace.

Another thing has, in addition, attracted my attention, but I do not wish to speak of it now, not having yet its full confirmation.

Certainly, for strangers who have not known the two little girls and have not lived on intimate [i.e., closely acquainted] terms with them the simple exposition of these facts cannot show what a perfect correspondence there is between the two little lives (Alexandrina 1 and Alexandrina 2). For us the resemblance is so perfect that, in order to express the impression of the whole family, I cannot do better than make this comparison: The development of the life of the present Alexandrina, as regards appearance, habits, and tendencies, is for us as though we were seeing again developed the same cinematographic film already developed in the lifetime of the other.

At all events, if strangers cannot feel and judge exactly like ourselves in the family, or like our intimates as to the correlation of these facts, and the general and peculiar mode of being, at an age in which the field of consciousness is still limited, they will, nevertheless, be able to consider how difficult it is to seek the explanation of the facts in fortuitous coincidences or in heredity, especially if they recall particularly the other circumstances which preceded the birth of the two little girls.

Dr. Carmelo Samona."

In the *Journal du Magnétisme* of September 1913, Dr. Fugairon published an article in which he criticizes the reports of Dr. Samona, asserting that this case is in not at all demonstrative of reincarnation. In the first place, because Alexandrina had said to her mother: " See, I have become as small as this, when showing her an embryo." In the second place, because the conception of the two twin-girls must have been anterior to the death of Alexandrina, by reason of the fact that the twins were born prematurely, and that, in short, if she had reincarnated it was impossible for her to manifest typtologically (i.e., through spirit-rapping) to her parents.

Dr. Samona replied to these criticisms in the *Filosofia della Scienza*, no. 4, of December 15th, 1913.

He remarked in the first place that it was in consequence of an erroneous French translation of his article that Alexandrina was made to say " See, I have become as small as this," whilst the text reads : " I shall become as small as this."

In the second place, concerning the conception of the two twin girls, Dr. Samona, in the double role of father and doctor, is better qualified than Dr. Fugairon to inform us exactly on this point.

The births of twins occur very frequently before the nine months of gestation is fulfilled. Now these girls were born in eight months, which is perfectly normal for multiple births.

Finally, the objection that the little Alexandrina would not have been able to manifest, if the reincarnation had commenced, is quite incorrect, for we know that the incarnated spirit can perfectly well give communications, and, with stronger grounds, when it is not yet completely attached to the body which is in the act of being constituted.

The habits of Alexandrina 2 cannot more reasonably be referred to the influence of environment and education, for her twin-sister Maria-Pace who was submitted to the same conditions of existence, differs completely from Alexandrina; it is indeed the latter who has returned, for physically and morally she is the resurrection of the first Alexandrina.

These legitimate inductions are further fortified and become certitudes when it is stated that a memory of the first Alexandrina has been awakened in the second in so clear a manner that doubt is no longer possible. ·

Here is the last document, which I again borrow from Mr. Lancelin, which definitely establishes the return to this world of the regretted daughter of Dr. Samona.

Mr. Lancelin, having been constantly in touch with Dr. Samona, has obtained from him information of the keenest interest concerning Alexandrina 2. These are a few passages published on page 362 *et seq.* of his book *La Vie Posthume*. It was written on March 20th, 1921:

> "My twin-girls, who have already exceeded by some years the age of the first Alexandrina, are well-developed physically and morally. They still continue to be very different from each other, as regards physique they even seem of different ages, since Maria-Pace is of a much taller and robust figure than Alexandrina. The latter continues to resemble the other Alexandrina in a surprising manner, and has even the same repugnances. She is still left-handed, to the great despair of her governess, who always strives to correct her of this defect.
> The two little girls, who are, besides, very intelligent, have quite different inclinations. Maria-Pace is more inclined towards domestic occupations, whilst Alexandrina has a passion for things spiritual. Maria-Pace still amuses herself with her dolls, while the other runs to her books. This little

one, though playful like the generality of children, loves to concentrate in a kind of meditation which often gives rise to reflections above her age. I mention this in order that you can form an idea of her psychical development.

I shall now narrate two facts, the only ones which I have remarked in the little one, capable of proving some reminiscence of her former life. Firstly, you know that the first Alexandrina died of meningitis; this illness began with severe headaches. Now the present Alexandrina has an extraordinary terror of headache. This fact, certainly, has only a relative importance. What follows appears to me surprising and alone, I think, proves in the child the persistence of a memory of her preceding life.

Secondly, two years ago we spoke to our twin-girls about taking them on an excursion to Monreale. As you know, we have at Monreale the most splendid Norman church in the world. So my wife said to the little ones, 'You shall go to Monreale, where you will see things which you have never seen before.' Alexandrina replied, 'But, mamma, I know Monreale, I have already seen it.' My wife then remarked to the little girl that she had never been taken to Monreale. But the child replied, 'Yes I went there; don't you remember that there was a large church with a very tall man (statue) on the roof with his arms open?' And she imitated the gesture with her arms. 'And,' she continued, 'do you remember that we went there with a lady who had horns, and that we met some little red priests?'

We are not at all conscious of ever having described Monreale; in fact, Maria-Pace had no knowledge of it. We can, however, admit that someone else in the family may have spoken to her of the large church and of the Saviour over the principal portal of the monument, but we did not know what to think of the lady with horns or of the red priests. Suddenly my wife remembered that the last time she went to Monreale was with the little Alexandrina a few months before her death, and that we had taken there a lady we knew, from the provinces, in order to consult the doctors of Palermo with regard to some large excrescences on the brow; and that, moreover, at the entrance of the church we had met a group of young Greek priests, who were wearing blue vestments embroidered with red. We then recollected that all these details had greatly impressed the little Alexandrina.

Now if we may admit that someone may have spoken to the present Alexandrina of the Church of Monreale it is scarcely to be supposed that anyone at all would for a moment have thought of the lady with horns and of the little red priests, since they were for us very insignificant circumstances. Such is the fact in all its childish simplicity, but as the little one persisted in her three memories in order to prove to us that she had already been to Monreale, we did not wish to press the matter further, because at that age it is very easy to suggestionize children by asking them questions. So we contented ourselves with listening to the simple accounts she gave us, and avoided making any allusion to her supposed connections with the other Alexandrina."

A FEW REMARKS

The phenomena concerning the prediction of a future incarnation are by now sufficiently numerous to impress us as realities. I could have multiplied them further if I had taken account of all which have been sent to me; but I have had to eliminate some, not only through lack of space, but also because, while presenting evident characters of authenticity, they were capable of being interpreted, either by autosuggestion on the part of the parents, or by transmissions of thought from the circle to which the medium belonged.

At this point it should be recognized that I have striven to cite only examples in which these interpretations appear to be devoid of foundation; it will be noted, in fact, that in the first case it is the little girl who predicts her early return to her mother; another time the spirit who has to return manifests to its first mother and to the second independently of each other, the sex and physical appearance of the new-born child corresponding perfectly with the image seen in dream. In the case of Captain Batista the remembrance of the soporific lullaby is an evident demonstration of the awakening of a memory which was sleeping in the child's subconsciousness. This account should be compared with that of the second Alexandrina Samona; it proves the perennial character of memory, in spite of the change in the physical envelope of the spirit. These spontaneous cases have great value, since those who reported them had no knowledge of the laws of reincarnation. In Spiritist seances we must evidently be on our guard against the cause of error which may result from the autosuggestion of mediums. I have examined in every case the value of this hypothesis, and I think I have demonstrated that it was insufficient to explain the phenomenon, especially as regards the accounts of Misters Bouvier, Toupet, Engel, de Reyle and Jaffeux.

Finally, we arrived at the very well-documented case of Dr. Samona. Here no reasonable doubt is possible; the identity of the two Alexandrinas, physically and intellectually, is affirmed with so much evidence that I deem it useless to insist further thereon. It is indeed the same being who has twice come to take her place at the family hearth-side; if all the other cases had been studied with such minute care and so precisely documented, we should be able to assert aloud that the scientific demonstration of successive lives is henceforth an accomplished fact.

If we have not yet reached that point, it does not remain less certain for all who will study impartially the examples related here that there is such a probability in favor of palingenesis that it constitutes a moral proof of the first rank.

It is scarcely doubtful that the future will bring us new and decisive confirmations, and that the great law of reincarnation will take a definitive place in the domain of science.

13

OVERVIEW OF ARGUMENTS IN FAVOR OF REINCARNATION

THE SOUL IS A TRANSCENDENTAL BEING · THE PERISPIRIT AND ITS PROPERTIES · WHERE COULD IT HAVE ACQUIRED THEM · PASSING THROUGH THE ANIMAL SCALE · ANALOGY BETWEEN THE INTELLECTUAL PRINCIPLE OF ANIMALS AND THAT OF HUMANS · THE EVIDENCE THAT WE POSSESS · THE HUMAN REINCARNATION OF INTEGRAL MEMORY · THE FORGETTING OF EXISTENCES IS NOT SYNONYMOUS WITH THE DESTRUCTION OF MEMORY · HEREDITY AND CHILD PRODIGIES · REMINISCENCES AND TRUE MEMORIES OF PAST LIVES · ANNOUNCEMENT OF FUTURE REINCARNATIONS · PALINGENESIS IS A UNIVERSAL LAW

As we reach the end of this book, if we take a look back at the road traversed, we will find that the great theory of successive lives, which originated at the dawn of humanity, has gone through centuries and civilizations with diverse fortunes; and that in modern times it has taken a new life thanks to the thinkers who studied it in the 19th century, and to observations and experiments carried out by Spiritists.

It seems that reincarnation must now leave the philosophical domain to enter that of science. Though observations and experiments are still relatively few, some of them are fairly well established, therefore they cannot possibly be ignored.

These are, as it were, the initial pillars of this edifice, which tomorrow's science will certainly build.

To fully appreciate the value of the arguments of various types that I have gathered by following the inductive method in this volume, it is essential in the first place to be well acquainted with the scientific demonstrations on which rests the certainty of the existence of the soul, as a principle independent of the body, and that of an immaterial substratum which individualizes it and of which it is inseparable.

THE SOUL IS A TRANSCENDENTAL BEING

Undeniably, it was found from the researches conducted for half a century by some of the most prestigious scientists in the world, that there exists in humans a transcendental principle which extends beyond the framework of official, mainstream physiology – since it is revealed through faculties which often makes it independent of the conditions of time and space which govern the material world.

This is what emerges from the work of the British Society for Psychological Research (SPR), which since 1882 has published over thirty volumes reporting the observations and experiments that its members have controlled (i.e., scientifically verified), after careful investigations. The names of Crookes, Sidgwick, F. W. H. Myers, Gurney, Barrett, Oliver Lodge, and many others, are sure guarantees of the authenticity of the facts which are related therein. Similar investigations have been pursued in the United States by the American branch of the SPR under the direction of Professor Hyslop and Dr. Hodgson. In France, they were held by a number of psychists and, in particular, by Camille Flammarion in the three volumes of his *Death and Its Mystery* (New York, 1922–1923).

More recently still, French researchers Warcollier, a chemical engineer, published a book called *Télépathie*; and Dr. Osty, two volumes called *Lucidité et Intuition*, and *La Connaissance Supranormale*, respectively; all dealing with the unknown faculties of human beings.

In Italy, the periodical *Luce e Ombra* collected a number of indisputable testimonies, and Mr. E. Bozzano published a series of monographs of the highest interest on this subject.

It is now absolutely certain that the thought of an individual can be exteriorized and act upon another living being independently of any sensory action, despite the distance that separates them. It is to this phenomenon that we have given the name of telepathy. It is no less certain that remote viewing, despite the obstacles interposed, is exercised whether in waking or sleeping state – without having recourse to the ocular sense faculty – which requires a power different from that which is purely physiological. Here again we find ourselves in the presence of a faculty entirely distinct from those which physiologists recognize in the nervous system.

Finally, it is established by numerous and indisputable examples that a phenomenon as extraordinary as the knowledge of the future, or premonition, has been repeatedly found. This proves that there exists in humans a being independent of the physical organism, which is rigorously conditioned by the laws governing the material world. A fact now so incontestable that a philosopher of the caliber of Prof. Henri Bergson did not fear, in a conference on soul and body made on April 28, 1912, to say:

> "However, if mental life, as I have tried to show, goes beyond cerebral life; if the brain confines itself to translating into movements a small portion of what is happening in the consciousness; then survival becomes so probable that the burden of proof will rest on those who deny it rather than those who assert it, because the only reason to believe in an extinction of consciousness after death is that we see the body disintegrate, and such reason ceases to have value if the independence of almost the totality of consciousness with regard to the body is a fact that we can see as well."

THE PERISPIRIT AND ITS PROPERTIES

The independence of this inner principle has been established through numerous and varied proofs. The soul is individualized by the perispirit.

But, better still, this spiritual principle is not a vague metaphysical entity, an abstract word, nor a function of the nervous system, but a concrete being having an individuality; for even during life, it is this being that has been given the name of soul or spirit that can disengage from the body and manifest its objective reality in the phenomena of duplication (i.e., out-of-body experiences).

Out-of-body experiences of the human being are now demonstrated by observations repeated a thousand times. On the one hand, the presence of the physical body has been found at a given place, while simultaneously the existence of its fluidic double at another place.

This phantom of living[211] carry with itself the person's sensibility, intelligence, and willpower. It has been possible to reproduce this phenomenon experimentally, which is a second demonstration of the independence of this inner being, which is usually called the spirit.[212]

After death, it is this fluidic body that survives and manifests itself objectively through materialized apparitions, which are in all respects similar to those of the living. Here we are in presence of a direct and immediate demonstration that:

1st) the spirit is not a product of the body, since it survives its disintegration, and

2nd) it always possesses the same fluidic organism which accompanies it throughout life, and which still individualizes it, after its separation from the physical body.

During life, knowing about the existence of the perispirit makes us understand:

1st) the preservation of the individual type, despite the incessant renewal of all fleshly molecules;

2nd) the repair of lesioned regions of the body;

---

211 [Trans. note] *Phantom of the living* or *phantasm of the living* are both expressions made internationally known and established by British scholars E. GURNEY, F. W. H. MYERS and F. PODMORE in the 19th century.

212 See G. DELANNE, *Les Apparitions Matérialisées des Vivants et des Morts* (Paris: Librairie Spirite, 1909), tome I.

3rd) the continuity of vital functions in an ever-changing environment.

Spiritists have long been aware of these interesting and curious phenomena, and they see with satisfaction that little by little mainstream science, through the voice of some of its representatives – and some of the most authoritative among them – has gradually sanctioned all orders of facts that make up this new science. It is therefore quite legitimate that we use this precious knowledge to try to solve the problem of the origin of the soul and its destinies.

It is perfectly shown[213] that in materialization seances, a being is formed which is foreign to all the sitters, and which is objective because everyone describes it in the same way; because it is possible to photograph it; because it leaves imprints or casting molds of its limbs; because it acts physically by moving objects; and because it can speak or write.

Therefore this being possesses all the physiological properties and psychological faculties of an ordinary human being.

This is not a duplication of the medium, not only because it differs from the latter in every aspect, but also because often many materialized spirits appear simultaneously. In addition, it was sometimes found that the awakened medium talked to the apparition. On other occasions, the same spirit materialized in an identical manner through different mediums; and lastly, quite frequently, its identity was controlled (i.e., verified) by those who had known it during its lifetime on Earth.

Since the perispirit possesses after death the faculty of materializing itself by completely reconstituting the physical organism it possessed here below, this allows us to suppose that at the moment of birth, it is it that forms its physical envelope, the body, which is nothing but a stable and permanent materialization; whereas in experimental seances the materialization is only temporary, because it has been produced outside the normal pathways of generation.

---

213 See *op. cit.*, tome II.

This opinion, which I had entertained twenty-five years earlier, regarding the evolution of the spirit is now accepted by a scholar as eminent as Sir Oliver Lodge, during a lecture given in England before an elite audience in 1922. He is not afraid of expressing himself in the following terms:[214]

> "Often for these kinds of manifestations, the forces employed are not of a higher essence: ectoplasm, for example, is one of those material manifestations which can be submitted to examination by our senses. These facts alone are already extraordinary: however, they are facts and we must study them, as we must study these voices that we hear, these direct writings that we see; and we should believe as we have believed in the sentences read on the wall by the guests at Balthazar's feast. There are immense truths in the 'legends' of the Bible. The materializations, the ghosts are not hallucinations. Would we, ourselves, not be materializations that can last seventy years like the others last seventy seconds?"

Where and how could the perispirit have acquired its properties?

It is one of the most beautiful conquests of the 19th century science to have demonstrated the fundamental unity of composition of all living beings, all born of an egg, all formed of cells whose protoplasm is substantially the same, despite their prodigious diversity. All beings are born, evolve and die. All organic functions are essentially similar: nutrition, digestion, respiration, reproduction, take place in almost identical manner. This is a demonstration due to the fact of this unity of Nature; and because intelligence, though different from matter, is associated with it. However, it is legitimate to think that their spiritual principle is fundamentally the same, notwithstanding the quantitative differences that exist at all stages of its development. We have found that transcendental faculties, such as telepathy

---
214 See *La Revue Spirite*, February 1923, p. 76.

and clairvoyance, and even ideoplasty, also exist in animals, which is yet another reason for admitting the common identity of all creation.

If this is so, if the soul has actually climbed the ladder of zoological species, it is no longer surprising that at each birth it reproduces in abbreviated form the whole history of its past, as it takes place during embryonic life for all beings.

All these inductions are legitimate, they follow one another mutually, and may be considered as proofs of universal palingenesis (rebirth).

It is still not clear how the intelligent principle, which drives innumerable billions of rudimentary and primitive organisms, can be synthesized into a unity of a higher order; no more than it can be explained clearly how this passage takes place from one species to another. It is nonetheless real that there is a permanent and continuous connection in all spheres of life, at all levels; and that if life is one in the universe, the same certainly applies the spiritual principle.

Therefore, we are obliged to ask ourselves where the perispirit could acquire its functional properties, and it seems logical to suppose that it fixed them in itself during its earthly stages of evolution, while passing successively throughout the chain of the animal scale, by integrating into its indestructible substance the increasingly elaborate laws that allow it to automatically animate and repair increasingly complex organisms, from the simplest forms to the human form. It is a gradation and involves a continuous evolution. If this hypothesis is correct, we must find in the animal scale phenomena analogous to those observed in humans. This is indisputably what actually takes place, since we have found that the animal soul also survives death.

In one of my previous books,[215] I tried to indicate how one could conceive of the progressive development of the spiritual principle; and I have shown that by placing the

---

215 G Delanne, *Évolution Animique* [*Animistic Evolution*] (Paris: Chamuel, 1897).

cause of evolution in the efforts of the intelligent principle to progressively freed itself from the bonds of matter, facts are better explained than by the materialistic theory which points out only to factors such as heredity and different environments.

Physical and intellectual progress comes from incessant, repeated efforts, and improvements almost imperceptible to each passage, but whose summation eventually leads to the human stage, which summarizes and synthesizes this great ascension. Once reaching any degree of the vital scale a being cannot retrograde, simply because it would no longer find, due to its current evolutionary state, the conditions necessary to reincarnate in the lower forms which now it has superseded. Cross-breedings between different species are generally infertile because hybrids cannot reproduce, and even more so across families and phyla.

Let me also remark that vital functions, such as nutrition, respiration and reproduction, and even sensibility and motricity, do not determine essential differences between animals and plants, which sets the great fundamental unity that exists under the veil of appearances.

Science shows that transformism[216] is only a special case of a general law. Everything evolves, whole nations as well as individuals, orbs as well as nebulae. Everything starts simple to lead to a compound; from primitive homogeneity one arrives at the prodigious complexity of current-day nature achieved by laws which require only duration to produce all their effects.

We have seen that in higher vertebrates, and more particularly in domestic animals, intelligence has developed sufficiently to understand human language, to formulate reasoning, and to solve certain arithmetic problems.

---

216 [Trans. note] In biology, *transformism* is the hypothesis that existing species are the product of the gradual transformation of other forms of living beings.

Although its degree is obviously very inferior when compared to human intellect, it is still of the same nature as ours, as can be amply verified.

I have also pointed out that so-called supernormal powers, such as telepathy, clairvoyance, and premonition, are often observed in the canine race. What makes it possible to assimilate the spiritual principle of the animal to that of humans is – I repeat and stress – that there are animal phantoms quite analogous in their manifestations to materialized apparitions of the dead.[217]

In summary, there are in all living beings, the same organic constitution, the same vital functions, the same thinking principle and the same perispirit envelope which individualizes it.

It is a magnificent demonstration of the great law of continuity which, as I said above, governs the entire universe.

HUMAN REINCARNATION AND THE INTEGRAL MEMORY

To approach experimental verification of the reality of successive lives, and to explain why the memory of previous existences is not kept, it was necessary to briefly study the different modalities of memory.

If the soul is really individualized in a substance which accompanies it during the whole duration of its evolution; if this spiritual body is the constant guardian of all previous acquisitions; we are entitled to ask ourselves why at each return here below we have no knowledge of our past.

To understand the forgetting of past lives, it was necessary to show that even in our current existence, there are profound gaps in a multitude of incidents that have happened to us, and even sometimes that periods go entirely out of our life's memory. Hence, it will not be extraordinary that it is the same for all that precedes our current life, since the perispirit has

---
217 See *Revue Métapsychique*, issue of January–February of 1923.

undergone very profound inner modifications by reappearing here below. Each time a new balance is established which necessarily modifies the state of our memory.

Therefore it is indispensable to show that, although memory is indestructible, it only becomes conscious again in specific circumstances that should necessary know well. Again this is not a theory imagined from scratch, but rather an extension of facts already known.

The experiments conducted by Pitres; Bourru and Burot; Pierre Janet; among others, have proved that everything that has penetrated into us has left an indelible trace. Without doubt, all these intellectual acquisitions do not present themselves simultaneously to the consciousness. The rule is that most of them are forgotten. But forgetting does not mean obliterating. The subconscious has forever recorded all mental states, and, what is even more remarkable, it has indissolubly associated them with their contemporary physiological states, so that by resuscitating the former, the latter are revived at the same time, and vice versa. As I indicated above, this regression of memory can occur spontaneously, or it can be induced by different methods and mainly by hypnotizing certain subjects who possess this power of mnemonic resurrection.

Spiritists, by practicing magnetic experiments, discovered this power of reawakening earthly memories during life, and they continued this regression to states prior to one's current birth.

I told why this method has not yielded so far, despite some success, all the results that might have been expected; but I am sure that it will be more fruitful in future, when we have eliminated the causes of error due to suggestions made by the operator, or to autosuggestion on the part of the subjects, and instead start acting upon the exteriorized spirit in collaboration with the spirit guides of the medium, which will know how to use the most effective means to give back memory to the perispirit in all its intensity. Moreover, this method was not always infertile, since Professor Flournoy, despite his well-known skepticism, was obliged to admit that he could not explain how the sensitive Hélène Smith could exhibit such knowledge and her command of the Sanskrit language, when speaking as Princess Simandini.

If I have some reservations about the narratives of Spiritist seances in which reciprocal recognitions have taken place, it is because no means of scientific control were provided to verify the reality of the events related by the subjects, which does not mean that their stories were inaccurate.

However, this is not the case in some cases where it was possible, to a certain degree, to check the accuracy of these recollections.

Indeed, when spontaneously that English lady, quite ignorant in the normal state of French politics, shows, during an out-of-body state, in-depth knowledge on the same subject, and she affirms to have formerly lived in France, we should take the utmost account of these statements since they come from an environment where reincarnation is not generally accepted even at Spiritist centers.

The same is true of the story of the Prince of Wittgenstein, where the spirit of his cousin claims to have lived at Dreux in dramatic circumstances as related earlier in this book. The writing of communications in pencil being in every respect similar to that of the living canoness, the identity of the latter seems to be well established and the reality of the memories is confirmed in part by the researches that a friend of the author has carried out to find the remains of the convent where she had been a clergywoman.

Finally the recognition of the bronze medal is also an argument that cannot be neglected. But with the case reported by Prince Wiszniewski, this time the proof is complete. A completely ignorant woman, speaking only a crude Low German dialect, expresses herself in excellent French, narrates the events of her past life, which one verifies and which are perfectly exact. Here we are in presence of a real case of reincarnation that no other hypothesis could logically explain.

The example of the madman Suciac is no less demonstrative, since after his death he remembers to have lived in a castle and then indicates exactly the place ignored of all in which documents were hidden, which could be found by following his directions.

Such verifiable facts are unfortunately still very rare, yet we have no right to neglect them, because they serve to establish experimentally the reality of past lives that we will see confirmed by other phenomena no less interesting and even more demonstrative.

Let me point out that the personalities, so diverse and so different from one another, that are observed at each reincarnation are not incomprehensible and do not infringe on the principle of identity, since we have already observed that the same individual, during his/her life, may present prodigious contrasts of character.

Louis V., for example, was sometimes gentle, honest, submissive, then, under the shock of an emotion or organic disorder, his neurological state changed completely, and he became teasing, thieving, insubordinate; each phase separated by the loss of consciousness of his previous intellectual state.

We observe the same contrast in the cases of Félida[218] and especially in that of Miss Beauchamp. It would seem that these various personalities are in a sense, allotropic states of an overall individuality.

Any reincarnation inevitably bringing about a vibrational tone quite distinct from that of the life on the spiritual plane and those of previous existences, it is natural in such conditions that, at each return here below, the being who has reincarnated differs more or less from what it was previously, while maintaining an unalterable individuality.

---

218 [Trans. note] The famous case of Félida X, studied by the French doctor Eugène Azam for seventeen years.

Heredity and child prodigies

Since materialistic science ascribes the intellectual faculties to the functioning of the brain, the continuation of the studies that I have undertaken obliged me, necessarily, to investigate to what extent the phenomena of heredity could furnish an explanation of cases of child prodigies.

We have seen above that by the word "heredity" I mean only the transmission of anatomical and physiological traits from parents to their descendants; as such, this is an indisputable fact.

But current science provides no valid explanation. All theories conceived by Herbert Spencer, Darwin, Nägeli, August Weismann, and others, are absolutely incapable of giving an account of this phenomenon, for gemmules, micelles, idioplasm, determining ideas, biophores, pangenes, etc., are just words that do not correspond to any objective reality. We Spiritists will therefore be allowed to use the knowledge we have acquired experimentally, for it allows us to formulate an explanation, which, at least, has the merit of being based on observation and experiments.

Since the perispirit has the power to organize matter, it is to the perispirit that we ascribe this function in order to explain the formation of the embryo and the fetus.

If the spiritual principle has slowly climbed the ladder of the zoological scale, if it has preserved in its substance the indelible traces (as atrophied organs) of this evolution, it is natural that it reproduces it in abridged form during the first months of gestation.

The secondary characters which belong to the parents can be attributed to a magnetic action of the father and the mother which modifies more or less profoundly the perispiritual type of the being who is about to incarnate to give him/her a resemblance to their progenitors. This physical heredity is neither general nor absolute; however, it sometimes exists, and this is not contradictory to my explanation.

It is quite different when it comes to psychological inheritance. There is virtually no such thing, and although we can sometimes discover similar intellectual abilities between parents and their descendants, such similarities are never the result of direct transmissions.

A mathematician, for example, will not communicate to his child the knowledge of algebra, any more than a linguist would be able to transmit to his child the command of one of the languages that he can speak perfectly well.

I have cited many examples which demonstrate not only that a great many individuals of genius have come out of the most obscure circles, in which it would be impossible to discover the cause of their eminent faculties, but also that the greatest among them often have only mediocre children.

Psychological heredity is so infrequent that a number of physiologists have been forced to imagine a law of innateness. In reality, that is what is happening. Each being, on returning to Earth, brings with it all the baggage of his/her past, and sometimes manifests, from their earliest childhood, such prodigious knowledge that it is materially impossible to attribute it to heredity or the functioning of the cerebral matter. which has not yet been able to develop all its functional properties.

All forms of intelligence have manifested themselves with incomparable brilliance in musicians such as Mozart or Beethoven, even before they knew the fundamental notions of their art.

It was the same with painters such as Giotto and sculptors like Michelangelo, who at the age of eight had nothing else to learn about the technique of his profession. What to say in order to explain the unlikely, but nevertheless very real, case of a Heineken who, at the tender age of two, knew three languages, and at 2 1/2 years, still suckling his nurse, was subjected to an examination on history and geography? Or William Rowan Hamilton knowing at the age of three Hebrew and, at seven, being more advanced than most candidates in a high-level exam for teachers?

It is quite certain that the brain of these children should only be used mechanically for the enunciation of ideas, for it would have been incapable of recording – due to its incomplete development – the multitude of knowledge and associations of ideas and reasoning that these sciences require.

As I have said, it was probably by a phenomenon of exteriorization that the incarnate spirit manifested its prodigious aptitudes, which it could obviously have acquired only in its past existences.

These phenomena are so embarrassing to materialistic science that they have been carefully ignored.

Reminiscences

I have already indicated the reasons why the memory of the past, which is so strikingly manifested among child prodigies, is not generally preserved. However, as there are no rules without exception, it is possible that sometimes the incarnate spirit, under the influence of different circumstances, momentarily recovers part of its previous memories by finding itself again in the places it once had inhabited.

These reminiscences may be vague, but sometimes they acquire enough intensity to impose on the one who feels them the certainty that he/she has already seen the country where he/she is and even where he once lived.

Neither the feeling of déjà vu nor clairvoyance is sufficient in some cases to fully explain this phenomenon. All that remains is the theory of past lives to account for it.

This is how we have seen, as expected, that reminiscences, although generally imprecise, are quite common in young age. But due to the impossibility of verifying the reality of such impressions, I have indicated them only in order to neglect nothing, choosing those authentic examples where the reminiscence has been checked.

With the cases of Major Wellesley, the clergyman, and Mathilda de Krapkoff, we took a step forward.

True recollections of past lives

It is no longer a simple feeling of déjà vu; each percipient has the distinct feeling of having lived there once and of not simply watching a vision that would resurrect the past. But how much more demonstrative is the case of the Russian lady: from her childhood she draws without models characters dressed as in the 18th century; and she recognizes the castle of Versailles and the ruins of Marly without ever having seen them before; she has a very clear feeling of having lived there at one time.

The same occurs with Mrs. Katherine Bates, whose previous handwriting is recognized as the one she once possessed; then the vision, the knowledge so thorough of the village of the British town of Broadway, are really demonstrative since, in her current existence, she had never known this place, and she did not know that her ancestor had lived there, which excludes the hypothesis that clairvoyance could have been the source of these very precise notions.

Dr. Gaston Durville's inquiry into Raynaud's previous life is quite interesting because of the exact documentation that has been collected so as to verify all the circumstances. This is really an example of a recollection of a previous life, because no other hypothesis can explain all the incidents.

As seen in my report to the International Spiritual Congress of 1898, many famous personages claim to remember having lived in the past. It is impossible not to take into account in modern times the testimonies of individuals such as Lamartine and Méry, so demonstrative in different respects.

The same can be said of Joseph Gratry, who declared that the genius of the Latin language was revealed to him all at once (from within to without). This is really an awakening of a science formerly learned. Indisputably, this is exactly what happened to Nellie Foster, who recognized a location she had never seen since her birth and designated the people with whom she had been related in her previous incarnation, when she was named Maria.

This cannot be a case of extrasensory perception, no one had ever spoken to the child of the town where his family had previously lived.

The same is true of the case reported by Major Mantin, where a girl named with absolute accuracy the Spanish localities which she had never seen during the course of her current life.

It is of the greatest interest to point out that cases of recollections of past lives can be observed in every country, in every race, in every epoch, and even in places where ideas of reincarnation are completely unknown. It seems, then, that these spontaneous phenomena are actual manifestations of the continuity of subconscious memory.

Their relative scarcity is not sufficient reason to negate those we have collected. Indeed, we have seen that in India the examples of memories of past lives are quite common; the cases reported by Dr. Moutin are well controlled and can only be understood if the idea of reincarnation is taken into account. Cases of reenactment of individualities quite unknown to the children who claim to have been individuals who really existed in the past are also of the highest interest.

The examples of Inspector Tucker in Burma and Major Welsh also in the same country, if better documented, would be entirely and completely demonstrative. I cited them for the record, but the stories of Mr. Courtain and the case in Havana were meticulously observed and prove the survival of the last incarnation's memory in some children.

I am well aware of all the criticisms that can be made of the historical method, and those regarding the validity of testimonies drawn from such different sources. It would have been necessary for inquiries similar to those made by elsewhere Moutin and Durville in order to verify these phenomena.

But it is not permissible to systematically neglect the examples I have collected. It seems inconceivable to me, that so many testimonies furnished by honorable persons, unknown to each other, coming from all walks of life, and having no interest whatsoever in deceiving, would be completely devoid of value.

They emanate from sources so diverse and yet have so many characteristics in common that it is impossible to attribute them to the fantasy of the narrators or to the imagination of the children. This is all the more so since sometimes they have occurred spontaneously in environments where any idea of an earlier life was absolutely foreign to both parents and children.

One would have to willingly close one's eyes so as to ignore the importance of similar findings: these are facts, and no one has the scientific right to neglect them. Until proven otherwise, to me they seem to be positive demonstrations of the indisputable reality of past lives.

Reincarnations announced in advance

If it is useful to carefully observe cases of resuscitation of memory; it is no less necessary to record the stories in which a future reincarnation was announced. Sometimes such predictions take place spontaneously; at other times they occur during sleep; and finally during Spiritist seances.

We have seen these revelations happen in the most varied forms. It is, first of all, the case of the little girl who, before her death, has such a clear intuition of being called back that she fixes the date of her new birth.

Then there is the case where the discarnate spirit informs in a dream both his mother and the woman who was his sister, that he will be reborn from the latter; and the newborn turned out to be physically identical to the one his first mother saw in the dream.

These are complications that no chance factor could have combined.

Again, it is with a vision that Captain Battista's wife learns that her beloved little Bianca will come back to her, and this is so assuredly a reincarnation of the first Bianca that she remembers the cantilena sung in French to which she had so often fallen asleep in her previous life.

Resuscitation of memory is even more complete in the case of Nellie Foster where all the details of her previous life were resurrected with complete fidelity. These are eminently convincing facts, which alone would be enough to solidly support the theory of successive lives, because really no other logical explanation could intervene.

I have shown that in Spiritist seances it has been very frequently announced by the spirits that they would be reborn in certain families designated in advance, bearing some characteristic traits; and that these predictions were exactly fulfilled.

It is useful to point out the moral character that emerges from some of these observations; in a general way, souls that come to take a body through incarnation do so in order to improve themselves, and they explicitly declare it to be a necessity imposed on them by immanent justice.

This is a common feature in the teaching of spirit guides, since we have seen it pointed out in England to Mrs. Bates and in mediumistic groups at Lyon, France. Such were the cases cited by Bouvier, Toupet, and Jaffeux.

They are in a way summed up and completed by the story of Dr. Samona, where the announcement of the future rebirth of the little Alexandrina is complicated by that of a twin sister with such an abundance of evidence that any doubt becomes impossible.

Not only the character, but also the habits of Alexandrina 1 are found in the newcomer, in addition to very accurate memories that leave no doubt that the little departed girl has returned again.

It would be offensive to our readers to further insist on the importance of these cases. Is it possible that such a set of phenomena of all kinds is the result of mere coincidences?

How could one explain the properties of the spiritual body that resuscitates its ancient form in materialization seances? If we cannot admit that they were acquired here below, who can give us a logical explanation of the memories and reminiscences of which we have encountered so many examples?

How can one refuse to believe the predictions made in Spiritist seances when they are fulfilled with such perfect accuracy?

All these phenomena, seemingly so different from one another, have a common explanation.

They are all explainable by reincarnation, which shows us the spirit slowly climbing the arduous path that should lead to happiness, the reward of such incessant efforts.

14

CONCLUSION

THE LOGICAL EXPLANATION OF INTELLECTUAL AND MORAL INEQUALITIES ·
THE FORGETTING OF THE PAST · THE PROBLEM OF THE EXISTENCE OF EVIL ·
PROGRESS · MORAL CONSEQUENCES OF PHILOSOPHICAL DOCTRINES

THROUGHOUT THIS BOOK, I have endeavored to present to the reader a large variety of facts which seem to prove scientifically the objective reality of successive lives. I deliberately left out the teachings given to us by higher-order spirits about the great law of spiritual evolution. I must now summarize them briefly, so that we can appreciate its importance and greatness.

They shed an unexpected light on the problem of human destiny by providing new solutions on our divine nature and the true destiny that is in store for all human beings.

In fact, spiritualistic philosophers of our day have not been much occupied with the origin of the soul; if its future has interested them, the same does not seem to be the case with its past. It seems, however, that both problems stand out, and that they are both equal in mystery. Theologians have been more zealous in developing this question, which is held close to the very basis on which Christianity rests, the transmission of original sin. Their opinions are relatively uncomfortable and can be reduced to two hypotheses. Some have admitted that all souls were contained in that of Adam, and that they were transmitted through generation: such was especially the opinion of Tertullian, St. Jerome and Luther. Leibniz and Nicolas Malebranche have rallied behind this doctrine. This has not been universally accepted and the common opinion is that it takes an act of the divine will to create a soul at every birth. But here we come up against logically insurmountable difficulties, for this hypothesis is irreconcilable with the goodness and justice of God.

To classical proofs concerning the demonstration of the existence of a first cause, Spiritism has added a new one, somewhat experimental, resulting from our relations with discarnate spirits. The study of spirit communications has conclusively proved to us that the rank of the soul after death is governed by an infallible law of justice according to which every being is in a condition of existence rigorously determined by its evolutionary degree and by the efforts it has made to improve itself.

Our rapport with the Hereafter has taught us that there is no hell, no paradise, but a moral law which imposes unavoidable sanctions on those who have violated it; whereas it reserves deep joys to those who have striven to practice good in all its forms.[219] The goodness and justice of the Almighty seem to be somehow lacking when we examine the formidable physical, moral, and intellectual inequalities that exist among all beings from the moment they are born.

Why, let me ask with Allan Kardec, if the goal we must achieve is the same for all, would the sovereign power favor some of its created beings while denying others the same faculties to reach future happiness? It is only too obvious that there are profound differences of mentality between the peoples that populate the Earth, and even within each nation, from birth, a tremendous inequality among all individuals. It is absolutely certain that the soul of a child shows from a young age diverse and independent learning abilities. Why do some people show abilities in the arts and sciences from an early age, whereas others remain mediocre or inferior throughout their lives?

Where do some of the innate or intuitive ideas that do not exist in others come from? How to accept that a brand-new

---

[219] See Allan KARDEC, *Heaven and Hell* (New York: SAB, 2003), where we encounter the justification for these statements. See also *The Spirits' Book* by the same author, in which all Spiritist teachings are condensed.

soul, coming for the first time here below, is already steeped in vices and shows an irresistible propensity for crime, while others, even living in inferior circles, possess very clear feelings of dignity and gentleness? What will be the fate of children who died in infancy and why does the infinite power of the Almighty create souls that must live in bodies of idiots or the mentally handicapped, without any social utility?

It is clear that education is powerless to give humans the faculties they lack, and that it simply develops those they bring from birth.

If our future immortality really depends on a single passage here below (which lasts scarcely a second in the immensity of time), God being the eternal, infinite, omniscient being, for which there exists neither past nor future, knows in advance what fate is reserved for each created being to whom It gives existence. We are therefore justified in asking ourselves why It creates these monsters, whose life is only a series of crimes to be punished by endless tortures. In the same way, knowing what must happen to each one of us, why will God favor one at the expense of others, which is contrary both to the sense of goodness and justice of the one which Jesus called "the heavenly Father," whose love must extend to all who come out of It? When a philosophical doctrine or a religious dogma leads to such inconsistencies, logically we can be assured that this dogma or this doctrine are manifest errors, and we are entitled to seek a better explanation of these apparent anomalies. Therefore, the explanation by successive lives acquires an incontestable value, since it offers a reasonable solution of all the problems which, otherwise, are insoluble. Indeed, if we admit that the current birth is preceded by a series of previous existences, everything becomes clear with a new light and can easily be explained. At birth, human beings bring intuition of what they have acquired; they are more or less advanced according to the number of lives they have lived. Creation being a continuous process, in a society we find at the same time beings whose spiritual age considerably differs from one another. Hence the moral and intellectual inequalities that differentiate them. Therefore we can say with Allan Kardec:

> "God, out of divine justice, could not create souls either more or less perfect. Given our multiple corporeal lives, the differences in qualities that we see around us is still consistent with strict equality because everything has roots, not in the present, but in the past. Is this reasoning based on any preconceived system or hypothesis? No. Instead it is founded upon the clear and undeniable fact that natural aptitudes, in addition to intellectual and moral development, are all different. This cannot be explained by any current theory, while the explanation is simple, natural and rational by using a new theory. Does it make sense to prefer a theory that does not explain this fact over one that does?"[220]

If all souls must go through all social situations and all physical conditions to develop morally and intellectually, the inequalities of all kinds that are found among beings in a society are offset in the series of successive lives. Each in turn occupies every step of the social ladder, which creates a perfect equality in the conditions of development of beings. By virtue of the law of justice, all are at every moment in the social condition best suited to their individual progress, for every rebirth is conditioned by the consequences of past lives.

Any fault entails unavoidable effects; I have shown how this distributive justice, which is infallible, operates in a way that is somewhat automatic.

Forgetting the past

The most common objection to palingenesis (i.e., rebirth) is the almost general forgetfulness of previous existences. Therefore, it would seem illogical, from the point of view

---

[220] A. Kardec, *The Spirits' Book* (2nd ed., New York: USSC/USSF, 2016), book 2, ch. v, question 222, p. 117.

of justice, to make us atone in an existence for the faults committed in past lives of which we would have lost memory. It is worth pointing out, first of all, that forgetting a fault or a crime does not mitigate its consequences, and that the knowledge of these faults would be, for many of us, an unbearable burden and a cause of discouragement that would rob us of strength to fight for our recovery. Moreover, if resuscitation of the past were widespread, it would perpetuate dissensions and hatreds which were the causes of past mistakes, and would represent an obstacle to any progress. So it is a good thing that we come back to Earth every time with our soul unburdened from the weight of the past. But it is also worth pointing out that all the unfortunate incidents of our current life are not necessarily atonements for previous mistakes. In fact, these trials and tribulations are indispensable conditions for compelling us to conquer our selfishness and to develop faculties or virtues we lack. Besides, this forgetting of the past is not permanent, nor absolute. We have seen it, since already on Earth we have cases reported in which the memory of past existences has been preserved. After reaching a certain degree of elevation, we encounter in the hereafter, between two incarnations, the memory of our previous lives, and this allows us to better know what we still lack to rise in the hierarchy of spirits, by developing all the intellectual or moral potentials that are germinating in our consciousness and whose fulfillment must lead us to the highest summit of spirituality. This panoramic view of our spiritual evolution gives us the feeling of our identity and of the perpetuity of our spiritual being.

Forgetting the incidents of our past lives is necessary so that we can more easily abandon the errors and prejudices that we made during those lives. Yet justice demands that we redeem our mistakes since we knowingly committed them. That is why, as Dr. Geley says:

> "Each of our actions, our labors, our efforts, our sorrows, our joys and sufferings, our mistakes and faults, has a fateful

repercussion, with mental reactions in one or another of our lives."

THE PROBLEM OF THE EXISTENCE OF EVIL

If Spiritism has conquered millions of adherents all over the world, it is not only because it brings to humanity the scientific demonstration of the existence of the soul and its immortality, but also because it proposes logical solutions for all the enigmas that religions or philosophies have not been able to solve until now. It does not content itself with comforting those whom the sorrow of losing the beings they loved had reduced to despair; it answers our questions about our origin and our destinies by means of theories that are in harmony not only with God's justice and goodness, but also with the demands of science.

What can be more agonizing than the issue of the existence of evil? How can an all-powerful being allow it to subsist, if it depends only on Its will that this evil should disappear? Why do natural blessings, such as health, strength, intelligence, seem to be distributed at random, as well as fortune and honors, while most often they are the prerogative of those who are the least worthy? Why are calamities ravaging countries and suddenly plunging into pain thousands of innocent people? Question the religions and they will answer you only by invoking the free decision of the Divinity which can, at Its discretion, make receptacles of virtues or impurity. The arbitrariness of such a doctrine is blatant. Unless imbued with a monstrous partiality, a just and good Parent cannot possibly make anyone predestined to abjection, while others will have to do nothing but be alive in order to arrive at supreme happiness.

The tenet of multiple lives gives us a glimpse of part of the solution of this problem. If we return a great number of times to Earth, the game of reincarnations will successively place us in all possible positions, and the real inequality that exists for a single life is offset when we embrace the multiplicity of physical and moral, intellectual and social conditions that we have by turns occupied here below. What would seem arbitrary disappears if all intelligent beings undergo similar trials and the sense of justice that each carries engraved in himself/herself is satisfied.

Progress

Evil is no longer an inevitable and malicious fatality from which one cannot free oneself; it appears as a sting, as a necessity destined to push humans into the path of progress. In spite of all the sophistry of demagogues, it is certain that progress is not a utopia. The existence of human beings, in the Quaternary period, wandering through the forests or dwelling in caves, is not comparable to that of the most miserable peasant of our modern countries. As we penetrate further the mechanism of Nature, we can use scientific know-how to improve our physical situation; this has occurred over the ages by a gradual transformation of plants that are useful as food, by the sanitation of unhealthy lands, by the recovery and regularization of rivers, thus suppressing floods, etc. In the same way, the natural scourges, such as cholera, plague, diphtheria, and rabies, diminish in intensity every day, as a result of the immortal discoveries of Pasteur and his pupils. We have the right to hope that, thanks to progress in hygiene, tuberculosis and other epidemic diseases which still decimate humanity will be, in a few years, nothing but a bad dream that the light of science will have obliterated.

Civilization gives humans a security that our forerunners did not know, just as agriculture and industry gave us a well-being that our ancestors would never have dreamed of. Rapid communications among all parts of the world have removed the periodic famines which have been the scourge of antiquity and the Middle Ages, as the progress of hygiene has reduced epidemics.

Morally, progress has been slower; the struggle for survival is still cruel, especially in the cities, but who would have the nerve of comparing current proletariat with ancient slavery? If wars are not likely to disappear anytime soon, they have lost some of their original horror. Whole populations are no longer ousted of their homes for them to be sold at auction, and the rulers no longer spend their time, as in Assyria or Egypt, to starve prisoners or erect pyramids at the expense of their mutilated limbs. After the horror of carnage, the wounded are now collected and cared for, the homicidal fury is extinguished when the human beast is satiated. We treat the wounded instead of finishing them. The feeling of solidarity is confirmed by the multiplication of hospitals, by pensions for old people, by the aid given to the sick, as well as by associations which guarantee their members against the risks of sickness and unemployment. We feel that a new state of affairs is being developed; if it is still rudimentary and too defective on many points, it is not forbidden to think that it will gather day by day greater momentum. The evolution towards the better appears as the consequence of the intellectual elevation of the social mass; that education, liberally distributed, begins to bring it out of the torpor in which it languished for so many centuries for the exclusive profit of its exploiters. One no longer waits for the happiness of a supernatural intervention. We understand that it will be the result of the collective effort of all people. It is necessary to leave to the amateurs of easy paradoxes the negation of progress, since progress emerges as the spiritual law that governs the entire universe.

Therefore It follows that we are creators of a subsequent determinism which will be the consequence of our past actions, while having the possibility of modifying our future existences in a more favorable sense, according to the degree of moral and intellectual freedom that we have already achieved in our evolutionary process.

Moral consequences

Successive lives have as their objective the development of intelligence, character, faculties, good instincts, and the suppression of bad ones.

Evolution being continuous process, and creation being perpetual, each one of us, in the course of our existence, is at all times what one has made of oneself. In fact, each of our actions carries with it an inevitable consequence which may not manifest itself immediately, but which, sooner or later, will have a definite repercussion in future lives.

Thus, moral and intellectual inequalities are no longer the result of arbitrary decisions of the Deity, and justice has in fact never been transgressed.

Starting from the same point to achieve the same goal – which is perfecting our being by going through all earthly situations – there is, in reality, a perfect equality between all individuals, differences being offset in the course of multiple lives.

This community of origin clearly shows us that fraternity is not an empty word. At all levels of development, we feel connected to each other, so that there is no radical difference among different nations, regardless of their skin color or degree of advancement. Evolution is not only individual, it is collective. Each nation by reincarnating in groups, bears a collective responsibility and an individual one. It follows that, whatever our position in society, we have an interest in improving it, since it is actually our future fate that we are preparing as well.

Egoism is therefore at once a vice and a miscalculation, for general improvement can only be obtained from the individual progress of each of the members which constitute society. The day these great truths become well understood, one will find less hardness among those who possess and less hatred and envy in the dispossessed.

If those who hold wealth were convinced that their next incarnation could happen amidst the poor, they would have an obvious interest in improving the social conditions of workers. Conversely, the latter would accept with resignation their momentary situation, knowing that later on they may be in their turn among the privileged.

Palingenesis (i.e., rebirth) is therefore essentially a renovating tenet; it is an energizing factor, since it stimulates in us the will without which no individual or general progress can be accomplished.

Therefore solidarity imposes itself as an essential condition for social progress; it is a law of Nature which can already be detected in animal societies which have been formed to resist the brutal law of the struggle for survival.

Evil is therefore not a fatal necessity which would be imposed on humanity; humans can and must be freed from it. It derives purely and simply from our ignorance regarding the physical and moral laws which govern the world.

In short, the theory of successive lives satisfies all the aspirations of our souls that require a logical explanation for the problem of destiny. It reconciles itself perfectly with the idea of a providence, at once just and good, which never punishes our faults by eternal tortures, but instead grants us at every moment the power to repair our errors by slowly getting back to our feet through our own efforts, by climbing the steps of Jacob's ladder, whose very first steps are plunged into animality, whereas the highest ones rise to the most perfect spirituality.

Speaking of reincarnation, we can say with poet and essayist Maurice Maeterlinck:

> "Let us admit in passing that it is very regrettable that the arguments of theosophists and neo-spiritualists are not assertive; for there never was a belief more beautiful, more just, more pure, more moral, more fertile, more comforting, and to a certain extent, more probable, than theirs. Alone, with its teaching of atonements and successive purifications,

it accounts for all social inequalities, all the abominable injustices of destiny. But the quality of a belief does not attest its truth. Although it is the religion of six hundred million people, and the closest to the mysterious origins, the only one that is not odious, and the least absurd of all, it will have to do what the others have never done: bring irrefutable evidence. And what it has given us so far is but the first shadow of a beginning of proof."

These proofs asked by Mr. Maeterlinck, I think have now been provided in this book.

It is now a positive demonstration that we have in our possession, which allows us to understand not only the survival of the thinking principle, but also its immortality, since for millions of years we have evolved on Earth, which we shall eventually leave when there is nothing else for us to learn here.

PHOTO CREDITS

P. 85: FIGURE 1. WILHELM VON OSTEN AND CLEVER HANS, DECEMBER 31, 1907, photographer unknown.

P. 91: FIGURE 2. PAULA MOEKEL AND ROLF, 1913, photographer unknown.

P. 149: FIGURE 3. LOUIS VIVET, APRIL 20, 1885, photographed by Godefroy.

P. 191: FIGURE 4. HÉLÈNE SMITH (REAL NAME CATHERINE-ÉLISE MULLER), LATE 19TH CENTURY, photographer unknown.

P. 217: FIGURE 5. PEPITO ARRIOLA, OCTOBER 1900, photo from Jean Boussod, Manzi, Joyant & Cie.

P. 275: FIGURE 6. LAURE RAYNAUD, date and photographer unknown.

P. 275: FIGURE 7. GIOVANNA SPONTINI'S HOUSE, 1922, photo from C. Lancelin.

P. 341: FIGURES 8, 9, 10. ALEXANDRINA 1, ALEXANDRINA 2, AND MARIA-PACE, 1922, photos from C. Lancelin.

www.ingramcontent.com/pod-product-compliance
Lightning Source LLC
Chambersburg PA
CBHW062146080426
42734CB00010B/1582